We are anti-fascist, anti-violence, anti-racist. We're against ignorance.

Joe Strummer

Photo 1

This is Joe Public Speaking

Anthony Davie

LUND CHOOS PUBLISHING

Published by:
Lund Choos Publishing
P.O Box 10781
Chandni Chowk
Delhi 110006
India

lundchoospublishing@gmail.com

First published in 2018

Text Copyright © Anthony Davie 2018
(unless where otherwise stated)

© Copyright warning
All rights reserved. No part of this publication may be reproduced or transmitted in any form or by any means without prior permission in writing from the publisher.
Lund Choos Publishing endeavours to ensure that the information is correct but does not accept any liability for error or omission.
If you require any further information on permitted use or a licence to republish any material please contact Lund Choos Publishing

Front cover artwork: Dave Spencer
Front cover photograph: Simon White, The Clash, **Rex Danforth Theatre**, Toronto 20th February 1979. Copyright © Simon White
Rear cover artwork: Amée Davie

Foreword

Joe Strummer was once asked at the height of punk if he'd ever been to the countryside. He replied, "I went there once and it made me puke!" Well, the idea of a book "made by fans for fans" sounds like a similarly vomitsome proposition, were it not for the fact we're talking here about The Clash, a band who profoundly touched the people who saw and heard them like no other rock group in history. To understand precisely why, would take at least 84,000 words written by those very individuals, whose experiences occurred in different countries and cultures across the world - which is exactly what this amazing and endlessly fascinating collection of memories is.

That Ant Davie has managed to pull this book together is the result of his own Clash epiphany, and deep connection with Joe, Mick, Paul and Topper, and the extraordinary things they achieved musically, culturally, politically and everything else-ally.

I first met Ant when I was compiling Clash reminisces for their From Here To Eternity live album in 1999. There was one amusing (and quite poignant) email from a guy in London who in 1980 climbed over the wall of the police training college in Hendon to attend a Clash gig at the Hammersmith Palais, thus ending a promising career wearing a silly hat and swinging a truncheon in the

Metropolitan Police Force. Instead, Ant Davie went on to deliver the city's post with a winning smile and to later work with Joe and the Mescaleros. And now he has brought all of us Clash lovers together via this great tome. Thanks Ant - you're a lovely guy with a heart of gold; and thank you to The Clash for showing us the way forward, now as then, in a complicated, tough and still-bigoted world.

I hope you enjoy these memories as much as I have.

Pat Gilbert
Author of Passion Is A Fashion: The Real Story of The Clash

There have been dozens of books written about The Clash & Joe Strummer.
I myself wrote one back in 2004!

I am sure everyone has their favourites, mine are Pat Gilbert's "Passion is a Fashion", Salewicz's "Redemption Song" is top drawer, Marcus Grays: "Last Gang in Town" / "Return of the Last Gang in Town" (I love it, where else could I have found out that my mum & Paul Simonon were born next door to each other? Albeit 16 years apart……………) and Tim Satchwell's work is also well worth a read.

You may well ask, so why write another one?
Well this one's a bit different, it's written by the fans…you/us!

I've also been fortunate that the following have very kindly contributed: Pat Gilbert has done the foreword. The Godfather of all Clash authors: Chris Salewicz and legendary Clash roadie: The Baker have both kindly agreed to contribute. Along with great input from Ralph Heibutzki & Mark Andersen co-authors of "We Are The Clash", Randal Doane: "Stealing All Transmissions", Tim Satchwell: "Combat Ready - The Clash". Plus other top authors: Marguerite Van Cook, Tony Beesley and Frank Moriarty have committed their writing talents.

Now, this is a fairly decent collection of top authors that have contributed and I will be forever grateful to these people but, the heart of it is written by fans telling or rather sharing their stories/memories of The Clash, the gigs, punk rock and all that was great about that time and in particular being a fan of The Clash.

Over forty years on now (we are all getting older!) and The Clash are still regularly featured in so many publications etc. Only recently, the Evening Standard did a feature entitled: **The 20 greatest British rock bands of all time** and they were at number 9 in that particular publication. In June 2018 another media empire, this time the BBC/Spotify, wanted to do 3 short films and a series of 8 podcasts on The Clash.

When I was asked to be involved, my main part was to contact fans asking for their memories/stories as the BBC wanted fan involvement, rather than the usual big names.

The Beeb had noted particular gigs of historical value (and the fact there is good footage available of all of them might have had something to do with it!) which included:

- Roxy New Year's Day - January 1st 1977

- Munich, Schwabinger Brau - October 4th 1977

- Anti-Nazi League, Victoria Park, London - April 30th 1978

- Glasgow Apollo - 4th July 1978

- Bonds Times Square gigs - May & June 1981

- Shea Stadium, New York with The Who - Oct 12th & 13th 1981

They later included Scottish dates in 1980 on the 16 Tons Tour as someone somewhere at the BBC must have discovered in the archives the BBC Nationwide programme from the same time which filmed the band whilst on the Scottish leg of the tour.

The emails flooded in from all around the world, quite a few weren't even about those particular gigs, but how punk rock and especially The Clash changed people's lives, influences them still to this day.

The BBC producers were totally over the moon with the fans contributions.

Now, I ain't a particular fan of the BBC, I often send in complaints about how biased the Match Of The Day football pundits are against my hero Wilfried Zaha and don't get me started about Radio 2, people who listen to that think they're "with it", if you listen to that crap you were never with it in the first place!

But, I must give credit where it is due, if it wasn't for the BBC contacting me, receiving all those great stories/memories would never have happened...etc. etc

And the BBC have indeed used some of these stories which has included filming fans as well as audio. And because every story/memory was really such a great read, I have put them all in kindle form for the world to also read and enjoy.

Many of the people who sent in their stories/memories I have known for nearly two decades….some even longer and even one good friend I have known since I was a 14 year old schoolboy, which makes it kinda close to my heart.

My main source of contact was with the extensive mailing list I have from a combination of the Joe Strummer & The Mescaleros old official site: strummersite.com & without doubt the best Clash website in the world: blackmarketclash.com

Which brings me round nicely to the fact that so many books on The Clash have undoubtedly used blackmarketclash.com whilst researching and very few acknowledge the site. So, as in all my previous publications I will carry on the proud tradition and say "Special thanks/acknowledgement to Blackmarketclash ".

Before I sign off:

I have deliberately left the stories/memories grammatically as I received them. It's what gives them their unique identity, their character. Anyroad, who am I to correct someone's writing that they've spent both time and effort on, especially on some occasions when it's not even in their first language?

One further note of particular importance: **all proceeds/royalties** from this book will go to the **Great Ormond Street Hospital for Children, London.** No one's making any money out of this.

I have had various suggestions as to where the monies from sales should go, but whatever I decided I couldn't please everyone, so I decided you can't really go wrong giving the monies for young children who are unfortunately ill and in need of treatment at this great hospital.

Out of the BBC's list of gigs, the one I did attend was the Anti-Nazi League rally at Victoria Park in April 1978, by the way I have honestly never met anyone who stayed behind to watch Tom Robinson Band that day!
So what better way to open the book than with this fascinating insight into the build-up and actual day from the bands point of view, courtesy of **The Baker:**

On a bright, sun-drenched day in Victoria Park in Hackney 40 years ago, the 'Rock Against Racism' demonstration met in Trafalgar Square, and then marched to Victoria Park where an extraordinary concert of immense proportions took place. In a seemingly spontaneous act of mass consciousness, many different factions united under one banner to protest the current state of race relations, police injustice, and revel in unbridled explosion of musical self-indulgence. It was a 'people's event,' with everyone from the organisers to the bands contributing their efforts for free and demonstrated the ability of music to try and bring about change with its supporters claiming that it eventually helped demolish the National Front.

It also proved to be a surprising spectacular milestone in the Clash musical journey, representing a quantum leap in their public exposure and political credibility. With audience estimates of up to 100,000 it was not eclipsed again for the band until the US Festival in San Bernardino, CA five years later. More importantly, it gained national media attention for The Clash and firmly anchored the band's flag to the left-wing's cause. After the disintegration of the original punk scene just a year before, the carnival offered The Clash an opportunity to align themselves with a more political national version of punk constructed very much in their own image. In a time before the emergence of 'Thatcherism' and it's jackbooted authoritarianism; the massive military build-up of the confrontational Reagan years, the enforced and bitter epoch-ending miner's strikes, and long before the Thatcher-contrived, manipulated Falklands War, it symbolized a fervent rejection of the right-wing agenda that was shortly to come.

Though not a great number by today's standards, with social media and instant internet access to world events reaching millions, back then it was quite an achievement for two far-left fringe organizations to pull together simply by word-of mouth and undoubtedly exceeded their wildest expectations. Viewed now, in hindsight, it can be seen as an anguished elegy for the post-World War II social system aspirations that Thatcher would so soon thoroughly sweep away. Played against a rising tide of tabloid press-inspired right-wing National Front popularism, it also had a significant socio-political impact, raising the consciousness of young people in the UK against racism, and unexpectedly turned out to be an ideal platform for the Clash to present their anti-racist stance, despite all the misgivings and doubts about the validity of the show beforehand.

I say surprisingly, because from the start, the prospect and outcome of the gig was mired in doubt, suspicion, and conflicting emotions. As true today as it was back then, safety is only assured when we take matters into our own hands and Joe Strummer was keenly aware of this all his life, hammering the message home in all of his lyrics. He had been originally approached by John Dennis of the Anti-Nazi League and Red Saunders of Rock Against Racism, after Saunders had been thoroughly declined by Bernie Rhodes who'd dismissed them as "a collection of students playing politics." Joe nevertheless was adamant and pressed for participation in the event despite the internal politics being played out. For Mick's part he had already shown himself quite willing to make friendly overtures to the likes of the Tom Robinson Band. But to many of us in the Clash camp there were grave doubts about the organizers' ability to stage such an event and wariness regarding any ulterior motives. Bernie was the big stumbling block against the entire venture and was extremely suspicious of the organizers, their political commitment, and what the band would eventually achieve doing a *'gig in a park'*. Bernie, saw them as a bunch of hippies and doubted their competence and their effectiveness.

I remember about a month before the gig, the band and crew all went to John Dennis's flat one bright spring morning to discuss the details with him and his committee. We got rebuffed on most of our requests and felt that there was needless obstinacy towards us, especially on the part of the Tom Robinson's people. So far from being assured, we came away even more unsure of what the band was getting itself into and keenly felt the growing contradictions: to be supporting a cause they fervently believed in, but was run and coordinated by a group of inexperienced politico's who had never initiated a show of its kind before. The organisers could never have attracted the numbers they did without The Clash (they'd originally Planned for 20,000) – they needed them – but were unwilling to bend to any demands. It was most definitely Tom Robinson's event and playing support to The Tom Robinson band hardly seemed a step forward either, merely rubbing rub salt into already open wounds!

Bernie grasped all of these intangibles and was already dead set against playing support to the Tom Robinson Band realising it meant giving up control of the event and its outcome. He wanted complete control. The last card up his sleeve was the band's backdrop and when Bernie discovered it would be virtually impossible to use the backdrop on-stage he flatly withdrew all participation in the event. To him the backdrop was, in some peculiar way, more important than any other facet of the performance and was something I never understood. Even at Mont-de-Marsan the previous year where we thought we couldn't

15

use the backdrop, he'd had me climb up a ladder and spray-paint in big letters 'THIS IS JOE PUBLIC SPEAKING!' (We did actually get one section up at the back of the stage before being stopped by the TRB roadies.) But all of this was denied and there were tense discussions and arguments on all sides from inside and outside the band. Had the eventual scale of the event been known beforehand, maybe there wouldn't have been so many doubts but no one could have foreseen or realised the ultimate impact of the 'gig in the park'. But at that point it felt like we were deceived in the name of a moral cause.

The trap was set. Conscious of the stitch-up that was being perpetrated in advance, the band nevertheless decided to spring the trap and run the gauntlet. Ignoring Bernie's advice, they determined the cause was ultimately larger than they were. And so, the opportunity was taken up, despite all misgivings and unease – the band braced themselves to, if nothing else, blow everyone else off-stage.

Come the day of the gig, Johnny Green and I begrudgingly loaded up a rented van with all the equipment in the very early morning at Rehearsals – only to find the back doors of the van wouldn't shut! Not a good start! We were already behind schedule. Of course, we blamed each other for not checking the van out beforehand and cursed each other the whole way to the park. The guitar roadie on that day was Mickey Abbot, an acquaintance of Joe's who worked at The Roundhouse Music Store and who Joe had originally approached months before to replace Rodent after he had seen fit to jump ship for the Pistols. Mickey eventually worked for the band throughout the recording of the 'Give 'Em Enough Rope' album at Basing Street Studios.

As Johnny and I drove into the park, the realisation of what actual kind of event it would be slowly dawned on us; our qualms and misgivings multiplied (especially mine). The band had only played in broad daylight a few times before, but this event was on an unimaginable scale. The crowd was already huge with a vast assortment of hippies, punks, rasta's, beatniks, hobo's and weirdoes. People with fuzzy gray beards and worn-out woolly jumpers selling copies of Socialist Worker were not our usual crowd and our wariness grew. Lines of cops were everywhere; blokes with collection buckets taking donations; massive trade-union signs; it seemed like chaos to us out front of stage. As The Clash bassist Paul Simonon later remarked, "I'm glad we did the anti-Nazi rally because it was important but it was a bit off-putting with all these hippies wandering about with a giant bucket, going, 'Put your money in here!' and shaking it all around. We wanted to make the left seem more glamorous because at the time it was all hippies."

Our anxiety notched up once we finally nosed our way through to the backstage area to unload the gear and find an even worse shamble. Five acts had to get on-stage, perform, and get off with all manner of instruments and equipment flying all over the place. There were no separate dressing-rooms; the old lido at the back of the stage was used by everyone. Even the PA had only been arranged at the last minute. Johnny spent the time leaping up and down the backstage steps three-at-a-time with arms flapping like an ostrich on speed.

Mick Jones breezed in unfazed with Tony James, wearing what looked like a leather bus conductor's cap. "Tickets Please!" everyone called out to him. The interaction and high spirits of the bands themselves only lent itself to the bizarre, carnival surrealism of the afternoon – it was just mayhem and you had to have eyes in the back of your head, especially those of us trying to get the show on the road. The TRB road crew were in charge of proceedings and gave us little consideration or attention. "You can't do this!" "You can't do that!" was all we heard that afternoon. Mickey Abbot ran a mains extension from the stage so the band could tune-up only to have the TRB road crew rip it out (a sign of things to come.) Maybe they knew in advance we were going to try to steal the show and had made their preparations accordingly which included making our lives as difficult as hell (again, parallels with the US Festival five years later). Our ritualistic pre-gig routine had to be forgotten.

By the time we were forced to take the stage at 2:30pm (ready or not), the crowd had grown even more enormous. None of us had ever seen such a huge and VERY animated audience before and even the band was gob-smacked at the sight and sound of such a huge mass of humanity. The band was dwarfed by more than 80,000 punks, skinheads, rasta's, long-hairs, and all-sorts by then all wanting one thing ….hard, fast, roots-rock-reggae music. The roar of the streaming, surging crowd was deafening and swept over the four musicians as they ran headlong on stage. The Clash gave them want they wanted in torrents – virtually non-stop, number after number. Fuck-ups were many. The sound was poor, barely carrying to the back of the crowd (when TRB came on later, the sound improved dramatically.) But the 'band played on' regardless, forced by sheer adrenaline, energy, and passion.

We played over our allotted time (as we'd intended all along), and finally Tom Robinson's road crew had had enough and pulled the plugs (much to the anger of the crowd.) The lights and music stopped and there was a mammoth jostling, shoving match backstage, with all of us trying to get to the power. Finally, through bluster and threats we got the power back on and Steve English, the Pistols' hulking security man doing double duty that day, was told to stand over the mains and guard it with his life! The roar from the heaving, uncontrolled crowd was earsplitting as the band went into 'White Riot' and it seemed like WWIII had erupted. I was too busy getting equipment working and plugging stuff back in to even react to the emotion of the instant but for many it was an iconic moment. Jimmy Pudsey ran onstage like a fixated berserker, taking the mike and screaming the words but that was just fine with all the Sham skinheads that were in the crowd. Youth was having its say that day no matter what end of the fashion spectrum they hailed from and the cops were left looking on helpless as over 80,000 did as they pleased in the name of Rock Against Racism. The authorities' underestimation of the mood of the blue-collar, dispossessed suburban kids was quite staggering.

In a master stroke, Bernie had convinced the organizers to let the film crew for the movie 'Rude Boy' shoot footage of several numbers. Masquerading as a documentary film crew, they were there to capture the pandemonium of the day and the undeniable success of the event. After it was all over and Johnny and I drove back to the studio to unload the gear, the adrenaline slowly subsided and the magnitude of that momentous and historic occasion we had just been part of started to sink in. It's peculiar how you can only realise afterwards in hindsight how great something had been. We'd doubted it from the start, become paranoid before the show, but it turned out to be one of the highlights of the Clash's remarkable legend. The organizers had tried to stitch us up that day but we'd mugged 'em and turned the tables – it could have so easily gone the other way. But luck favors the foolish (or naive), and the band took home the ultimate prize.

In retrospect, who can say what the RAR gigs' eventual impact was on the politics and culture of the day. In years to come, Mick Jones said quite rightly that, "The event transcended petty in-fighting." Red Saunders summed it up: "The lesson from Rock Against Racism, is that we can all intervene, make a difference and change things: nothing is inevitable." A number of people in the crowd who would never have attended a Clash gig were, in time, inspired to stand up and subsequently make their own contributions, Billy Bragg and a young Tony Benn being among them. For a many of us it's still a most important reference point. The immediate effect of RAR was to incite the anti-NF supporters to come out and make their presence felt. Just one year later, Thatcher would become

Prime Minister, her uncompromising agenda creating schisms in Britain not seen since the English Civil War. With Thatcher on the way, it was if nothing else, a statement in time; a reminder that given a uniting influence, there was at least another voice in Britain, not just the UK's right-wing tabloid press.

In summary, only haphazard scenes and random images remain in my memory now – the individual minutiae of the show is currently the property of everyone who made the effort to be there and be part of it, not the journalists who chronicled the event years later. You, the audience made such memories possible – 80,000 of you.

The Baker's blog:
https://thebaker77.wordpress.com/tag/clash/

Iku, Japan

When The Clash came to Japan for the first time in January 1982, it was at Shibuya Kokaido Hall in Tokyo. I was over the moon to see the Clash because I hadn't expected that they were coming. My cousin, a friend and I were waiting for them to see them in a car, because just very quick glance made us very happy. It was very cold and then snow started falling, about 70 fans waiting outside were little by little leaving for home, and finally only

10 fans there including us. Having waited for a while in the snow, a security guard boy was running to us and shouted "Band members said that let fans waiting outside come in the dressing room because they are pity freezing out there. Just follow me, quick quick!!" We were in the hurry to their backstage. When we were in the hall, there were famous Rock journalist on both sides, it made us nervous too. I didn't expect that I would be able to see the Clash and get autographs, so I was shaking myself having my Hello Kitty notepad, there was only papers that I could ask for autograph.

We were the last fans waiting for, firstly I saw Cosmo Vinyl. Woooooow he was very cool!! I felt like I would have nose bleeding. The Clash members were at the corner of the dressing room, I straightly went to Mick. I said hello and made a lot of bows saying "thank you thank you", Mick also nodded many like me, and he was burst into laughter and gave me kind smile. My impression on him on the spot… his mouth was big (sorry LOL). Then I saw Pearl Harbor who was very busy putting her think make up. I passed her and went to Paul. His legs were too long!! He was drawing something on Hello Kitty while writing autograph. I said "Oh that's pretty!" and he smiled and said "Yeah?" His missing teeth was actually scared but later I thought it was lovely. Then I went to Topper, he signed very quickly, no word. Was he in a bad mood? And finally, it was Joe!!

I had a lot of nerve, and my first impression on him before talking to him was "What a beautiful skin he has. Beautiful white and his skin is something like transparent." I asked him autograph, and I told him with my broken English "My dream was to go to the concert of The Clash." He said "Yeah!? I don't believe it!" he smiled and looked at me from below, he looked like I said joke. I became very serious and enthusiastically said "Joe, it is true, very true, please believe me it is true!!" May be I was stressing too much, but actually it was true. Joe stopped smiling and his face became very serious and said face to face "OK I believe you"

I just returned to myself and said "Anyway you said on the stage that you had a cold, this candy is very good for throat, please try it". I passed him Halls honey lemon flavor. He was pleased saying "Oh good idea, good idea" while writing his autograph he also write "good idea" with lots of xxxx (LOL). Then, I said bye to Joe and we left the dressing room. We were totally lost in abstraction, it was the biggest ever up to then. The Clash were extremely kind, also the loadie of black guy, he was very nice as if he understood what fans were feeling (later I knew his name was Ray).

We were quite empty (can I say it is "pretty vacant"?) We

were walking like zombies on the street, and one car was passing by. The car stopped at a traffic red signal, I saw Ray in the car. He told something to somebody in the car and pointed out at us. The guy who was told looked at us, it was Joe!!! When Joe noticed us, he waved his hand to us, forever and ever until we were not seen .I do remember it quite well, even though it was in 1982, 36 years ago. It was one of the happiest things of my life.

Angelique Haswell, England

Coming from a small market town my punk was very main stream, articles in the NME or records that they would play on the radio. I don't remember the Clash especially standing out for me, I'm sad to say now. Of course I knew about and especially the Sex Pistols, who didn't they were so outrageous! I remember more The Damned, they being the only punk band I ever saw live (in those days, I've seen plenty since).

With strict parents I wasn't able to go off to gigs with my school friend Jo who would come home after midnight from gigs. I simply wasn't allowed. I also remember being a big fan of The Stranglers playing them on a battery powered tape recorder laid on the back seat of my little Austin 1100. Where I definitely was a punk was in my dress, clothes from the Charity Shop, ripped, splattered with paint, altered, I liked looking different and hearing older people say "look at that dreadful girl". Albeit I had to take my clothes and makeup out the house in a carrier bag and dress at Jo's. I used to buy mascara that you spat in and applied with a brush, I used it around my eyes as well as on my eye lashes. I did manage though to have pink hair on the pretence I was training to be a hairdresser at the time and it was just an experiment. I also remember being asked to leave the Crown pub once if I didn't remove the safety pins I had through my ears, how rebellious!

Then I met my husband to be, the hair went back to blond, out came sensible clothes and punk was over all too soon......only to be resurrected in the past few years, where there are still many of us out there.
(Use it, trash it, that's my rendition. Unfortunately nothing as exciting as singing "Oh Bondage Up Yours" on your parents front lawn). Once a punk, always a punk at heart.

Tim Satchwell, England
Author: "Combat Ready - The Clash" & "All The Peacemakers"

The Story of The Clash.....

"*Don't ask me to be your hero, I will only let you down*" sang Patrik Fitzgerald on his 1979 *Grubby Stories* LP. I suppose it's not very punk rock to have heroes. The

Stranglers said there were No More Any More. But Joe Strummer wrote that *"You can be a Hero is the age of none."*

The Clash…well it's been a strange journey for me. I wasn't immediately a serious fan. There was so much great music coming out in 1977/78 and I was totally hooked on the explosion of new music. I even picked up a bass and had a crack myself.

I wasn't at The Black Swan, the Roxy or the 100 Club. I lived in rural Shropshire, I had Jersey cows for company and a loving if somewhat detached family. We all did our own thing, and were brought up to be independent.

My insane obsession with The Clash developed later in life, it kind of crept up on me. A work mate of mine commented on this as Luke Skywalker had commented on R2D2…. *"I've never seen such devotion in a droid before."*

Looking back now, you realise just how important they were and for many still are. Although criticised for this and that, they did stand up as Paul said, "For what's right and what's wrong." Where they could, I think they stood by what they believed in and performed and presented themselves with an open honesty and passion that seemed to be lacking elsewhere, then and now.

So yes, they got caught out, made mistakes and got hauled over the coals for their sometimes contradictory statements and actions. For me perhaps unlike Bonnie Tyler, I'm not holding out for mine…I found them.

Let's not forget that they were human, with all that goes along with that; strengths, weaknesses, bad moods. Egos, vices and guilt.

Much as I don't want to drag Bono and U2 into the conversation, he did say that The Clash were used by U2 as a reference point. (Although he has said that about a number of other bands) But I take that on board, The Clash were and are a reference point. What would Joe Strummer do? Is a phrase I have come back to in my head at times in my life, sometimes in jest, others not.

I shouldn't forget the music, because that's what The Clash were really about. Strummer/Jones was an incredible partnership. The lyrics and songs just hit the mark. *White Man in Hammersmith Palais* seemed to hit the spot for me. After all the other great stuff they produced, I always come back to it.

Everyone has a favourite Clash album, but ask me which one is my favourite and I say all of them (OK maybe not *Cut The Crap*, there's a whole discussion there to be had) It's impossible to point to one and say, that is the definitive Clash album. That has got to be a good thing. They were all different, and every one had its flaws, highs and lows. But they were a lesson, don't get yourself hemmed in, but try and stay true to yourselves and your beliefs, Oh! And go out and find out about this or that subject if you are interested.

I don't feel let down at all.

I just want to say that over the years, I have met a lot of Clash fans, and for me there is a "Bond". Everyone has their own experiences, you talk to them, and they "get it." You don't have to explain too much. What is perhaps most important, is that they all have a story to tell....What's yours?

Peter Pakvis, Holland

This is the story of my life, The Clash

I can remember from the first week of august 1977 I was only a week on my new school when I was doing my homework, that on the Dutch radio Hilversum III played punkrock for the very first time during prime-time late at the afternoon on a VARA's radio programma on a tuesday. It was like I was hit by electicity of 220 volt when I heardm "Complete Control" from the Clash for the very first time and I knew immediatly this was something I never had experience before and after. It was liked I was strucked by lightning, I knew everything I heard before The Clash was vanished in the past! When I compared the music in the charts with The Clash it seems it was something like a different world to me. Bye the time of october 1977 I had cut my red hair very short with a safety pin in my right ear and in several safety pins in my leather jacket and I was the only punk not only on school but also in my village and the whole area around me.

Nobody seems to understand in the area where I lived what punkrock was! For me it was complety freedom and I understand immediately that you do not have the do the job after school which you don't like but that you also can live and earn your money with doings something creative, art or fashion or music. I become a photographer in later years but without the punk explosion and The Clash this was never happed!

They where I eye opener for me.....for the future...It was the first time I heard a band who has a message in his music. Another thing was I discover reggae music and reggae artists thanks to the Clash and I went to the concerts like Steel Pulse and UB 40 about
the time they where totally unknown, before they hit the charts in 1980. After that I got involved with a Rock Againt Racist Festival, the first one in Holland and went on supporting the Shandinista movement in Nicaraguay, which got a lot of suppprt from Holland in 1979 and 1980.

I always liked the musical development of The Clash from the very first time I heard them with "Complete Control" in august 1977 till "Combat Rock". If they did only played punk liked Sham69 always did and they still do in 2018 I think I quit with the Clash after a year of two but I am glad their music had has a incredble development and that is why the music of the band is important and sound so fresh today in 2018.

During the spring of 1982 The Clash should played in Holland on the Lochem festival in may 1982 but on BBC Radio One, Mick Jones, Paul and Topper has a message on the radio that nobody knew where Joe Strummer was and they asked Joe the comeback with the band for the gig in Holland. Even on the day in the afternoone when the Lochem Festival was hold it was uncertain if the Clash should play there. Eventuelly on the last minute they did played their on the 8th may 1982 and it was one of he best gigs they
ever played, but the very last one with Topper Headon....

After that gig I had a feeling that something was wrong in the band and when I heard that Pete Howard did join the Clash instead Topper Headon who was a heroin addict unfortunally, I knew it would never be the same again... Soon after that Mick Jones was sacked by the band…

The following is a review Peter did 34 years ago for the Dutch Clash fan Club:

The 21th of February 1984 was one of the finest days of mylife, on that day I travelled from Den Hague in Holland by train to the Brielpoort in Deinze in Belgium to see the Clash. It was a very cold and sunny day and at four o clock we arrived at the Brielpoort which lay nearly a great river.

The security controlled every Clash fan with a camera or tape recorder with them and if they discovered it you must gave it to them till after the concert was finished. On the outside of the Hall Belgium Clash fans hold a protest against The Clash and gave the fans flyers with the message "Strummer" sold out the Clash and turned rebellion into money" Af course we did not like the flyers.

Somehow I was lucky to get a camera inside. The gig was in a large Hall and I remember that nearly everybody frontstage was drunk and that on stage where The Clash started to play was filled with a lot of TV's The Scabs a Belgium band opened before the Clash. From the first beginning when the Clash started to play the band got a very good response from the public which came from Holland, Belgium, England, Germany and Italy. Nearly everybody fronststage started to dance and pogo.

I can remember that the clash sounded very fresh and the band was in a good shape. The setlist of songs was a mix of Clash classics like Londen Calling and Guns of Brixton and a lot of new songs like Dictator, Three Card Trick and This Is England ware received by the Clash fans very well. After nearly two hours and several gifts the band was finished and left the stage. After the gig I got the setlist part One from a Clash roady and on the setlist you could read 23 songs but they played 33 songs, there was a second setlist a small one filled with the second and third gift but I did not get that one.

After the gig Marcel my Clash friend and me walked away in the cold outside and forgot to buy the Out of Control 84 Tour shirts but I got the Tour poster which I picked up from the wall and I still got it with the setlist and the gigticket.

After that we fell asleep in a cafe which belongs to the local Deinze sport club where they played the Clash the whole night till we left at eight o clock in the morning and get by train at home the same morning.

Note:

On the 12th of October 1985 The Clash gig at Vredenburg in Utrecht in Holland was cancelled at the beginning of October 1985. I have seen advertisements in the daily news

paper called "The Hague Courant" where they spread the

news that they start to sell the tickets within two weeks. I phoned with Vredenburg at that time in september 1985 so I know that the advertisement in the Daily Paper is true.

Craig White, Scotland

good evening, i have heard through a friend that you are looking for individuals who were in attendance at the clash event on 4 july 1978 at the glasgow apollo. this was one of 4 or 5 times i saw the clash, and for many reasons, the most memorable - the incredible bill, for one thing, the clash, suicide and the (coventry) specials, honestly, who could have wanted more? the latter two performing awesomely (and in suicide's case challengingly) before being booed off the stage. the incendiary performance by the clash - even before knowing all the surrounding facts of the night, it was very apparent they were angry as hell. the street riot outside the apollo, which spilled all the way down renfield street. as i say, memorable!

Brandon Prince, England

When i see bands, there will always be comparisons. The Who at Charlton. U2 supporting Echo & The Bunnymen. The Magic Band. A Certain Ratio, Durutti Column & Ultravox @ the ICA. But most of all for sheer excitement, and a feeling we could, and would, change the world, the

Clash were difficult to beat. Has any band looked more Rock & Roll? Compare with Duran Duran or the Stones, nobody has had more visual impact. It isn't just because Simonon is an artist. The stage sets were often memorable. And the variety of looks, and genres absorbed into the music. Even having a resident cartoonist on tour, crossing into graffiti art, R&B, Dub, Cumbia, Jazz, Funk & Hip Hop. The Mescaleros albums make interesting listening. How sad that Rachid Taha passed away recently. He was an artist greatly inspired by the Clash. And that Ellen Foley album deserves a better appraisal. I also recall the gig at Crawley Sports Hall, where Suicide were attacked, also featured a support band called the Coventry Specials. A cover of the NME once featured Strummer in an overcoat & Homburg hat, with shades, making a V sign, smoking a cigar. A Churchillian figure, one Boris Johnson couldn't imagine. The article encouraged our naive thought that if someone like Joe Strummer was made PM, the country would somehow get sorted out. They were the gang (no, never Gary's) we wanted to be part of before 'gang culture' took on much more negative connotations. And if anyone looks for the Hammersmith Palais, they will be disappointed. That song is one of the main remembrances. I should also comment that in London, before the smoking ban, i well remember the air heavy with particularly fragrant smoke, which we hadn't smelt in the provinces.

Hope any of this helps paint a picture.

Tony Gravestock, England

I was always a good boy at skool, but didn't succeed academically, and the world was a real mess - no travel or anything on Sundays, or any ability to meet your mates during major holidays like xmas. So life was very boring in Greater London. Even talking to your mates you had to go to a phone box to get some privacy.

When we went to gigs, if it was cold we wore 2 T-shirts ...My mate still tells the story of hearing the Pistols at the end of our road - blaring out from my room.My Dad got so fed up with it that he cut though the wire of my record player, while it was still on, and got a bolt of 240v - I still remember him getting the shock, and trying to get downstairs to the phone. Luckily he was fine by the time he got down there !Greater London wasn't the suburbs, but trains stopped so early, you often had to leave before the end to get home, and you had to dress for sleeping in the park in case you missed the train

For me the draw was to get off your arse and do things for yourself, rather than wait for others to do it for you.

David Poudrier, United States of America

I am responding to an email that I received from you concerning the BBC project about the Clash and Punk Rock. I might suggest that you pour yourself a cup of tea and grab something to snack on if you intend to read my entire email and the effect that Punk in general and the Clash in particular had and continue to have on my life.

I was 17 when we started to hear about something called punk rock in America. The news was not good. It was said that the bands couldn't play, they beat up the audience and they vomited in public. It was also said that it was dangerous to go to a punk concert because the bands would beat up the audience. It must be said that Malcolm Mcclaren was a master publicist as his publicity stunts and stories about the Sex Pistols carried all the way across the Atlantic Ocean reached a small town called West Townsend, Massachusetts. In short, everybody I knew hated punk rock before they even knew what it was or had heard the music.

I was a teenager growing up in an unhappy family. I was into the Beatles, Stones and Bowie, but the Beatles had broken up, the Stones seemed like creatures that inhabited another dimension and although I loved his music, I didn't really know what to make of Bowie other than the fact that it drove my father crazy when I left photos of Ziggy around the house.

My first exposure to the Pistols came via the TV, we were watching some variety show and for some reason they stuck a video of the Pistols playing God Save the Queen at the end of it. I was immediately intrigued. this was the band that everybody knew about but that nobody had actually heard. Best of all, my parents found them totally repulsive. In short, they were perfect.
Fortunately, I lived about one hour from Boston and I was just old enough to be permitted to take the bus to Boston just to explore the place. I wandered around Boston going thru the record stores and the book stores, looking for anything related to Punk. I managed to find a couple of books which had just recently been published that were loaded with photos and lists of the Punk Bands. the most important of which was Caroline Coon's "1988 the new wave/punk rock explosion". This book was loaded with articles about the Sex Pistols, the Clash, the Stranglers, the Slits. It also contained photos of bands like the Buzzcocks, Subway Sect, the Jam etc. All the greats. With this book I felt that I had found the keys to a great kingdom of which only few people were aware and even fewer had the keys. I had a list of bands that were supposedly a threat to western civilization. I made a list

and was determined to find all the records I could by each of these bands.

the first punk album I bought was Nevermind the Bollocks. As I brought it to the counter of the store to purchase, the salesclerk had a look of horror on her face. She seemed to be thinking "what kind of a person would buy this?" I took it home. Played it on my cruddy, little record player and was assaulted by the opening chords of Holidays in the Sun. I must admit that it took me quite a few listens before I could make heads or tails of the music. It contained an attitude, an energy and a life force that I had never heard in any other music. It sounded like I was listening to a person who was a pissed off as I was about his living condition and the state of his existence.

I memorized the interviews with the Pistols and the Clash that were in Coon's book. the words of the Pistols and the Clash opened my mind to a concept of existence which I had never even previously considered; rebellion. Not doing exactly as I was told and not thinking exactly what I was told to think. I will always be grateful to Punk Rock for opening up my mind and introducing me to the concept of personal freedom. If I had never listened to punk rock I would have become either a mindless factory worker or I would have joined the military. Once I became a punk, there were other options, the possibilities were limitless. I could do whatever I wanted. I didn't have to listen to what people told me. Many of the things that Joe Strummer said were in direct contradiction with what I had learned and what I had been told. I quickly learned that somebody was lying. Either my boss, my teachers , my parents, or Joe Strummer and Johnny Rotten. The difference between the two groups was that one was telling me to do what they wanted me to do. the other was saying that I should do only what I thought was right. Clearly, Johnny and Joe were the truthtellers. Life would never be the same at my high school there was a music appreciation class which consisted of the stoners of the school bring in there stereos and presenting the latest offerings by Zeppelin, Free, Foghat and other mainstream big bands. One day I decided to bring my copy of bollocks, a 12" 45 of anarchy and the Clash's single Remote Control and demanded that it be played. the reactions was immediate; complete anarchy. nobody knew what had hit them, people started to throw stuff at me and tell me how much these bands sucked. I played the live version of "londons burning". People were puzzled; where was the big solo, why was it so fast? why was it over so quickly? It was great. Punk rock became my total identity.

I started to make more frequent trips to Boston in search of records by punk rock bands. Finally I found a copy of the Clash's first album. I quickly grabbed it and ran to the counter and studied the cover the entire bus ride home back to my small town. I will never forget the first time that I listened to that album. something about that music spoke to my soul and every fiber of my being. In the 70s, cheap record players had a spindle which allowed you to stack a group of records on top of each other and they would play one after another. however, if you only played one record and moved the arm to the left, that one record would play forever until you turned the record player off.

I was home alone that saturday night and I let that record play for hours. I could not get enough of it. I have been collecting records for over 50 years and have a collection of thousands. the only record that I have ever listened to 40 times in a row on the day I bought it is the first Clash album. that is the album that changed my life, formulated my world view and convinced me that I knew something that nobody else around me did.

I learned that Johnny Rotten wore a suit that he had razored to pieces and put together with safety pins. I did the same thing but I added masking tape, and staples to my attire. At that time I was working in a factory at night to pay for college. When I started to wear my new punk "uniform" the kind elderly ladies thought that I was so poor that I had to wear rags. The started to bring me clothes which their children had outgrown so that I wouldn't have to walk around looking like that. I patiently explained to them that I had done this to my clothes on purpose. They smiled back in confusion.

the first punk band that I saw was Chelsea. they played at a small club in Boston called the Paradise. The band were late. we were told that they might not play. suddenly some guys came on stage and started to set up amplifiers and drumkits. I thought, "well somebody is going to play because these guys are setting up equipment for some band." To my utter amazement, once these guys had finished setting up the equipment, they put on the guitars, sat behind the drumkit and started to play. This was the band. this was Chelsea. A band that set up its own equipment and then played immediately afterwards. this was frikkin amazing.

When Chelsea were done playing, they left a setlist on the stage. I copped it immediately. I saw one of the guys who had arrived with the band. It took me five minutes to ask him "hello, could you have Gene sign this? Hoping to get Gene October's autograph. The guy said "ya, wait a minute and just walked away." I was convinced that I was getting the blowoff by musicians who thought that they were too good to even recognize my existence. I waited several minutes and was about ready to take off when the guy returns and said "come on". We walked up a flight of stairs, entered a small room and the guy says to me; "Gene's over there, go ask him." I couldn't believe it. what? me talk to a musician, to a punk rock star, he's going to talk to me? I don't know how it did it, I was only 18, but I approached Gene and asked him to sign the setlist which he gladly did. James Stephenson was also standing there, so I decided to push my luck and ask him for his autograph. He somewhat less enthusiastically gave it to me. Despite being in a total daze, I managed to have a brief conversation with Gene. He was the nicest guy in the world and actually seemed glad to talk to me. It was late, I had to drive home and go to work the next day. I said thanx Gene and got ready to leave. Before I left, Gene reaches into a plastic bad and pulls out a chelsea badge and gives it to me. he then says, "you got any mates with you" I said, yes, one. He then hands me another badge. To this very day, I still treasure that badge.

I staggered out of the Paradise in a daze. I couldn't believe what had just happened. I was euphoric. I swang from the lamp posts along the Boston streets as I walked back to my car. It was like meeting God.

anyways, I don't want to take up more of your time. If you think that I could make a contribution to your project, please don't hesitate to let me know. If not, thanx for taking the time to read this. I went on to see the Clash a couple of times, and several other punk bands. the first time in a movie theatre in Cambridge, Massachusetts. It was the greatest show I have ever seen!!

Simon Warner, England

Although I saw Joe Strummer in action many times, I only met him once and, embarrassingly, confused him with someone else. In early autumn 1976, as term at Sheffield University unfolded, news of the arrival of the most talked about gig of the year filtered through the underground grapevine. The Anarchy in the UK tour, bringing the nascent fury of British punk to the nation, wended its uncertain way through the country, uncertain, because where-ever the entourage set up camp, there was imminent danger of the local council denying the potential hell-raisers a performing licence.

And so it proved in the northern city of Sheffield. Hours before the concert was meant to proceed, with Sex Pistols, the Clash, the Damned and the Buzzcocks due to deliver their psychotic symphonies for a new age, the authorities pulled the plug on the event.

We were in the student union bar, early that evening, barely a soul around in fact, the garish fluorescence of beer pumps glimmering and the ring and chatter of the pinball arcade, where I all too often made my home, competing with the crackle and creak of the Wurlitzer jukebox.

The era of the hippie was far from over. Long-haired and duffle-coated, a head with beatnik trimmings, I had begun to absorb the sound and fury of the battalion of young bands that were leading the charge against progressive rock and heavy metal. In recent months, we'd seen Daniel Adler's remarkable band Roogalator and, on a couple of occasions, the raw and raging rockabilly of a group called the 101'ers.

A venue called the Black Swan in the town centre had, for a year or so, been giving space to a series of London acts with small yet growing reputations, largely linked to the pub rock revival -- Kokomo, Chili Willi and the Red Hot Peppers, Graham Parker and the Rumour and others -- and Roogalator and the 101'ers seemed to be part of that scene.

But when that bar embraced a combo called the Sex Pistols it became evident that a fresh wave of, principally metropolitan, agitators were shaking off the dust of the good-time bar bands and forging something more sinister, more dangerous, more thrilling.

It wasn't long before Joe Strummer, the frenetic frontman of the 101'ers had re-emerged in a band destined to challenge the Pistols' ascendancy in the punk cavalcade. When the Clash were included on the Anarchy bill it was plain that Rotten and co were not the only shock troopers ready to take on any establishment -- political, musical, media -- they could identify.

But the establishment, in any its guises, was not willing to roll over quite so passively and the evidence was there to see on the Sheffield campus that long ago night. In the student bar, we were idling away the time, knocking back a drink or two, contemplating a night without the rock'n'roll apocalypse we'd been promised, when we spied, half-way into the deserted stalls, a pair of unlikely looking figures, refugees from A Clockwork Orange, close-cropped aliens in a land where long locks and flared jeans still ruled the roost.

I walked over and chatted to the one I thought I recognised. Johnny Rotten, it had to be. We exchanged a few words. He was quiet but not sullen, introspective but actually polite. He confirmed the gig was off, explained why he thought it had been called off, and found some kind of gentle solace in a pint and this impromptu conversation. He looked intimidating yet he was not unresponsive, willing to share his thoughts, the intimidating armour of combat jacket, pencil thin Levi's and Doc Marten boots misleadingly menacing.

In the days that followed I became a minor celebrity among my student mates -- the one who had engaged with Rotten, the anti-christ, the demon, the force of darkness, and survived to tell the tale.

But the truth, when it slowly emerged, was, in the end, just as interesting. It had, in fact, been Strummer whiling away the moments, swallowing his pint and his disappointment, in the deserted calm of that bar. In retrospect, it's hard to believe that Rotten, all snarl, all spite, would have been quite so civil to the Lennon lookalike in the battered Jesus boots.

The revelation that I'd been wrong didn't make me an instant Strummer fan but it wasn't long before I'd been convinced that it was the Clash rather than the Pistols who were the torch-bearers of potential transformation.

The Pistols had their incandescent moment, but the Clash burned brighter, longer and I probably saw Strummer's crew in their classic form three times, at least, after that and added everything they did to my record collection. They certainly became my favourite punk band, maybe my favourite band for some little while.

As my shoulder length hair was chopped back to new wave proportions, as my billowing loons straightened, the night in the Sheffield student bar had been a sort of Damascene encounter. Strummer, not Rotten, had opened my eyes to the punk insurrection.

Brook Duer, United States of America

I was in a band that opened for The Clash at Carnegie Mellon University in Pittsburgh PA in October 1982. They were the reason I even was in a band. However, it was disillusioning, as the band was falling apart. Terry Chimes was the only one who spoke to us. He was totally separate from the rest. Joe and Paul were together in a back room. They never spoke a word or even looked at Mick and Ellen Foley (who stayed at a different hotel; showed up seconds before the set and just walked on.) Never once onstage was there a smile. It was sad and broke my heart to have made it so far to be opening for my heroes and to see it so dysfunctional.

Fred Mills, United States of America

I'm sure you're being inundated with Clash info, so I'll keep this email brief. While I did not see the band in their initial prime, I did see them as the 5-piece Cut the Crap version on their US tour in Columbia, South Carolina. Years later, in 2001, I interviewed Joe Strummer twice, once by phone from England and then again in person in NYC (October 2001) for Magnet Magazine.

I subsequently republished the interviews in 2013 as part of a longer Strummer piece for my publication Blurt - link is below in case you want to take a look - I've still got pretty vivid memories of Joe. (Ironically, there's a couple of clips of me talking to him in the Dick Rude film "Let's Rock Again" about Joe and the Mescaleros).

I also interviewed Paul Simonon at one point when Legacy was doing the remastered CDs, although I can't get my hands on that story immediately as it's on an older format floppy disc. But I probably have it in hard copy form somewhere. And lastly, I interviewed Ari Up of the Slits and she talked a little bit about touring with the Clash.

On December 22, 2002, unexpectedly and tragically, Joe Strummer died, apparently from a previously undiagnosed congenital heart defect. I had interviewed Strummer twice in 2001, once over the phone from England and then again in person when he appeared at New York's Irving Plaza for an October concert with his band The Mescaleros. Portions of those interviews subsequently saw publication in the Phoenix New Times and Magnet Magazine, and in a surreal twist, a few video snippets of me interviewing Strummer in NYC would turn up in the 2005 Strummer documentary Let's Rock Again! by filmmaker Dick Rude (who I vaguely recalled having been present with a camera during the interview).

Around the time of the summer 2001 release of his latest album *Global A Go-Go* (Hellcat Records) Joe Strummer brought his band the Mescaleros to America for a promotional tour of record stores in Chicago, San Francisco, Los Angeles and New York. The Mescaleros played one-hour sets then stuck around to meet the fans who, needless to say, were in ample supply and eager to meet the former punk firebrand and ex-Clash vocalist/guitarist. This was to be the mere tip of the Strummer iceberg, however, because the band returned in October for a full concert trek, and I was lucky enough to see the band play and interview Strummer while I was in New York for CMJ. You'll read what the man had to say shortly.

To backtrack a moment, however, a common misperception about Joe Strummer is that he exiled himself from the music industry after the Clash folded in the wake of a critical savaging of the post-Mick Jones Clash album *Cut the Crap*. (There are several books available that can give you the whole poop on the Clash including former roadie Johnny Green's hugely entertaining *A Riot of Our Own* and journalist Marcus Grey's controversial but authoritative *Last Gang in Town*, recently updated and reissued as *Return of the Last Gang in Town*.) However, while having a markedly lower profile than during the tumultuous Clash years, Strummer hardly puttered around his garden shed, collecting royalties and regaling neighborhood kids of tales from the Great Punk Wars.

Strummer *did* lay low a bit for the next few years, but when his Sony woes finally ended and he was free to sign with a label that not only represented artistic freedom but practically demanded that he make up for lost time no matter what direction the muse might steer him. Coincidentally, the tail end of '99 saw the release of the first-ever official Clash concert album, *From Here to Eternity Live*. Accompanying this were UK screenings of filmmaker Don Lett's riveting Clash documentary *Westway to the World* and a surprisingly good VH1 "Legends" episode devoted to the band, followed shortly after in January '00 by the Clash back catalog being remastered and reissued by Epic. Strummer and his former Clash partners willingly participated in the inevitable Clash media retrospectives, fueling speculation over an impending Clash reunion. Unfounded, it would turn out; after making the promotional rounds, Strummer went back to what turned out to be a busy Mescaleros touring schedule. (Worth noting, however: this past May, when the Clash received the Ivor Novello award for making an outstanding and lasting contribution to British music, all four members were on hand for the ceremony, once again setting the Clash reunion rumor mill spinning. However, Strummer told *Rolling Stone* that while such a move would set them up for life, financially, "You have to ask yourself, 'Would it turn out to be good music? Would it be worthwhile in terms of making a brilliant record?' But as long as I can keep grinding away and doing really interesting things [with the Mescaleros] I feel I'm vindicating what I'm doing.")

The positive response to *Global* and *Rock Art* has been a pleasant surprise for Strummer, who additionally remarked to *Rolling Stone*, of his relatively slow-starting solo career, "I realized what I've done is save the best for last, which is a brilliant maneuver. I did it by accident, though. Rather than burn out earlier, taking [time] off has turned out to be a not bad idea at all. When the Clash broke up it sort of all fell apart and perhaps that was quite good for my artistic ability, which was a good thing for me at least."

Well said, Joe. Needless to say, I was thrilled to talk to the man, having ranked both Mescaleros album in my annual top ten lists without reservation. (Long-time Clash fanboy alert here too. Bootleg collectors and traders, get in touch.) Okay, let the games begin.

FRED MILLS: What are you listening to lately?

JOE STRUMMER: Strokes.

Any hot tips out of England?

No. [*laughs*] I don't know, I'm out on the road.

One of the things I'm interested in is the artist-fan relationship — the way fans invest a lot emotionally in their heroes, and how kids in particular emulate them. Patti Smith, for example, told me that she felt the one of the artist's responsibilities is to offer a shoulder to lean on, to illuminate the common threads in our lives. That's a role model viewpoint. Yet a lot of public people – sports figures especially — are uncomfortable shouldering that responsibility. How do you feel about the role model issue?

I don't agree. Just because you're good in some particular area and you excel in that area, you're not walking around as if you had a big jacket on saying, 'Do as I do. Do as I say. Follow me.' A sports guy's good at shooting the hoop. I don't see why he can't go downtown and get harebrained outta his box like everyone else, y'know? Why are you hogging it all for yourself? There was a rugby guy in England, and after a tour they were busted taking Ecstasy and cocaine in a nightclub. I looked at that and thought, after 25 matches, and they won 'em all, at the end of tour, why can't they? Everyone else does! If it were some annual company jamboree, people get pissed out of their heads.

And the kids? You're a parent yourself.

You're talking about Keith Richards and heroin, aren't you?

Yes, to an extent. However, recently there's been a heightened industry sensitivity regarding artists in rehab, responsibility towards kids, that sort of thing.

It's complete bollocks. Look. [*leaning forward, putting guitar down*] You're born a certain way. You inherit it from your father. If your folks were great drinkers, ten to one you're gonna be a great drinker yourself. So all of this is a load of bollocks. People are a lot more complex than, hey, they see someone doing it, why don't they do it too? I can see the point when heroin was chic; before people realized how dangerous heroin was. Maybe there's quite a few junkies in the world who thought, "Well, I'll try that because heroin looks hip."

Did you have a hero?

Bo Diddley. He's the one, yeah.

Did you ever subscribe to the notion that to some, you're a spokesperson for the Punk generation? People continually ask your opinion of British politics in interviews.

[*dismissively*] I'm not a spokesperson. Never was to anybody. They can hose off, man. I mean it. That's a load of horseradish. And I don't have any opinions about British politics. I resent being asked about anything. I'm quite happy not being asked about anything. [pointing to guitar] I'm happy to get that box and figure out something to do with it. I get rid of my opinions! Because some clever guy said, 'If you have opinions, you cannot see.' Meaning that opinions will kind of horseblinker you to see the truth about any situation. [*laughing*] Opinions aren't worth the paper they're written on!

What about issues that hit closer to home, then? Artists' rights and contractual matters are a hot topic these days, and you've had your battles with Sony, solo and with the Clash.

Our fault. We signed that paper.

But how old were you when you signed it?

Maybe 21.

That's not necessarily something you think about at the time.

There's plenty of smart 21 year olds, man, I'm telling you. There was no one grabbing my hand and saying, "Sign that paper." I could've gotten a decent lawyer to read it. Hey, any intelligent man would have done that. Not us, man. That was exceedingly dumb, but that was the way the world was. Maybe they capitalized on our eagerness and all that, y'know? But on the other hand, they got our records all around the world.

Perhaps we've reached a point now where genuinely artistic, creative people shouldn't expect to find good homes with majors — at Sony you basically went on

strike and waited things out – so would you tell musicians to go with indies like Hellcat?

Yeah, [with Sony] I waited it out until my hot potato had grown cold. [laughing] And so they went, "Ahh — pffft!" You gotta look at the small print, y'know? Hellcat's sympathetic to my cause – it's a label where the people there actually like music. It's not just a commodity. You've gotta go for the [artistic] freedom. Without it you're scuppered. And I already spent enough time trying to get out from under deals, which are quite complex with a corporation. Just to even get 'em to address the problem takes a few years! Nevermind getting the paperwork out of it. So I wouldn't be at all into getting back to that. If there is a young musician reading my guff, he'll get the picture because I put it pretty straight.

It's the George Michael argument that every musician should know about – there ought to be a book about that case! — which is basically, THEY are gonna want you to stay at whatever lucrative part of your career where they signed you. THEY are not interested in the development of the artist or having him change. So George is saying, 'You can't expect me to stay at my 18-year old songs now that I'm 34.' And yet THEY want to force him to stay where he's most well-known so they can make some bucks. The point is, you can't force someone to do something like that.

You know, in that case, I did wonder if someone got to the judge. Because the whole industry would've unpeeled if George had got out of that contract. It would have led to a huge unraveling! I wonder why the judge found for the label, because George had righteousness on his side there, y'know?

Now what if you'd gone to Hellcat and said, "Guys, actually, I'm gonna pull a *Sandinista!* here on you. I want to put out a triple LP, 2-CD set…" Would they have done a CBS on YOU?

[*laughing loudly*] That's a great question! I dunno… if you had a double's worth of tunes to back it up, maybe they'd go for it!

Is it true that if you, Mick and Paul set foot in a studio, it's called The Clash and you're automatically on Sony.

Yeah, that's a contractual thing. [*disgustedly*] And –it – will – never – expire. Because it states if two or three of us get together… that's The Clash. No choice.

What's your opinion on Clash and Mescaleros bootlegs? You should take charge and market your archives over the Internet like Pete Townshend does.

Yeah, that's a good point. Thank you! If you heard some of them and you liked what you heard, you could recommend it: "This is pretty good…" I'm in touch with this guy in Italy who's sort of the king of collectors, if you like, and I'm quite pleased he has all these recordings when it comes down to it, you know what I mean?

Tell me what it was like when the four of you from the Clash jointly received the Ivor Novello 2000 award for "Lasting Contribution to British Music" and Pete Townshend presented it to you.

Yeah, yeah, Pete was there. And Pete Townshend to give you the award, that made it really mean something, you know? It wasn't like some fat cat. He said, 'Your music sucks but here's your award anyway!' No, he said, 'Well done, lads.'

Was that Pete namechecked in the middle of "Minstrel Boy," on *Global*, kinda low in the mix?

That's it! You must have ears like a bat! You're the only person apart from me that knows it's on there!

I missed it the first few listens. Also, when I got my advance of the CD for review, it had no credits, but of course I spotted Roger Daltrey's voice on the title cut

and at the time I wondered if that was a Who sample or if you'd blackmailed Daltrey into appearing on your record!

In the end it was a breeze. We'd been booked to support the Who on a British tour in November. Roger began to hang out with us as we ran up and down. He knew we were recording, so one night he said, "Hey, if you want me to come by I'd be more than pleased to do that." I said, "Sure, come on down, and let's get out the mics and sing!" So it was an invitation from him – he made the offer.

That was great. That makes all the people who are too cool to like a so-called dinosaur band like the Who kinda scratch their heads and go… huh?

True yeah. We can't have any of that kind of purism. Let's give the kudos to where they're due, c'mon! The Who in anybody's books must be great, with a body of work that fantastic.

The October *Mojo* included two Clash songs in their "100 Punk Scorchers" list, with "White Riot" at number four behind the Pistols' "God Save the Queen," the Ramones' "Blitzkrieg Bop" and the Damned's "Neat Neat Neat."

Goddam it! Insulting, ain't it? [*smiling*] No, I like the Damned, really!

When the media drags out its perennial Punk retrospectives, do you groan and go, "Reporters will be calling again, wanting to know about 1977…"?

I have to ignore it! Yeah, because every time an anniversary comes up, they always get around to the old [in pinched, nasal voice], "So, what does Punk Rock mean to you?" I did have an answer at one time, after 58 times. Can't remember what it was now. Yeah, you just want to scream.

Um, that was my next question. Nevermind. I'm leaving now… On another topic, what did you think of your ex-roadie Johnny Green's Clash book, *A Riot of Our Own*?

I LIKE Johnny Green's book! It seems to capture to me the feeling in the air like it was. You're reading the story as it happened, and it's nice how it actually conveys what it was like at the time. That book somehow captures something. It's entertaining for starters. And it's short! [laughs]

The *Westway to the World* movie comes off as very honest too....

Yeah, that's Don Letts there, who was part of the scene anyway at the time. He was perfectly placed to do that and I think he did great. I wouldn't have liked to try that!

I noticed that *Westway to the World* is now coming out on DVD with extra footage, with the *Clash on Broadway* film included. That originally hit the British theaters around the same time as the live Clash album, and shortly after the Clash remasters appeared too. Was it coincidence that the first Mescaleros album was released around then too? Because it was fortuitous from a standpoint of promoting your record. When doing the Clash-related interviews, did you want to say, "Oh, and guys, I got this little solo album too..."

It was totally accidental. That live album had been simmering on the backburner for two-three years so it just happened to lurch out. And in the interviews, I don't bother. You just gotta fight your way through.

And right now there's this new Clash book by photographer Bob Gruen, who I met yesterday. I

brought these photo samples from it that *Q* magazine ran this month.

[*looking at the photos excerpted in current issue of* Q *pointing at a stage shot*] Yeah, that was a good one. Great shot. Bob is lovely, isn't he?

Will you ever put a boycott on the Clash inquiries?

No, no, just carry on. [*grinning at me*] Don't you want to know when the Clash are going to get back together?

I know the answer... Back in, say, 1966, we didn't think rock 'n' rollers should be playing past age 30 — now there's a book out called *Rock 'til You Drop*, and one of its main theses is that 50somethings look ridiculous hopping around onstage and maybe they should just go sit on barstools and play the blues.

Not a bad idea! That's what Johnny Ramone thinks! No, I think you should just get on with it. Look at Paul Newman. And the Sufis think people get better, y'know? Why should we assume people get worse? Just because everybody makes loads of cruddy albums, hah-heh-heh!

I was watching old Clash videos and noticed how the three of you would form this frontline, shoulders all

kind of moving in the same rhythm. Is that same kind of onstage chemistry coming through for you now? What do you get out of being onstage in 2001? Do you have needs or expectations different from two decades ago?

Erm, every day is a new day, isn't it? So I just look forward to it. It's the same as in the old days. I narrowly missed the other night getting hit by a twizzling mosher, you know when they hold him up in a ball over the crowd, then they twizzle and their legs kick out frantically. But it's more or less the same as it ever was. I did a gig once with just one man in the room. So since that gig you're just glad that people are there, you know? Once you've done a few gigs like that with one man in the room – and that man was asleep! – you appreciate the crowds.

Every day's a new day, really. And you can't walk around with expectations. I don't like to know where we're going, actually. Because you always end up somewhere interesting. If you have a specific aim or target, and then you arrive at that point – whatever, the creation of a project, some sort of – it's like, boring! You're gonna end up there – and finally you end up there! There's no fun in that somehow, is there? There's no surprise in it. There's no chance in it. This is a construction of chaos, really. We shamble around; God knows how we put it together! But I think we've got something good rolling along here. We enjoy playing live, and we all get along. You get your juices going, you get out, you gather 'round the world again, you see the people you meet and you talk to people – it's a very stimulating experience in total, y'know?

One musician told me being on tour was like being in a fishtank, and when he gets home the tank is drained of water and he's left standing there trying to remember how to breathe.

It is strange. There should be a detox unit, a decompression chamber for about four days in some camp. Maybe I'll start up a camp!

Captain Joe's...

...Decompression Camp! Four days. Put 'em in a black room with a television.

What kinds of people are coming to your shows? I picture grey-haired punks in Mohawks...

Mostly they're truck drivers, a-hah-heh-heh! Yeah, any people, really. Quite a cross section are digging the music. Quite a wide age group.

When you look at the audience, what do you see in the faces looking up at you?

Hatred. [*laughs*] No, just people grooving around, you know? I did a gig once with just one man in the room. So since that gig you're just glad that people are there, you know? Once you've done a few gigs like that with one man in the room – and that man was asleep! – you appreciate the crowds.

Are there times when you're ill, or in a bad mood, and you really have to work hard to gear up to the point where you can give these people something they paid for?

Yeah, and that's one of the real – then you feel like you've learned something, when you can overcome something like 'I don't feel like it.' If you can overcome that AND do a good show, then you're really learned something. Mood has a lot to do with it.

I noticed last night you were fretting about the time left before the venue doors were to be opened and that The Slackers might not get a proper soundcheck. You told your road manager to hold the doors until they did. Yet some musicians take the attitude, 'Five

years ago I got treated like shit, now it's their turn to get treated like shit.'

That's idiotic. People are nuts. See, when you're being crudded upon by others, you say to yourself, 'One day when it's my turn, the support band's always gonna get one.' Because you live and learn what it's like to be in that position. 'Sorry, you can't get a check because Waffleface has got [*in whiny/superior voice*] to mend his fuzzbox!' You know? So you think – pffft, when it's my turn, I'm gonna make sure. There's lots of aimless soundchecks. They could go on for days if no one didn't go, 'Cuuuut!'

The back design of your album reminds me of the X-Ray Spex album cover *Germ Free Adolescents*. Just a kind of subliminal thing...

Oh yeah, I remember that. I must find that and have a look.

And of yourself? You've got one of the most distinctive voices in rock, like Dylan or Neil Young.

No, Neil's got a pair of pipes on him. You couldn't put him in the growling category. [My voice] is so out of tune it sticks out. I'm the sore thumb of larynxes. It's awful. It stinks. Once I was phoning up some friends in LA in 1988, this long list because I was doing a show, of people I'd met. I rang Jesse Dylan's number and went, 'Ahh, Jesse…' And he went, 'Oh, hi Dad.' It took me by surprise – otherwise I should have said, 'Go and tidy your room.' [*laughing*] But "distinctive" is code word for "cruddy," admit it.

PBS had a special on songwriters recently, and practically every classic song from the '50s and '60s era it covered was penned by a duo.

Yeah? Well, all right – Lieber and Stoller. This is good. There are geniuses like Hank Williams or Bob Dylan, these people who come along once in awhile. But for the rest of us I think it's really good when you have the two, three, four, five guys working on it. It's always different. Whereas if you leave it all to one person, after awhile it'll be in the same box.

With two albums and several tours in two years, does it feel like you're on a creative roll?

Yeah, I think so. Just show us a studio and we'll be in there like wrapped up a drainpipe. If we can keep it together I think we could do it and really hit some music. That's what I hope, anyway. Going with the vibe seems to be the way we do things. It suits everyone. Maybe that's why we're still on the road even two years after we started, which is quite an achievement.

A lot of musicians claim to be mere vessels through which music is channeled from some higher energy or power: do you think of yourself and an "artist," in quotes?

[*standing up*] I don't think along those bollocks, man. You're out of your mind! Horseradish. You gotta think of it, you gotta beat it outta your brain! [*slapping his head*] You can't sit around thinking like that! What are they – they've had too many crisps! I think of myself as a hack. Because, one, it's true. Two, it stops you from getting hi-faulting' notions – above your station. And three, you're just a hack anyway! I look in the mirror and go, "Hack! Hack! Hi hack! How's it hanging today!" Honestly, the people out there who are true geniuses, they are the ones putting little circuits together, operating on people's brains, you know? I mean, we're kind of on the level of crossword puzzle writers. Compilers of crossword puzzles. And no one ever goes to them and gives them an award. Do you think they've got a crossword puzzle writer's dinner and annual award? Do you think all the crossword puzzle writers get together in Florida once a year? If they do, I wanna be there! [*laughs*]

There's probably an Internet newsgroup of them at least...

Yeah, let's dial up the crosswords — www.crossword.com!

At any rate, people listening to your music do attach an emotional component to it.

Okay, that's true. But what I mean is that it's like a knack. Some guys can play helicopters, but they can't play football.

So should we strive to bring artists down to earth? You've said that in the Clash you guys had become 'corporate revolutionaries' or something to that effect?

Well, if people's platform heels get too high, yeah. There are some people that are probably geniuses, like we mentioned Hank Williams or Bob Dylan. But yeah, that's why it had to stop. Because, you begin, right? And it all makes sense – "Yeahhh!" But then five years later you're kinda professionally paid to be a rebel, which is insane. Isn't that a conundrum? It's truly insane.
And I realized that it was only going to get worse. Say we'd gotten as big as U2 – we would have been insane! I could certainly see that life from now on would only be – "Photo shoot. Do the interview. Go to the video shoot. Go

do another interview. Fly to Rio. Play the Asshole Stadium. Come back in a helicopter." And all the time you're suppose to try and write something real, or think real, or get through to real people – or "keep it real," as they say. In-fucking-impossible. I've had plenty of time to think about it.

There's a myth that says you spent a long time in the wilderness, yet you actually stayed pretty busy after the Clash…

JOE STRUMMER: With a lot of weird little projects. Mainly I wanted to play out of the eye, out of the spotlight. All the films I worked on were sort of off-off-off-Broadway. Way off, *heh-heh-heh*. It seemed to be good to lie low for awhile. Mostly I felt uncertain as to what to do, and that sort of breeds perhaps a lack of confidence. No direction home, so to speak.

Your film career wasn't exactly invisible. Alex Cox's *Straight To Hell* has just come out on DVD. Will that revive your acting aspirations?

Um, hopefully not! [*laughs*] I was in Los Angeles on the last tour for the last record and this guy comes up to me, like a one-man video crew, camera on the shoulder, microphone strapped on, and he asked, "Do you mind if I

interview you about *Straight To Hell*?" I said, "What, are you pulling my leg?" Because the movie died a death back when. Although everyone who was in it secretly loves it! But you couldn't say it went down well with the public or the critics. So this guy asks me, and I thought he was having a little jest. But the made a documentary and it's on the DVD. I think he interviewed anybody that he could still find that was still standing up.I
 was giggling to myself, hoping that one day there'd be a director's cut. The producers, when they saw what a crazy movie they had on their hand, I think they influenced a lot of the cutting. But I can dimly remember some really funny scenes that made me laugh, and one day I'd like to see them back in the flick.

For that matter, you've been in enough movies that someone could put together a box set of your classic screen moments…

It would be a thin box! A pamphlet… but no, I had a go at it, if you know what I mean.

I'd like to see *Walker*, too, because I never got to see that.

Do you think that would come out on DVD? That's the only place it could come out I guess.

A couple of years ago you did a film called *Docteur Chance*.

Oh yeah, now this has just come out on DVD because no one would dare play it in the cinema. No distribution guy's ever gonna dare book something like that. *Docteur Chance* is quite a wild movie. At the London Film Festival, they showed it, right? And myself and F. J. Ossang, the French director, had to get up. There was about a thousand people that had seen the film. "So here's one of the actors and the director to have a question and answer session." The usual sort of thing. We got up onstage and — dead silence! Everyone was sitting on their hands. Frozen. Nobody could think of a question because the movie, erm... what's it about, well, it's a kind of road movie, and, erm, it's very interesting! F.J. Ossang is really quite a character. And it is quite a movie!

I know what you said about having opinions, but I've got to ask: Suddenly, with the September 11 attacks, the world seems a much more dangerous place – smaller, too, if you're American. You're European – how do you feel? Or even simply as a parent?

Well, everybody's freaking out all over the world. That could happen on any airliner. So you gotta try and find a sort of bright side to the cloud. So now maybe, for example, just talking about airplanes, they'll be sealed off and there's gonna be a plainclothes sky marshal on every flight – and these things are probably good things for the safety of everyone.

As a parent I guess I might in the middle of the night worry about whether the real IRA's gonna blow up Shepherd's Bush tonight or not. But it's something you kind of learn to live with. I'm trying not to get too freaked out – keep it in hand. I reckon as time goes by we'll be able to get it into more perspective, take a more steady view of things, maybe. And maybe you can say, this might be too heavy for the piece you're gonna write, but it's really brought a lot of nations out that weren't previously into or down with the international community, like Iran and even Pakistan. Which is really a big leap forward.

Both your music, with its global sound, and your occasional deejaying on the BBC World Service ("Joe Strummer's London Calling") with everything from blues, African music and reggae to Dylan, Small Faces and the Pogues, which is really all over the map, seems now to have a different social context.

I guess I've been too shocked to think about that lately. But I've always been keen on hearing stuff from anywhere. I always liked that feeling where you don't know what's going on, and this is a feeling I actively like to search out –

say, you wanna find some music to hear at home or in the car. You know when you get tired of rock 'n' roll and you need to find something. So I often like finding music where you don't know what the hell is going on or what's gonna happen next. That's a great feeling, because you feel like you're being educated somehow, or you're learning something, or something new is coming in. But I ain't no expert, and [on the BBC] I just thought I might as well make hay while the sun shone. Because I've got a free hand, and that's kind of rare in the modern world, to be on the radio broadcasting and have a free hand to play the music that you want and that you like. I'm determined to make the most of it.

What, then, would you program off your new album if you were on the BBC tonight?

I might play "At The Border Guy"! [*laughs*] That would be weird. Or I could always play all of "Minstrel Boy" and go and have a sandwich.

Like the old underground deejays would put on a whole side of the Grateful Dead and go outside to smoke a funny looking cigarette…

[*laughing*] Brilliant!

Doug Deacy, England

I never got in to Eric's until late 77. First band was The Pirates. Also saw Iggy Pop, The Adverts, Ultravox, Steel Pulse, The Skids, Adam And The Ants, Magazine, Robert Gordon w/ Link Wray, Pere Ubu, Rockin Doopsie And The Cajun Twisters, The Selecter, Secret Affair. Some I went to see cancelled. When bands got to big to play Eric's they played Liverpool University. Saw The Buzzcocks with Joy Division supporting, The Undertones, Deaf School, Stiff Little Fingers, The Jam, The Specials, The Damned, Siouxsie And The Banshees with Human League supporting. More I can't recall. Secretary of Students Union allowed me to sit on balcony where road crew were only allowed. I bought my bondage trousers from Pete Burns who had a little shop at the back of Probe Records. I modelled my self on Joe Strummer. Had leather biker jacket I got from Motorbike shop in London Road, old jumper my dad had in sixties and red Airwear I dyed black. Probably best time of my life being a punk as it gave you an identity. I used to go and see rock bands at Liverpool Empire who had punk bands supporting early 77. First headline punk/new wave gig was Stiff Tour with Elvis Costello, Ian Dury and others. First attempt at punk dressing with tie and safety pins and denim studded jacket. Liverpool Echo did an article on Best Ever Punk/New

Wave Gigs In Liverpool. I attended 5 of them. Missed out on seeing The Clash as spent a lot of time in hospital in my teens. They never played Liverpool that much either. There is a Liverpool Eric's site on Facebook and am sure a few will have memories of seeing The Clash there. I also know there is a recording of The Clash playing Eric's on YouTube.

Colin Adkins, England

I was one of the first punks in Morden (see bottom of the Northern Line). I recall having to dodge the Teddy Boys who used to seek to ambush us for wearing their gear (brothel creepers), bootlace tie etc.

There was very little original music out in the early days mainly the American bands and UK groups like Eddie and the Hot Rods. The first real UK punk record released was New Rose by the Damned. Then followed the Pistols and in turn in various order the Clash (White Riot), the Buzzcocks and the Step Forward singles.

I bought the first Clash LP on the day of its release down the King's Road. I wanted the red sticker which you sent off on a coupon to the NME for the Capital Radio EP. From the opening drum beat of Janine Jones to the closing anthem of Garageland was like a shock. It all made sense and fell into place.

I first saw the Clash at the Rainbow supported by the Jam, the Buzzcocks, the Subway Sect and the Prefects.

I recall the Rock Against Racism gig at Victoria Park. Most of the punks from that area hung around on Wimbledon Broadway on a Saturday where there was a record shop called Cloud 7. There was a big black and ethnic minority community many of whom we knew from school. They called us the punx.

All of us arranged to meet at South Wimbledon tube station to go to the gig. Lo and behold many of our black friends attended as well. We are arrived at the assembly at Trafalgar Square and not knowing the protocol of these things jumped into the front. By the time we arrived we were near the back as we had stopped for 'lubrication' on the way. I recall me and one of my black friends Frenchie stopping for a piss break in an East End pub to find it full of NF.

By the time we arrived at the park Patrick Fitzgerald was on stage followed by Black State. When the Clash came on we rushed to the front. At that time many were given to sitting down at gigs. In getting to the front I unfortunately stood on a bunch of hippies' picnic. For me it was a metaphor for the times. A great gig and one of the best live bands ever.

I then decided to follow the Clash around. In all I saw them 32 times. I recall seeing them on Hastings pier supported by Richard Hell and the Voidoids. On that evening the pier remained resolute as another pier on the south coast got blown down!

David Sawicki, United States of America

My "history" with the Clash:
I grew up in the heart of the punk movement, 1978-1984 were my Junior High thru High School years. Punk was not mainstream, and growing up in rural Maine, there were no radio stations bringing us the good news. My friend Greg played The Clash and London Calling for me at his house when I was a young teen. The LP's belonged to his college age brother. The hard edge guitar based rock sound immediately caught my attention. The raw energy and genuinely impassioned vocals came across in their music in a way that was a sharp contrast to the bland 70's rock of the day or the emerging techno new wave music. Jenny Jones and Clampdown were my two favorites at the time. I could not understand how the band that made Train in Vain (the only Clash tune on the radio at the time), had golden treasures like these two rockers that were not on the air.

When I was a young kid learning to play guitar I wanted to one day be in a band like the Beatles. After getting to know the Clash (and Sex Pistols, Damned, Buzzcocks, etc.) I wanted to be in a punk rock band. So, as a senior in high school, I knew I needed a way to get on stage with a band. I approached the band director (as I played trombone and cello) and asked to organize a school wide music talent show to end the school year. They bought it. I formed a band with the friend/drummer who introduced me to those Clash albums, along with a bass player, and "lead" singer (who had never sung in public before). As it was the Reagan Era, we called ourselves "Evil Empire". In true punk fashion, we opened with the Sex Pistols "Bodies" (getting the f-word out there in song one!), moved into Psycho Killer, threw in a punk version of The Brady Bunch theme song (great response!), and closed with I Fought The Law. It is very safe to say, Evil Empire was the very first punk band to ever play Oxford Hills High School! (probably the last too...)

In the Spring of 1984 Joe Strummer brought his Clash to the Portland, ME Expo! I was 18 years old. This was a small field house style brick building, that housed a basketball court with riser type seating. Very small. But the brick walls were great for reverberating the raucous sound. Strummer came out on stage sporting a bright orange mohawk. Seeing the band live (despite the absence of

Mick) was a musical religious experience. I had never seen a band play with such energy, with Strummer's jackhammer leg bopping, buzz saw guitars, and locked in bass and drums.

I ended up watching from the floor, stage center, about 20 feet from the edge of the stage. I was surrounded by biker's with "club" insignia, tattoo's, leather coats, beards. The floor was slam dancing all around me and pushing me into these big burly guys who were much older than me. I remember doing everything I could to block the slam dancers from the biker dudes for the entire show. It was as much a physical contest as it was a concert experience. The show ended with a Tommy Gun encore (amazing!). As the crowd dispersed, one of the biker's said "Hey man, thanks for keeping the jerks off of us. You're cool dude. You wanna come outside and have a beer with us?" Shocked, yet relieved, I said "No thank you. I actually have to get home because I have a calculus final exam tomorrow."

My parents were not happy when they found out later, after giving me the OK to see the concert on a "school night", that I had a calculus final the next day. Somehow, and to the surprise of much better students in my class who went on to Ivy League schools, I had the highest test score. I give full credit to the blessings of the Clash!

Dean Platts, England

I remember seeing the Clash In Sheffield at what is now the Lyceum Theatre when it was a rock venue. I was 15 at the time, I am now 52.

It was my first ever major gig. The band and atmosphere was fantastic. There was a man wearing a suit and tie waving me my friend and I. The next day we found out it was our English teacher. Still listen to all the albums to this day. A very happy time

Randal Doane, United States of America

Author: "Stealing All Transmissions - A Secret History Of The Clash"

In 1982, I was 13 years old, living in Stockton, California, which was, population-wise, among the largest dozen cities in the state. Culture-wise, it was agricultural through and through. At the local high school, on game days for the school's American football team, the cheerleaders wore their uniforms of pleated skirts and matching sweaters. Muscle cars were the objects of choice of young men who parted their hair down the middle and feathered it back across their ears. Led Zeppelin and Van Halen dominated the after-market speakers of their Chevy Camaros and El Caminos. Local radio was an abomination.

That summer, I toured Europe with the Boy Scouts of America, and we stayed in Coventry for nearly three weeks. My host family had two boys, including Paul, who was 17, and Paul made me my first mix tape. The hissy TDK C-90 included songs by dozens of bands I had never heard before: The Specials, Captain Sensible, Madness, The Bodysnatchers, The Selecter, Echo and the Bunnymen, and The Clash. Side A opened with "London Calling." That bass-guitar slide of the opening riff told me that life could be otherwise, and I wore the iron oxide of that tape's first three-and-a-half minutes brittle and thin. Soon thereafter, I quit the Boy Scouts, parted my hair on the side, and fashioned a second-hand wardrobe that would have made The Specials' Terry Hall proud. I picked up London Calling at my local Tower Records—the best album, and the best-priced album, ever—and 30 years later, as a modest thank you to Strummer-Jones-Simonon-and-Headon, wrote a book about them.

Brian Young, Northern Ireland

I started the very first punk band here in Belfast (Rudi) and met the Clash for the first time when they tried to play here in October 77. met them all next morning in the Europa (the swankiest flashiest hotel in Belfast – but in clash propaganda double speak 'the most bombed in Europe' oh c'mon!!!) . Earlier they'd gone out to get those corny barbed wire and barricade pics which even Mick Jones admitted were totally embarrassing. (I have a lot of time for Mick Jones still..)

Our paths crossed several times after along the way but I wasn't at any of the gigs listed. best gig I saw them was in Dec 77 when they did return to play in Belfast on a rickety stage and I managed to get onstage to singalonga White Riot at the end..

One of my best mates stayed with Joe in the Europa that night in Oct 77 and when he moved to London was always on Joe's guest list. In 78 we moved to London and were promised support on the clash's upcoming irish tour by Bernie Rhodes..but the band sacked him and the support fell through. The Clash remain my fave UK punk band despite the moronic sloganeering and cliched tripe Bernie made them spout simply as they were the best songwriters and live performers – and much of that is down to Mick Jones – not Joe Strummer. (Thunders Heartbreakers were simply **the** best punk band worldwide full stop..) I'm not slagging Joe as he was an intense, captivating front man and a really genuine guy – but I saw the Clash live without Mick and they were abysmal. Joe had a silly mohawk and the band were like a bad showband. The Mescaleros were even worse. In contrast Mick's BAD were very good live – but the best post Clash combo was Paul's Havana 3am who were brilliant.

the Clash's first album is still my favourite – and their best songs are Complete Control and White Man. The carefully constructed mythology has gone into overdrive ever since Joe died...and it's like he's been sanctified now – which surely is everything punk was supposed to be against. But then, in hindsight, punk ..at least major label punk with all that entails doesn't really stand up...

The Clash just wanted to be the new Rolling Stones....I'm not criticising them for that as it was obvious from day one...but there's no excuse for releasing self indulgent rubbish like Sandanista. london calling is pretty great – but kinda over rated. Combat rock is iffy and the last album isn't the Clash. Rope is much maligned but not as bad as people thought at the time..the material just isn't as good as the debut and they kept their best songs for 45s.

The best thing the Clash did in their latter years was NOT reforming. I believe it was down to Paul and more power to him. he was always the most stylish member of the band and their secret weapon. he also had the best look and the least baggage....

As for punk..i'm kinda fed up with all this phoney punk nostalgia....and spurious claims that punk basically saved the western world..absolute tripe! Most of the punk nostalgia bears no relation to what it was actually like to be a punk from 76 –81/82 (then it really hit rock bottom) Same old cliche after cliche (example all punks supposedly liked reggae..no they didn't!..most were ex glam rockers! And no one ever mentions that most rastas hated and distrusted punks... mind you 90% of the UK punk bands were old timers who lied about their age and who had a quick haircut and jumped on the bandwagon simply to further their failed musical careers...they all religiously spouted the same old punk PC slogans and cliches in public but in private behaved like the BOF's they supposedly detested...believe it! For sure it was very different over here in Belfast...but then we had the hard rock bandwagoneers too...SLF for one..laughed all the way to the bank too...go figger!)

And judging by the mag covers and acres of cut n paste books the Clash are the new pink floyd (punk floyd?)..again NOT what they – or punk – was supposed to be about?

 But,paradoxically, back in the day, despite their many faults the Clash were undoubtedly the most exciting, intelligent and inspiring of the UK punk bands. And they made some of the best records ever in my book...tho again punk was musically VERY conservative...basically glam rock mixed with old 50srock n roll riffs and poses...(which i like!) Still,it's a pity they ended up selling levi jeans and supporting dinosaurs like the Who......

this probably ain't not what you're after...but I'm sick and tired of the same old whitewashing and revision of history by flabby middle aged ex punk rockers...yaaaawn!

Feel free to use any/all of the stuff I sent ya. It probably won't get me on the Christmas card lists of any of the diehards/true believers..but there ya go!

Just to clairfy for ya..my mate Wee Gordy Owens was the guy who stayed with Joe in the Europa...he's the guy Johnny Green mentions in his book ringing the Clash up from Belfast night after night in rehearsal rehearsals – tho Johnny said he came from the (nationalist) Falls Road which was wrong as Gordy was from (loyalist) Sandy Row..! I met Gordy originally as his stepdad used to work on building sites with Ronnie (from Rudi) and he mentioned that Gordy loved the same sort of music we did. Gordy never went to school and he and I used to just hang round town all day, checking out the various record shops etc. He used to haunt this phone box in Sandy Row and ring up the likes of Tony Parsons and get the phone numbers off him for the likes of Joan Jett in LA...then he'd ring them....If we ever went to a house party he'd make straight for the phone and sit there all night ringing round his contact list! (gawdhelp whoever got the phone bill!)..then he'd nick whatever records were lying around before we went home..lol!

His all time fave was Iggy (he had a homemade 'Iggy' tat on his hand) and The Clash!...tho I think the Clash overtook Iggy in his affections after he met Iggy one time and showed him his tat and Iggy didn't look too impressed!.. When Terri Hooley opened his shop in mid 77 it was a couple of hundred yards from where Gordy lived so we hung out there..and it was Gordy who dragged Terri down to see Rudi play in Jan 78 as (er?) immortalised (as the character 'Fangs') in the Good Vibrations film etc . Gordy (like most Belfast punks) moved to london for a while in the late 70s/early 80s and hooked up with the Clash again..Joe always stuck him on the guest list and we're both still good mates all these years later. He still rings up out of the blue and first question is always 'got any new Clash stuff?'.....

We (Rudi) moved to london in August 78 and lived in the back of transit van for a couple of weeks – pulling up at various public toilets and other places (like rehearsal rehearsals) to get washed/perform our ablutions etc...we ended up squatting in Clapham with a load of other punks from both northern and southern Ireland and had an absolute ball. Gavin Martin (from Alternative Ulster zine was over with us on his schoolholidays sort of 'trying out' for the NME.. He brought us down with him to the Carnaby

St offices to meet Tony Parsons. Through Wee Gordy he knew some of us loved the Clash and took great delight in showing us all those pics of Mick with hair down to his arse..lol!..(common knowledge now – but kept a closely guarded secret back then!) How we laffed! Then he got Gavin to do an article on us. The photo shows a band who look as if they'd just clambered out of the back of a transit van in which they lived...oh dear! We'ed met Micky Foote and the other Clash folks at rehearsal rehearsals and we got to meet Bernie and later Malcolm Mclaren by simply going up to them and asking if they could help us out... Both seemed kinda underwhelming as we were already used to the full on bravado and bluster of the mighty Terri Hooley (a full on force of nature) but Bernie promised us rehearsal space once the Black Arabs had finished doing stuff for the Swindle film and also support on the Clash's upcoming Irish tour... Topper and Johnny Green were always hanging out at the Music Machine which we were at almost every night (they had books of free tickets most nights or if it was a big band to avoid paying in our great buddies in the Raped had showed us how to climb in over the back roof and down through the upper balcony...just watch out for the bouncers!). Anyways we told everyone we'd got the tour ..and then Bernie got sacked and the tour went ahead without us...oh well!.... (Mclaren also promised us rehearsal space..but he was caught up n the film at the time and that fell through too..). Another Alternative Ulster alumni Dave mcCullough was also over in London then and had started writing for Sounds . His best buddy at the mag was Gary Bushell and they both adored the Clash. I've no Dave/Clash stories..tho he did get me and Liz (my wife who was over in the van with me) into lots of gigs free..best of all being Thunders Lyceum bash and better still the after party where we got to meet Johnny for the first time and saw the London punk elite make utter fools of themselves thanks to a free bar....

We had a ball in London – before falling foul of the SPG and having to come home or else two of the band were doing 6 months in jail (another story for another time)... Phew! Ok that's got very little to do with the Clash I know – but it kinda sets some of what I wrote in context...rememebr too that i was 18 when we went to live in London...many of the UK punk bands were like old men to us! lol! As the main guitar player and joint songwriter in Rudi the whole way through I do gotta say that Mick Jones was a huge influence – not that I ever tried to copy him (that woulda been utterly pointless..) but in that he always wrote guitar parts that ultimately served and improved the actual song...and the songs themselves were stunning. In contrast many of the other punk guitarists tended to stick with that traditional rawk/sub pistols wall of guitar soup and old fashioned guitar histrionics...Mick was waaaay beyond that ...... I'm always sceptical when the BBC decide they want to do a retrospective on some one or something – cos they so often get it completely arse about face. I'm fed up with programmes telling me punk happened like this....as if there was one 'correct' history and everyone has to fit into it. And its always London, Mclaren, Don Letts etc...yawn...

I was probably a bit blunt in some of my comments too...I'll fess up..i'd not have bothered even replying if it wasn't a band whose music I loved and who I kinda idolised albeit briefly lol! But my opinion of the Clash has been diluted by the flood of self serving arse licking books and retrospectives that have poured out ever since poor Joe died tragically young... I guess I kinda over react when I see the same old tosh tarted up and knocked out for the fast buck. And I do gotta admit the Clash lost me musically with most of sandanista and we'll have to agree to disagree on the post Jones Clash. I saw them only once but they were embarrassingly bad. like benny hill punk panto. Only Simonon retained any kool lol! I saw an early line up of the mescaleros (i think) and it was basically Joe with some younger session men who stared all night at their fx pedals and looked as if they'd rather be watching TV at home. Most of the crowd that night had never seen the Clash but weren' t remotely interested in Joe's current/new songs and kept yelling for old Clash songs..and again that band really couldn't play then a tenth as well as the 'proper' line up... I was bitterly disappointed…

Still, even today for me the Clash's stuff stands up a lot better than 99% of the other punk bands from back then..frankly I have trouble listening to a lot of the old punk records now..tho there were dozens of great 45s but very few killer albums...unlike glam rock which was my first love and I think still stands up much better than punk. Electric Warrior or Crossing the Red Sea with the Adverts? Ziggy Stardust or the Suburban Studs album..ditto! No contest! But each to their own.

It's more the rewriting of history by self appointed punk experts (who invariably weren't at half the gigs they claim to have been at!) now that galls me...not the Clashs fault by any means – but sadly people tend to use them in particular as a backdrop on which to project their personal theories and diatribes on todays gullible sheeple.

What irritated me about the Clash too was that they made so many promises in public and followed through on so few... in contrast, to pick but one, Paul Weller put his money where his mouth was - funding record labels and publishing books out of his own pocket...Rudi were the first band on Jamming! and the Jam folks couldn't do enough for us..when we toured with them we got paid, got soundchecks, and had the full support and backing of their entire organisation.

Anyways I'll wrap this up as I'm rambling...again none of this is an attack on you or what you believe...just a bit of good honest debate about a subject that still energises me...(to my surprise actually) The fact that I could take the time to type this i guess shows that deep down the Clash still have a very special place in my heart... and i certainly can't blame them alone for punk becoming the lumpen toothless parody it became in the early 80s..(and remains today..?)

Ewan Butler, England

I was 7 years old when I bought my first Clash record "White Riot". My brother, a teenager at the time, introduced me to punk and the great bands of the time but the Clash were the ones that always stood out head and shoulders above for me. I was instantly a convert and I followed them religiously until their breakup. At 10 I saw them play at King George's Hall in Blackburn, they blew me away. I waited with many fans after the gig and got my photo taken with them and my Armagideon Times booklet signed by the band. I saw them again several times at Brixton academy as my brother later moved to London (my brother actually saw them at the Victoria Park RAR gig with the local ANL contingent from Blackburn).

When I left school I formed a band called Bradford, who were heavily influenced by the Clash. We went on to support Joe Strummer on the Rock Against the Rich tour and got to hang out with him back stage. Jammed clash songs and chatted. He was such a warm and beautiful human being. He watched us play and complemented the band. Encouraged us to record an album which we later did entitled "Shouting Quietly".

I later moved to London and met Strummer one last time at the George Robey in Finsbury Park in November 1995. It was a all-nighter my friend used to promote called "the Farside"; underground techno music. He turned up with a small entourage of very cool looking rude boy types, his wife Lucinda and some members of a band he had put together at the time he said were called Radar. I had the nerve to say hello and having supported him had an "in" to chat. We chatted all night in the beer garden, he was so genuine and happy to chat. I was devastated when he died; I felt a huge part of the person I am had gone. I grew up the son of a working class socialist so the Clash spoke directly to the politics I had come to accept from childhood. Strummer's knowledge of history and culture introduced me to the Spanish civil war, Allende's Chile. I have since visited the grave of Vitor Jara in Santiago whist travelling in South America - would I have done that without the Clash...?hmm.

Zäta Zettergren, Sweden

My meeting with the Clash was on August 4, 1979. I was less than two weeks from turning 17 and had travelled from Sweden to Finland to see the Clash playing the Ruisrock festival in Turkku. The band were in the midst of recording the London Calling album and this was the only concert they played during this period.

Before the concert, the crowd tore down a fence and thereby managed to get very close to the stage. And could actually walk under it, which some of us did and met up with the Clash backstage. They didn't mind, they all greeted us and took time talking to us.

Of course they played a great gig, with "London Calling" and "Four Horsemen" included in a strong set that started with "Clash City Rockers" and ended with "White Riot" as the third and final song of the encore.

After the concert, a lot of us Swedish punks found our way to Hotel Ruissalo where all the bands from the festival stayed. We managed go get in, much to the annoyance of the hotel manager and guards, and were invited by The Clash + crew to party with them. We occupied the bar where I conducted an interview (well, sort of) with Paul Simonon, for my fanzine "Innocent" (edition: 25). I also had the band members write greetings to my readers. Mick, Paul and Topper kept it short, Joe asked me "is it for the punks?" and aafter I answered "yes" he spent quite some time writing something more serious.

After spending time in the bar, the band decided to go downstairs where there was a discoteque. All Swedes joined them but for some reason I wasn't allowed to go downstairs according to that hotel guard. Maybe it was my green hair. Anyway, I stood there by the stairs hoping for a chance to sneak in, or for something to happen so that I didn't have to be alone in the hotel lobby. Next thing that happened was that two Fins came up to me and started harrassing me. One of them pinched my earlobe and as he snatched my earring there was blood and pain. At that point some hippie type of guy turned up and asked, in English, what was going on. One of the Fins answered "we're gonna beat the shit out of him". The hippie guy said, in a serious voice "well, you can try". As it turned out, he was part of the Clash crew and the two Fins buggered off as he made it clear he would take them both if they didn't.

Not so much later I saw rapid movement downstairs. First, I didn't notice what happened. Then I saw one my Swedish friends running in the corridor. Immediately I ran down to find out what was going on. It seemed there was some kind of commotion in the bog so I went in there and found ¾ of The Clash, plus manager and a Swedish guy I knew a little bit. And two other angry Fins. Big guys. They were quite loud and aggressive and Joe was trying to calm them down. Topper and Mick + manager behind him. Me and the other Swedish guy at the other end of the room. The Fins wouldn't calm down and suddenly one of them took a hold of me, lifted me up and threw me across the room so that I crash landed on The Clash. Luckily Joe kept his cool and finally managed to get the Finnish guys to explain what had happened. He pointed first at Topper and then to his forehead. And said "he kicked me in the … what do you call this?". Again, he pointed to his forehead and to be more precise he pointed to a small cut with some blood coming out of it. Joe answered "A cut" and the Fin continued "Yes, he kicked me in the cut!". Joe looked at the guy in disbelief. The Fin was like two meters tall while Topper was quite short. Joe expressed his disbelief and as a reaction, the guy leaned down, caught Toppers leg and lifted it up hastily so that Topper fell over into the urinal. Then both Fins got more aggressive again but luckily the hotel manager and a guard came in and put a stop to the situation. The Clash took the lead out of there and told us to follow. On our way we picked up the other Swedish punks and escaped to Topper's hotel room. There, he told us how it all began:

As Topper walked into the toilet room he suddenly felt someone grabbing his ankle. He turned around and saw that big guy lying on the floor, with a firm grip around Topper's boot. Topper tried to get free but the guy wouldn't let go. Finally Topper got pissed off and kicked backwards. As he had a spur on his boot that's why the Fin got the cut. As Topper gave us his story the news had spread and Graham Parker and Bram Tchaikovsky came to Topper's room to hear about it all. Both had been on the same festival bill.

As we were talking the hotel manager turned up and told us the Fins were still around and gathering reinforcement. This lead to Joe getting very active, running out of the room and returning with a toolbox in hand. He opened it and made sure there was a hammer and other heavy tools for us to use as defence weapons should the Fins attack. Then the band made sure all of us Swedes had somewhere to stay. Me and a couple of more guys stayed at Topper's room, I don't know about the rest. We were at least 10-15 Swedish punks there and the band was amused by being in Finland and only meeting Swedish people.

When we woke up the next day Joe and the others made sure we all got breakfast and were safe and sound. After that we returned to Sweden by boat, all aware we had had one of the best adventures of our lives.

JUST MAKE SURE YOU
ARE NOT NARROW
MINDED, SOUL HAS
NO SHAPE, FORM OR
COLOUR. SOUL IS
SO DON'T GO SEERING
AT WHAT YOU
CANNOT UNDERSTAND
OR ELSE WE MAKE
The MISTAKE WHICH
WE LAUGHED AT
WHEN THE STRAIGHT
WORLD MADE IT.

Photo 2

To Innocent
remain
So.
Mick

Photo 3

Photo 4

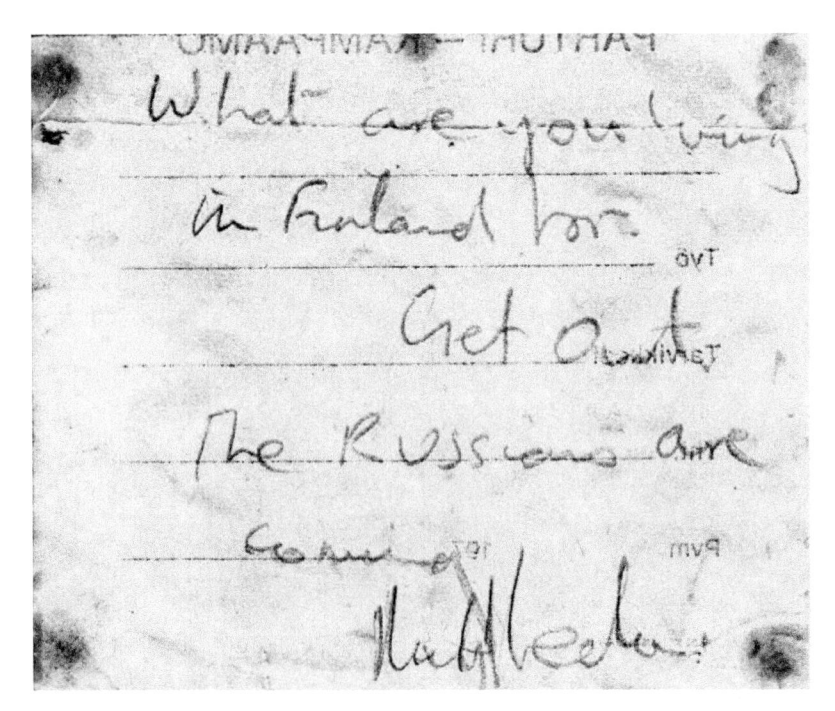

Photo 5

Stefan Tews, Germany

My english is only school english, but i think you understand it.
1977 - i was 12, hearing gary glitter, suzi quatro, what the older boys in my school heard.

1978 - my older cousine came early this year back from london and was out of order! he told me he saw the damned and it changed his life (for only one year...) but, he gave me the first clash single and the roxy live album. i was now 13 years old...the artwork from the roxy album...i saw the pictures and my blood began to pump...i knew, this was something that changes my live! than i heard the album...this beginning with all the voices and the breaking glass...and then...hello, we're slaughter and the dogs...and it blows me away...'til today! then the clash...again this artwork...terrorists (remembers me to the german RAF)...the music...white riot/1977...i don't understood every word, but there was a feeling of: i found someone who told me what was going on and...oh man...some new friends!!! they changed my life - 'til today!!!
there were other punk records that gave me a special feeling, a political understanding,a kick in the mind for another understanding...i never saw the clash live...the whole punk movement inspired me a lot, i worked with

some friends on a fanzine, played drums in a chaotic band, went to demonstrations...

the day joe strummer died was for me...one of my friends died...one of the "last gang in town" was dead!!!

today i'm 54, happy married, got a job, a dog, support two animal organisation, live vegan.i love my clash records, especially the boots, and my whole punk records. they are not every day on my turntable (save the vinyl!), today i listen to a lot of music...but, when I kick the old turntable...and he goes round and round...and i hear those voices and the breaking glass i know: what a wonderful life!!!

ok, those are my emotions to punk in germany from england!

Photo 6

Mat Berry, England

I grew up in Oxford and was 10 when The Clash released their first album. Suffice to say it didn't reach my ears.

At that time, punk was viewed in the same way as pornography – it was dirty, it was not to be spoken about, and it was to be kept away from children.

I remember visiting a record store in early 1978, age 11, with a school friend of mine whose musical knowledge already surpassed the rest of us; this was Laurence Bell – later to become founder and supremo at Domino Records. My aim was to buy one of the latest pop hits being peddled by the radio (I forget what) and I really had to think hard when Laurence advised me that this was on EMI, the same record label as Sex Pistols – I had no idea what a record label was, but the connection with the Pistols was enough to make me think I might get in trouble. I didn't make the purchase.

Back then, radio meant Radio 1 and the only music on TV was Thursday's Top Of The Pops; The Clash's music featured rarely on the former and never on the latter. John Peel would, of course, provide an opportunity to hear punk, but the AM radio signal after 10pm was absolutely shocking, and listening to the radio post 10pm was not really something done by pre-teens.

I seem to remember the first record I heard by The Clash was Tommy Gun – I was now 12. At the time I don't recall it changing my world; it was an incredibly exciting time for music – Top Of The Pops in the week Tommy Gun came out featured The Rezillos, Buzzcocks & Blondie – but the fact that I can remember hearing it means it clearly made an impression.

It all changed in 1979 when The Cost Of Living EP was released. In the same way (and the same year) that Sex Pistols had got regular radio play with the post-Rotten releases of their Eddie Cochran covers (Something Else & C'mon Everybody), The Clash were suddenly on daytime radio with I Fought The Law, a cover version, presumably being considered "safe" enough to play. The power and energy of the performance (not to mention the title itself) just grabbed my attention… and didn't let go – this was the first Clash record that I bought. I was still just 12.

I played the record incessantly – not just I Fought The Law, but the whole EP; these were great songs with often quotable, and often indecipherable lyrics – it introduced me to the idea that you didn't have to be able to hear and understand all the words of a song in order to like it, it was about how it made you feel.

Later that year London Calling was released and it felt like The Clash were everywhere. I remember spending most of the school Christmas holidays loitering around the records and magazines in WHSmith in Oxford where there was a huge display of that iconic album artwork, and where they would regularly (constantly?) play an entire side of the LP – I didn't have the money to buy the record, but I grew increasingly familiar with all the songs.

The Clash were far from universally popular among my peers; now, everyone who grew up at that time seems to like The Clash or at least has a favourite Clash song. I don't begrudge them that – there are plenty of bands from that time who I actively shunned then, but now love; instead it makes me proud, vindicated even, that a band I regard as "mine" has now gained this sort of appeal.
But then occasionally I'll be fortunate enough to meet someone who "gets it", someone for whom The Clash mean so such: the music, the politics, the attitude, the fashion, but always most importantly the music. They may have been around during the band's heyday, they may not; they may have seen The Clash live, they may not – that's not what is important. What matters is that, like me, they have found a band whose music in its depth & variety can stir, challenge, uplift, educate and sometimes simply entertain. I've been lucky enough to meet a few such people, and many years of friendship have followed from this initial common bond.

The Clash never played in Oxford.

Luca Lanini, Italy

I run into The Clash by chance when I was a 13 years old boy. I was visiting some relatives in Bologna and a friend of a friend told me there was a free concert in the main square (Piazza Maggiore). The band was a menacing band from London, UK, they were called The Clash. I was quite frightened, I've never attended a rock concert, actually I was never exposed to r'n'r music, let alone punk rock. It was 1st of June 1980. Italy was a quite depressing, awful place in late 70's early 80's: recession, terrorism (2 months later a bomb exploded in Bologna central station and killed more than 80 people) but there was a very creative and radical "Movement". Bologna was the epicenter of it all. 100.000 people gathered at the free concert, we (i was the youngest of the lot) were there very early and befriended a group of roman fans that called themselves Centocelle City Rockers (Centocelle is a working class neighborhood in Rome), part punk rockers, part mobsters. They roughened up some anarcho-punks who were there to contest the Clash ("we're The Crass, not The Clash"). The Clash played the first part of the set with the support band drummer because Topper went AWOL. When he arrived they start all over again. I was mesmerized. It was the light on the road to Damascus. Two songs in and I was a believer. I had never ever experienced that intensity, that ferocity, that commitment to a cause: I saw my entire future life pass me behind my life: long line to get in a stadium or a hall for a concert, record hunting all over the world, crazy sum of money burnt to buy a rare 45 of an obscure garage band...

I missed the Impossible Mission Tour 1981 (their finest hour IMHO), but I caught them in the Out of Control Tour (1984). A lot of things have changed: Mick and Topper were thrown out, some Carnaby street punks (sorry guys, it wasn't your fault) were in. I was a seventeen old guy turned in a rabid r'n'r fanatic running a fanzine. Two dates in Milan were booked. The first one was pretty miserable. The new guys wasn't gelling and the performance was subpar. The second one was pretty good but you couldn't avoid the feeling that something was wrong. We gathered at the hotel to "talk" with the band in the morning. No one showed up until 1 p.m. when a bored Joe strummer shaked some hands. We handled the fanzine ("Messy Band") to him and he asked to scribble our phone numbers on the back of it. Quite a let down.

September 1984, just back in town after summer holidays. My heart jumped: giant posters all over town, The Clash will play in Cava de' Tirreni (a little town between Naples and Salerno) the 6th of September (oh, those pre-internet days). There's a rumor mounting: Joe Strummer is already in town, alone, running around with some mobster guys in vespas... Never Mind, I said, that's bs... Afternoon, my junior brother knocked at my room: "there's someone at the phone asking for you. In english". I picked up the phone: "Hi, Luca. It's Joe Strummer of The Clash speaking. I am at The National Archaeological Museum but they won't let me in. Can you talk with those guys? I just want to see the mosaic of the battle of Issos". It turned out that Joe wanted to enter the Museum sporting a blonde mohican haircut, a lion tamer jacket and his stage combat attire. The janitors thought he was a lunatic and stopped him at the gate. I secured him the entrance ("Look guys, he's an international artist, a superstar, he won't harm anything"). The concert was their last hurrah: the band in its final days, but they went on with the force of desperation and bring the house (a stadium, really) down. After The Clash mk. 2 disbanded I met Joe a couple of times. The last one he hugged me and said: "Thank you for coming. I've never thought so many people would have remember me". I miss him so much. I met Topper in Naples with his ill fated band in 1986. The signs of addiction were quite evident: he barely spoke with me and never put off his sunglasses. I saw Mick with the BAD, supporting U2 in 1987. Me and my friends all thought that it was sad: it should be the contrary.

Have The Clash influenced my life? You bet! They open up to me an entire world: jamaican music, bank-robbers,

Martin Scorsese, hip-hop, cool dresses, sandinistas (never heard of them before). What else could a poor boy do?

Joe Ree, England

The Clash, focusing mainly on how the band changed my life. First and foremost, I wasn't around at the time and having been born in 1999 (I'm only 18) you could say I'm a bit of a late starter to the Punk movement, however my passion for the band knows no bounds.

The Clash changed my life in so many ways. It all started primarily when I discovered a clip of Joe Strummer playing with his later band, The Mescaleros, at Glastonbury in 1999, on an old VHS tape i found. The song was Rock The Casbah. I was 14 at the time, and having heard the song before years ago on a rerun of The Simpsons, (oh the little things in life) it kick started a revolutionary path in life for me. Within a few days I was listening to the studio version by The Clash and it was the only song I would ever listen to for a solid month. Eventually with encouragement from my dad I took it upon myself to invest in more of their music and bit by bit I listened to practically every official release they had done. (Give 'Em Enough Rope quickly became my favourite album by them and it remains so to this day) I read up on countless magazines and books and it's safe to say I have an almost encyclopaedic knowledge of the band now (I could name all their UK single releases, the dates they came out, and where they ended up in the charts for good measure!)

I of course watched several clips of footage and within 9 months of getting into them, I started to learn guitar. Rhythm guitar. It was Joe Strummer that had done it, and the man is one of the most important people in my life and I never even knew him. I was simply transfixed by his style, the way he dressed, the way he aggressively tore at his guitar with all the violence and ferocity of an atomic bomb about to implode, and that's just one member!

Reading up on interviews, it was amazing. I just couldn't believe how much my ideals on politics and work and society in general seemed to correlate with mine and the fact their music is still as incendiary now, over 40 years on, and relevant too I might add, just goes to show how incredible a force they were. They made me feel so much more confident at school and it's always nice having an in-depth conversation about The Clash with your history teacher!

The influence of their music on me knows no bounds. I have played guitar and sung vocals in tandem with over 225 CD bootlegs of taped gigs from over the years, ranging between their lifespan as a band from 1976-1985 and it made me all the more better at singing and playing, with my goal still to get in a band someday and be even a shred as influential as Joe Strummer and The Clash were.

As a young Clash fan it saddens me that I'll never see them live,(the footage of the climax of Complete Control from the Music Machine in Rude Boy gives me chills whenever I watch it, it's THAT powerful) but it's something I (and countless other fans my age) will have to deal with, but I still cling on to the hope of meeting Mick, Paul or Topper someday! The influence they had though, they practically shaped my career path for me. I am currently studying Music Technology at college in order to get more intelligent on the whole aspect of recording and producing music and I even laid down vocals for a couple workmates on a mix of I'm So Bored With The USA, something I was very, very proud of. I even played London Calling at my end of year Summer Concert in my last year of high school in 2016 and it was simply amazing. All because of The Clash.

I don't think this planet will ever see a more important, innovative, talented or simply musical band again, they literally mean everything to me and from the second I first heard Rock The Casbah and properly started getting invested in The Clash over 4 years ago, I haven't looked back. Such a crucial, crucial band and I hope wherever

Joe Strummer is or any of the surviving members know just how important they are actually regarded, because I and many other young fans are existing proof that their music is still as inspirational and encapsulating to kids in 2018 as it was back in 1977, it really is.

I know this is probably aimed more at people who were actually around at the time but I just couldn't pass up a potential opportunity to give some insight on how much I love this band (easily my favourite band of all time, no one comes close really) and it would mean the world to me to have some people hear how much I, individually, like the band that is such a crucial part of my existence on an actual radio series dedicated to The Clash, it really would mean the world to me.

I hope you read this with some interest as I'm excited to be writing this email and can't wait for the upcoming radio series.

Carl Schumann, United States of America

Hello, my name is Carl Schumann, and I saw The Clash [The only Group That Matters] three times within the space of a year, from 1981 to 1982. Twice at Bonds in NYC, and again the next year at the Dr. Pepper summer music festival at Pier 84 , also in NYC.

The concert at Bonds was the greatest live concert I ever attended.

I don't say this lightly.I grew up going to classic rock concerts in New York City. When I was 15 years old I began going to the famous Fillmore East seeing The Faces {twice},Jethro Tull,Ten Years After, The Allman Brothers[twice, including the one of the nights they recorded their fantastic concert 'At the Fillmore"]Johnny Winter, Delaney and Bonnie, BB King, Albert King, and Frank Zappa.

I have seen The Rolling Stones 12 times including their seminal concert at MSG in 1969[which I would considered the second greatest concert I ever witnessed.Saw them in 1972, 1975,1981, etc...I saw David Bowie at his first New York concert in 1972 at Carnegie Hall, and then a few months later, at Radio City Music Hall. All in all saw Bowie about ten times. I saw George Harrison and Friends at The Concert for Bangladesh at MSG in 1971. I have seen Roxy Music, four times. I saw Led Zeppelin at Carnegie Hall in 1969. Also saw the original Who, twice.I've seen Cream and Eric Clapton solo, five times. I've seen Bob Marley as well as Peter Tosh. I saw Jimi Hendrix twice,but, the best of them all to me, was The Clash at Bonds in the early summer of 1981.

I was working at N W Ayer advertising agency in NYC, when it was announced on the radio that they would begin selling tickets to see The Clash at Bonds that afternoon. My friend and I took a short walk over to Bonds and bought tickets for the May 31 show[I still have the ticket stub somewhere in my house} and the Saturday afternoon 'kiddie shows'. The Saturday afternoon show was only $5.00 !

The day of the concert my wife Joyce and I got there right when the doors opened. Hardly anyone was there. There was a long bar to the left of the stage that began right where the stage itself was situated. This is where we camped for the rest of the evening.

Since there was nobody there yet, we ordered a few drinks and began to speak to the bartenders. They had been there for every concert so far. They told us that the best sound men and lighting people in the business were doing the show. Some for free as they just wanted to be part of The Clash Experience in NYC. They also told as Frank Sinatra had been there as well as Martin Scorsese and Robert di Niro. Jesus, this was going to be some night!

Finally, the lights dim and the four members of The Clash{ along with keyboard player, Mickey Gallagher} came on stage to the strains of Ennio Morricone's score from the spahgetti western's of Clint Eastwood movies, then BAM, right into London Calling.

The crowd leapt as one. We were one pulse.

My wife and I were about ten feet away from the boys, right by Mick Jones and Topper. Fantastic!

These are the elements that made this concert so great to me-Proximity. This was the closest I ever was to a group. You could see the spit flying out of Joe Strummer's mouth throughout the night. I think this was before he had his teeth fixed.

Set List- Great mixture featuring songs from "Give "Em Enough Rope", London Calling and Sandinista, plus a few early surprises.

Great Players- Topper, to be was one of rocks great drummers. Mick, though not a guitar hero on lead had is own distinct sound. Paul was much better on bass then I expected. I had always read that he could barely play, but he layed down a solid bottom. Joe wasn't much of a player. He seemed to scrape and beat the crap out of his rhythm guitar, but what a passionate singer!

And finally the Look-The four of them looked like an ideal group from this time period. Haircuts, boots, you could have starred them in a movie about Rock 'N" Roll.

We saw them again the next year at Pier 84 and they were not as good. Almost a let down. Topper wasn't in the group then, and he was greatly missed. Tory Chimes was more of a "plodder" to my ears. Not as exciting.

Anyway, I am lucky enough to say to my two sons," I saw The Clash, at their best, up close and personal!"

Stuart Green, England

I was 15 when The Clash was released. It was the soundtrack to my life. Career Opportunities mimicked word for word my interview with my school's careers advisor. I loved The Clash. Went backstage when they played Leeds University where Strummer autographed my student bus pass. Started to hitchhike to Derby only to hear to the gig had been cancelled, but I saw them on every tour.
I was at Victoria Park. I had travelled down on a coach from Leeds laid on by RAR/Anti Nazi League. I remember two young black kids sat on top of a gate as made our way into the park, one turning to the other saying, 'wow, look at all them punks'.
Punk burst into my life and has remained an influence. I can wax lyrical on punk, The Clash and the impact it had on my life and politics.

Rick Hind, Scotland

The time was 1977 and I was a disillusioned, angry young kid. I knew nothing about music and then, about the middle of 1977, I heard this album of pure guitar-driven music. This was my introduction to The Clash's first album (thanks to my older brother). I had to find out who they were and where this band were playing. All I could ever find out about them was from the music papers and John Peel playing various tracks of theirs on his late-night show. Months passed and I'd found out lots more about other punk bands, 999, the Lurkers, Stranglers, to name a few. Even the Sex Pistols but to me The Clash spoke to me. They were the band I had to follow.

Bingo, I found them through the NME playing the Glasgow Apollo. I had no idea how I was going to get there but once again, thanks to my older brother who could drive, he fitted seven of us into the car and off we went. From what I can remember, the gig was fantastic with many punks in different home-made attire and this to me was fascinating and I wanted to be part of this scene. Even the bouncers couldn't control the crowd with many fights breaking out between the punks and the bouncers and punks and themselves! This was because the kids in 1977/8 had nothing and now they had punk, more so The Clash. You could never see the Pistols play live, so this is what made The Clash rise above all other punk bands. This made me want to see The Clash even more, so, after getting home very late and missing work the next day it was off to Aberdeen to see The Clash play there. I found out Joe and Paul had been arrested after the gig in Glasgow and waited around the back of the venue after the gig, as I had no way of getting back to Perth from Aberdeen. Luckily I got speaking to the roadies and even met Joe for the first time! They offered me a lift back to Perth as they were travelling to Dunfermline for a gig the next night. I said to them that I would definitely be at the gig but didn't know how I would get there as I couldn't drive. Once again, thanks to my older brother he borrowed the family car and off we went. I vaguely remember Joe and the crew laughing at me when I said I would definitely be there. Joe said he would put me on the Guest List but I didn't believe him until we got to the gig and I chanced it and barged my way to he front of the queue, argued with the bouncer that I was on the Guest List, he laughed but checked and yes, my name was there. This made me want to follow the The Clash even more.

Through time I bought/stole anything punk. Work commitments got in the way as I was an Apprentice but I had to see the band again. Yes, they were playing Edinburgh in November. I jumped the barriers at the train station in Perth as I had very little money, got to Edinburgh and found the gig. I had to pay at the door, bummer! Once again, this gig was guitar-driven mayhem. The punk crowd could not be controlled, there were fights everywhere but was was now my calling....I loved it. I nearly got sacked from work for going to the gig on a Thursday night as I missed my work on the Friday but it was worth it.

I went to many other punk gigs but none compared to The Clash. Unfortunately they never toured in Scotland for ages after that. Very few of the so-called punk stalwarts toured Scotland.

1980 – The Clash announced the "16 Ton Tour". I was now a 4 th year Apprentice and on more money. I bought tickets for one night in Edinburgh, 2 nights in Glasgow and one night in Dundee. This would be their first gig in Scotland. This would be my first gig in my mini tour. I booked holidays in January for 6 days and with travel plans all in place, off we went.

The Caird Hall gig in Dundee was a mix of their punk classics from their first album and the dreaded "Give 'Em Enough Rope" album. I hated that album. The gig was mayhem. The fixed seating had to be removed during the gig as the punks were wrecking everything. We didn't care as we thought we were rebels with a cause but, in hindsight, we were rebels without a brain! I stood looking at Paul Simonon trying to work out what notes he was playing on the bass, as that was my instrument of choice. I had no idea how to play it though! The band had to keep stopping to tell the crowd to stop fighting and wrecking the place. More so for the spitting as Joe and the band were covered in it. It was a disgusting habit carried on from 1977. Paul Simonon spotted me in the crowd and told me to come backstage after the gig when they were going off. I could only think "why me?". Once backstage Paul told me Joe and him recognised me from the Aberdeen gig, way back in 1978! He said they couldn't believe the amount of crap I spoke on the way down from Aberdeen to Perth. They asked what I was doing and I told them I was following them about from gig to gig. This is when my life changed....big style! They put me on the Guest List for every gig of that tour.

I followed them right the way to the end of the Scottish tour. I was not sure what I thought of the gigs as I hated the "Give 'Em Enough Rope" as it wasn't punk enough for me. The last gig at Glasgow Apollo was another night of fighting the bouncers. This seemed to be a recurring theme in my life whenever I went to the Apollo. I went backstage and spoke to them all, saying that I would be at any gigs I could get to, thinking to myself it would be impossible as I had to go to work. I went back to my humdrum life then the last day of January came and I was now a fully fledged mechanic and was told I was on a month's notice. I said bollocks to this and I left.

I went to find The Clash and caught up with them at the Electric Ballroom in London. Good to their word, I was still on the Guest List. In I went, argued my way backstage, met up with them all again and told them my woes that I was now unemployed but who cares. They put me in touch with the company they hired PA and vans from who gave me a job driving a van for them. I did a few gigs with The Clash and had a right old laugh but they were going over to America and Europe and me being the new boy, there was no way I could go so I thought that was it. By this time I had relocated to London living in squats and sofa-hopping. I did a few driving jobs for other bands. I heard nothing from The Clash until about June 1980 and was suddenly told by their management company I think, to make my way to Derby and pick up a tour there and make sure I had a valid passport. Err, what was a passport?! Could have been Johnny Green, who pointed me in the right direction on how to get a passport. What a rigmarole but I got one. Off I went and did the tour. I finished the tour with not a clue as what was happening now. I bummed around London, squatting and not doing much. Popped my head into Rehearsals Rehearsals, The Clash's base in Camden and then Joe asked me if I would be up to going abroad and doing the European tour with them. Me, with no fixed abode said "sure".

We toured through Europe in 1981. The Clash's music

was changing, attitudes within the band were changing and there were a lot of arguments between themselves but they carried on. They never took a break, always rehearsing, recording or playing gigs.

Off we went to America after Europe. Once again they were trying to crack America and were booked to play a seedy dive called Bonds Casino. The gig was so oversold. The Promoters ripping everyone off, even the band, or trying to. The cops threatened to shut Bonds down after the first gig. The band argued with the Promoters about money and about the fans going to miss out but the band held all the cards. They threatened to cancel the atmosphere was so hostile from the promoter, cops and even fans who thought they had been ripped off and wouldn't see the band, but they decided to play and so they did for the next 17 days. Over the days that I saw them, it was a highly mixed guitar driven sound with hints of reggae and ska thrown in. Joe's stagecraft had grown in leaps and bounds and he was now communicating with the fans, telling them not to believe the hype, etc., and that The Clash would be here until all the fans had seen them. Sadly, I didn't manage the whole American tour but this tour opened my eyes to all types of music. I even fell in love with the Sandinista album. I returned to the UK somewhat dismayed thinking that was it, I was going to get the bullet. I heard nothing until about October and told to get my ass up to Glasgow and pick up the tour there, which I duly did and counted my blessings. We toured all over the UK and Europe. The crowds were getting bigger and some gigs were guitar driven pure punk, other gigs were very mellow. They changed their set-list like they would change their socks. The end of that tour was about the end of 1981 but it was a very hazy time in my life due to issues.

The band announced they were going over to Japan at the beginning of 1982 and they didn't know who was going and who was staying...it was all down to money. There was a lot of arguments within the band. They were not gelling together. From what I could gather, it was down to Mick wanting to go in a different direction with the music and Joe wanting to stay true to the fans with the music they had grown up with. Luckily Joe let me go to Japan (God knows why as I'd let them down on the American side!). The venues were getting bigger and bigger and the crowds were becoming more varied, but The Clash juggernaut kept rolling on. The crowds were amazing wearing all the leathers trying to emulate Joe and Paul. To me, it was not an enjoyable tour. We got back to the UK in May and like I said, it was a very hazy time for me again. I decided I was leaving London as I hated it and went back up to Scotland.

I got a call at my parents house in May from Joe about Topper being sacked. I was gutted. The guy was brand new, I liked him and partied with him a few times. I vowed that that was it for me but the call of The Clash was too strong. Off I went on the "Combat Rock" tour. I hated the album, hated the tour and now hated The Clash. I did the whole of the UK right the way up to Inverness and said that I needed a rest as I was burnt out. I had mega issues in my life.

Off they went to do some other parts of the tour, I just wanted to get my life back together. I heard there was a big falling out in the US. I think some of the roadies and management had had enough and left, so Joe called me at my parents house and asked me to go out to America (he paid for the flights God bless him). I can't remember where I picked this tour up in America. They were going through their American 1950's gangster look. Mike Jones was getting into very early sampling of Grand Master Flash stuff but I didn't pay much attention to Mick as we didn't get on. The only good bit of the tour that I can remember was Shea Stadium. The Who were the headliners and I was getting to see them from the side of the stage! This gig was epic! The crowd were worked into a frenzy by Kosmo. The Clash came on and I think the first song was "London Calling". The place went wild. They ran through quite a bit of their back catalogue and new songs. They then finished with "I Fought The Law". This made me laugh as every time they played this song it reminded me of the very first time I saw them in Glasgow and they got arrested. I wonder if they did fight the law then, as the Glasgow Polis took no shit from punks! LOL. I think The Clash at Shea Stadium outshone The Who in my books.

By this time the in-fighting was getting too much. Joe and Mick were hardly speaking, Paul Simonon was jumping between camps and I'm sure Johnny Green was back on the scene. From what I could see and was told by various people in the crew the band were on a downward spiral. I did the tour and called it a day after that. I'd had enough of all the backstabbing and decided that that was it for me.

I saw The Clash a couple of times when they came to Scotland, met up with Joe from time to time as he came to Perth quite a lot and then suddenly in 1983 Mick Jones was sacked. I wasn't too bothered about it and had a few pints with Joe in Perth after the sacking but basically his head was up his own ass. He was going to carry The Clash on with wannabe Mick Joneses. It was a wrong move. He asked me to go out on tour with them but I said no. My days with The Clash had ended but my association with Joe hadn't. I was not shocked or saddened when I heard The Clash had split but in reality they just stopped touring. They never split up, even after getting rid of two of the founding members. Joe got in touch with me in 1988 as he had been press-ganged into doing the "Rock Against The Rich" tour but it wasn't the same for me. The crowd loved it though. Punks seemed to crawl out from the woodwork just to see Joe. Zander and Joe fitted like a glove playing guitars together. The whole tour made a lot of money for who?....I don't know. I don't even think Joe knew who made the money. It brought back lots of good and bad memories. I had responsibilities now, I had grown up. My days in the music industry were finished.

I was sitting in my Internet Cafe in Perth when my eldest brother phoned me. It was the saddest day of my life. The 22nd December 2002 was the day that I lost a good friend. I hung up the phone and wept. Joe had died.
I had met up with him sporadically since 1988 but now I'd never ever meet him again. Later in my life I nearly did meet up with him again but the Crash Team in the Perth Hospital brought me back. I still miss the guy. Love playing his music, even fallen in love with "Give 'Em Enough Rope" album. I can stomach "Combat Rock". Love "London Calling" and "Sandinista". These four guys changed my life. I was a young, angry youth. They taught me how to love

other cultures and not to judge everyone. The saddest thing is The Clash lost their values once the money came rolling in. After The Clash stopped touring they found themselves again but it would never be the same if they ever reformed and I'm glad to say, God rest Joe's soul, they will never reform.

The Clash didn't know what they had. They took disillusioned kids and adults to a place where no other band could have taken them. Between 1977 and 1979, if Joe Strummer or any member of The Clash said "let's riot", they would have had a serious amount of people behind them to take on anything. But that wasn't The Clash ethos.

Eugene Butcher, England
Editor: VIVE LE ROCK

I have a fairly good Clash story. I was living in Christchurch New Zealand and the Clash announced a one off show in NZ's biggest city-Auckland. We thought this was not on-so 2 of our student friends got a petition together for the Clash to play Christchurch-and they listened! They played a sold out show in Christchurch to 2500 fans. This is where it gets interesting.My punk band Desperate Measures were picked to play at the after show gig for the Clash. However the club was run by a psychotic former bouncer who didn't like us punks. Every band played, including the world famous indie band the Bats. We were last and set our gear up on stage. Then the bouncer said-"Ive decided I am not going to let you play" and actually hit one of our fans with nunchukkas. It was pretty heavy and violent. So, reluctantly we took our equipment off stage, and carried it down the almost vertical, dangerous staircase.We were dejectably loading our gear into our car when a van pulled up behind us. It was the Clash!!! I went up to Joe Strummer- "Hey Joe-this guy won't let us play!" "Hang on boys, I'll see what I can do" Joe said, and within 5 minutes we were on stage playing to the Clash-our heroes!!!! Afterwards we had a good chat with the band and they were very cool and supportive. Needless to say it was a dream come true-and possibly the most rock n roll experience of my long and varied life!I met Joe twice later on and he said he remembered, although I am not sure he did. He was genuine and down to earth.

Howard Young, Scotland

Music has always been important to me. I can't envisage a day without it. Growing up I was influenced by my Dad who was into classical music and by my sister who loved the Beatles and the Stones. However, I wanted something I could call my own, something special to me. That band was the Clash. Punk arrived at the perfect time. In 1976 I was 19, at university with a little bit of disposable income to go to gigs and buy singles and the odd album. The Clash weren't the first punk band but right from the start they stood out. The look, the swagger and attitude, their political stance but above all their music.

At that age you get influenced by various things. Politically I was still forming my own views and the Clash were fundamental in looking left rather than anywhere else. The mid to late seventies marked the rise of fascist organisations. Their outlook was anti everything that seemed decent and from being fairly neutral I got involved and motivated including Rock Against Racism. That was largely down to the Clash.

White Riot was the first single and I couldn't wait for the first album. Forty one years later it is difficult to describe the absolute joy of hearing the debut album for the first time. Every track is excellent. The album version of White Riot was better and faster than the single. Police and Thieves was a revelation to a boy from Scotland who had heard only a few reggae tracks. Remote Control and Career Opportunities were stunning and I still quote 48 Hours even to this day, especially on a Sunday when work looms large and "Monday's coming like a jail on wheels." With early copies of the album (10,000 as it turns out) there was a red sticker inside. If you peeled it off and sent it to the NME they would post back the Capital Radio E.P. I still treasure it to this day.

Getting to see the Clash was the next imperative and this was duly done at the Apollo in Glasgow: a legendary venue now, sadly gone. The first show with Richard Hell supporting passed in a blur. The second in 1978 was different. Rumoured to be closing the scene was set for a wild night. As always I went up early to make sure the gig was on. As I headed up the stairs to the foyer a bouncer had a fan in a stranglehold and was hitting him with his other hand as he marched him out. I then went round to the back lane to witness support band Suicide arriving. It was always difficult to get backstage at the Apollo and so I thought I would chance my arm and see if Suicide wanted help bringing stuff in. Thankfully they did and I duly got into the dressing room. After chatting with them I asked them to sign the book I was reading at the time. It was the follow up to All the Presidents Men. I still have it to this day. More importantly I also got to meet the Clash. It was only for a few minutes but Joe was great and asked me how I was. Just as I was going to leave he gave me 4 cans of Tennents Lager.

Gigs by the Clash were always exciting but the febrile atmosphere made it even more intense. After that I got to see them a further three times, each of them special. Musically the band moved on very quickly. Some fans weren't happy with the second album particularly the sound but it is classic Clash. London Calling was a further step forward and their Apollo show featuring the album was special. I prefer London Calling to Sandinista but there are few bands that could make such a massive transition over such a short period.

The Clash are gone. But their legacy continues to inspire. I am no longer that spotty youth but I still care. For me the Clash meant great nights out. More importantly my politics, outlook and viewpoint is still influenced by them. The Clash taught me to question and challenge orthodoxies. To care about the world whether it be people or the environment. They were on the side of the angels and have kept me from turning into a boring old so and so. The music doesn't date and the live version of I Fought the Law will instantly brighten my mood. A few years ago I met Sonny Curtis who wrote the song. He said he loved what the Clash brought to it. Can music change the world? I don't know. However, the Clash changed me and for the better. What more could you ask for?

Roy Ferguson, Scotland

Where do you begin to unravel the years and pick out specific moments and memories of a time and a band that were so crucial to your growing up, defining yourself, discovering what you wanted to be and cared about? The questions of youth, and being from a small town outside Glasgow and one of the relatively small numbers of early punks, wore many badges of pride. My Complete Control button one of the absolute faves, but who know where that has gone now - all these years later.

The search for straight, let alone drainpipe type jeans in Glasgow almost impossible until word got out that a department store I have long forgotten had these shiny black skinny things. Brilliant. Wore them till they fell off, knees wore out and back seam split! With my trusty selection of home made T's, lovingly stencilled and sprayed vivid with car spray, borrowed from my dad's business and a mouth spray from art class. Think most only lasted one wash or a few wears but who cares. There was always tomorrow and a new burst of creative ideas waiting.

And that is a great deal of what this 4 piece band from London meant to me… and so many others. They opened doors. The made things possible. They had values, attitude and they cared about us. I bought the Sex Pistols first and New Rose on the same day from a record shop in Queen St and took them home to play non-stop. Pouring over the NME weekly to find out what was going on, where were they all coming from, chatting and bursting with enthusiasm told my long haired fellow musos that this was what it's all about! Few believed, few listened and that was all that mattered. The music was happening, vital, urgent and the look matched the DIY thoughts forming in my brain. The streets were alive with the sound of...

White Riot - first single, the album and the free single from the NME - all safe and sound in my collection today... along with every other since. And sad poignant moment two weeks ago when I extracted the London Calling album from its sleeve only to find out some CBS shoddy vinyl had gone crackly over the intervening years. Is that not typical of Obie and his cronies? Anyway, working in a screen printers during the summer of '77 I had access to all sorts of useful stuff and knocked out a poster culled from bits of posterised bits and pieces demanding if anyone wanted a riot of their own - then call me. I was ready. Needed to play and picked up my Woolies guitar, plucking and strumming with passion and defiance of those other school kids who loved Wishbone Ash and sneered at my lack of ability. It didn't matter - we had the power.

Too many associated members come and go through that period, strange parties, gigs around Paisley and Glasgow. Anyone from that time will know the Bungalow Bar, Mars Bar, Listen Records, the first punk gig with the police cordons at the City Halls and the legend that was the Glasgow Apollo. The home of so many's first experience of live music from the outside world. The bouncing balcony and the bastard bouncers who only wanted blood and when they got spit they gave back venom… so yes, I was at the fated gig mentioned when the boys were arrested. The surging forward as they came on - the line up of thugs ready to repel in anyway they fancied. Seats ripped, bloody lips, calls for calm from the stage.

We had witnessed the front line in all their sonic assault and devoured the new tunes, leapt to the old faves and burst out, ears ringing into the Glasgow dark. They were round the back - we knew and tried to get near but it was already going off. So we ran down Renfield st with everyone else. Some windows were lost in the scramble to follow Jones, and the city's streets echoed to many an anthemic holler. It's dark in my mind but I think I ended up in the east end and collapsed at a friend's house with tales of all sorts being swapped and those vibrant moments that the Clash brought to us. In those days before all the social media instant meaningless waffle, we only had each other and those we bumped into for more tales - no doubt being built and exaggerated in being retold. Glasgow police were not our friends! The reputation for heavy manners was legend.

Glasgow was burning that night and as a town for inspiration and music love it is well known. The nascent punk scene gave birth to many who strived for that knowledge and understanding. I remember Jim Kerr and, with some friends of mine, stopping him from being beaten up at a West End party. Way before the Minds became great and influential. And I'm not taking about "Don't you forget about me"! Stadiums beckoned for many and America called for the Clash but they remained the 'truth' of what they stood for. Bonds being a prime example of that...

I had already seen the Clash a few times and still have a ticket stub from the previous year but the one for the 4th of July one is missing! Along with my button badges, much cherish biker leather jacket and boots. There is a connection that cannot be underplayed from them to us and I will never not hear myself shouting "you're my guitar hero" when Complete Control is playing.

My musical journeys went on for years, taking many meanders but always never quite getting the sound or time right, but that is all history that I would never change. Picking up a guitar, plugging it in - standing in front of the mike, the count in of sticks and the launch of like minds such a feeling... Early days of 77, my band of merry man played the first punk festival at the Custom House Quay bandstand - a saturday that was wet. chaotic, full of enthusiasm and my lasting memory is walking to central Station with my guitar thinking I was terrible, but that was ok. It will get better...

Was at the 16 tons tour too and graduating from school to college to art school they were always close, even though I don't think I understood all that Sandanista was exploring at the time. I still wanted things to be honed with no surplus! And when Jones was given the marching orders it was a moment of change that signalled much to me and those I know who loved them. Though there were plenty of others who didn't care and had moved on to other acts and dull jobs. Dull jobs were never meant for me - I know that and the absolute creativity and dedication the Clash stood for, I believe, is mine too.

I sign off this memory outpouring with 2 final anecdotes.

Glasgow Art School - the busking tour. We bought them tea and they played in the canteen. After all the years they were our size, our people and there they were. In a place that has now sadly burnt down and another key part in my pride in being 'outside'. Who else would have wandered around the UK, being humble and playing their souls away? Henry Afrikaas - crappy pretentious nightclub run by a quite unpleasant individual who was typical city club owner. BS to the max and surrounded by hangers on. Can't remember which band I had gone to see there. But Paul and Joe were there too on this night after the Art School busk, so might have been some CBS shindig. I bought the bass player a pint and told him in some semi-coherent way how much they meant to me and he said a thanks and we chatted for a bit about things and I something to the fact that the record company owned him and there was no escape!

A few years later I found myself in London designing record sleeves and vividly remember going through the doors of CBS Soho Sq. Smiling at the knowledge that they all had done the same, climbed the stairs, got in the lift, sat in reception, chatted in the graphics dept, abused A&R… and one sunny day I left the building with a copy of the limited ed 12" Medicine Show, having had the summer soundtracked by E+Mc2. They were still with me and still relevant.

And you know, they always will be. "At the top of the diaaaallllll…"

A tightly knit unit that forged the way through the vagaries of the punk movement. Beginning with the toughness and then it all loosened up to absorb so many multi-cultural ideas and behaviours. An important thing for a young man from a small town like Paisley. Heavily violent and pretty polarised impoverished. Though I escaped the shit school to a Grammar at 11+ and forged musical mayhem friendships via Bowie - of course, Reed, Eno, Roxy so the die was cast and the heart open for the Clash.

James Leftwich, United States of America

I attended the last Clash concert in July 27, 1985 in the Olympic Stadium in Athens, Greece. I was 15 years old and went with my Mother! The opening acts were Talk Talk, Nina Hagen and the Cure. I remember it well must have been 60k people there. Anarchists outside burned cars and I recall got into the show free. Several encores we left after 2am and they were still playing.
I ripped a poster of the show off a wall in Glyfada, Greece and now have it framed in my apartment.

Photo 7

Johnny Haeusler, Germany

At the end of 1983 my first Berlin-based band "System" had dissolved, my new combo called "Plan B" was just starting out.

Even as we were rehearsing our first songs, I got wind of the fact that the only concert in Germany of The Clash's current tour would take place on February 19th, 1984, specifically at the Philipshalle in Düsseldorf. Sold out, weeks ahead. 5.000 people? 6.000? Never mind, I had to go to Düsseldorf to see them for the third time. Especially since I had yet to experience their new lineup which as it turned out would be their last and most inglorious one.

As I got on the phone (there was no internet back then ... I am not even sure there were push button phones then ... was it even a phone? Maybe I was using drums ...?) to organise tickets, I was struck by a splendid idea to save some money: Plan B from Berlin would play their second gig ever as the opening act for The Clash! Then surely we wouldn't need to pay for tickets.

Keep in mind two things: Firstly, in spite of their separation from Mick Jones The Clash had turned out to be a pretty successful band that got platinum in the US, worked with huge tour promoters and played in pretty big venues as far as punk rock goes. In a nutshell, they were a band that seemed every bit as much out of reach in the mid-eighties as those bands of the mid-seventies that they had once revolted against. And secondly, I couldn't care less. The Clash were the most important band in the world for me, I was 19 years old, there was nothing I couldn't achieve if I wanted it badly enough. And I wanted this badly. I wanted to play with Plan B as support for The Clash in Düsseldorf. With eight half-finished songs if memory serves.

So two weeks before the Clash gig in Düsseldorf I looked up their tour dates in the NME and found out which city and which country the band was currently at. At that time I was only vaguely familiar with the concept of tour organisation. I knew, however, that the band always (really always?) were with their personal manager and press spokesman Kosmo Vinyl. I also knew it would be futile trying to contact the band directly. So the one person I "knew" other than the band members, Kosmo Vinyl, would be the one I was intending to reach.

But how? And where? In a hotel, of course, a pretty big one. In the city they were playing that day, obviously. On the first day of my research (and also on the next few days) that meant somewhere in the UK.

It is one thing if an insolent, naive 19 year old picks up the phone, convinced of his sufficient grasp of the English language to drive home a support gig during an ongoing tour. It is something else again, if that tour leads through Ireland and Scotland and the telephonists of the big hotels there have their very own concept of said English language that differed considerably from my own schoolroom and punk rock English.

It was easy to identify the five biggest hotels in each city. But it was next to impossible for me to understand the people in those hotels. Many times I simply couldn't find out whether the band didn't reside in the respective hotel, or the staff had been instructed to deny they were there, or nobody understood me, or I had interpreted their sentences wrongly. And after several days of research I had no idea how huge my phone bill would turn out to be.

By now my band was laughing at me. That won't do. That will never work. Let it be.

Then, after a great many frustrating phone calls, two days before the Düsseldorf gig on February 17th, 1984, I dial the number of a hotel in Sweden, since Stockholm is on the tour plan that day. Brilliant: The receptionist's English is just as bad as mine. I reel off my by now well trained sentence with an intonation that leaves no room for doubt that the band and I are old chums and that this call takes more of my valuable time than I can really afford:

"Hi, can I speak to Mr. Kosmo Vinyl, please? He's with a band from England called The Clash and he's staying in your hotel."
"Sure, just a second."
Unfortunately the earphone melts at that moment (with coiled cable, since back then there weren't any … oh, never mind). At least it feels that way. In fact it is only sweat by the litre that all of a sudden and without warning is pouring down my entire body including my hands. Furthermore, my muscles have decided in a spontaneous act of rebellion never again to bow to the terror regime of my brain and, damn it, it's been a long, long time since I last went to the loo.
What the hell? The next line in my script is "Okay, thanks anyway, have a nice day!" as I said it each of the days before. I am not prepared for "Sure, just a second".
"Hey", it chimes fiercely from the receiver.

He is in a foul mood, I better call back later. No, it isn't him at all. It is another telephonist, a male this time, who is about to inform me that Mr. Kosmo Vinyl, who is with a band from England called The Clash, is not a guest in their hotel after all. And what about that lump in my throat?

"Am I talking to Kosmo Vinyl of The Clash?" – "Yes, you are."

Now it's over anyway, he's completely stressed out, I can hear these things, three words are enough for me and my lump and my brain-freed muscles and already I have also lost three kilos.

"Hi. Er. So. We are a band from Berlin we are called Plan B we like The Clash very much we wanted to ask if you have a support band for the concert in Düsseldorf or not we wanted to know if maybe it is possible to play before The Clash we could come to Düsseldorf we don't need money we like The Clash."
Silence.
But he's still on the line. And he hasn't started laughing yet. He says:
"How do I fucking know that you're not a fucking heavy metal band with fucking Flying V guitars?"
Fair question. Not really posed in a friendly way but I decide not to get caught up in matters of style right now. The problem is, though, that I have no answer prepared for such a question. Then it goes "click".

Not on the phone, but in my head: The man is a punk rocker! That's his way of being friendly! I decide to stake everything on one card and answer with the same kind of friendliness.

"I would hardly call you in Stockholm and ask you to let us support The Clash if we were a fucking heavy metal band with fucking Flying V guitars", I answer in a trembling voice, surprising myself with the unexpected grasp of the word "hardly". And I quickly add a "would I?" which even today is at the very top of the list of my personal linguistic triumphs. Kosmo sighs.

"Tell you what, we actually haven't got a support on this tour, so here's what we can do. You'll be there at six with your own amps and drums. Bring a tape so I can listen to it. If I like it, you can play."

"Good!", I say, even today at the very top of the list of my personal linguistic failures.

So that was that. I did it. We would be the opening act for The Clash, all the Clash fans would love us, we'd receive a golden record and become famous. Only we didn't have any records or even demo tapes for that matter, just a horrible tape recording from our rehearsal room. And I couldn't possibly tell my band mates that we'd be travelling to Düsseldorf on spec to maybe support The Clash.

So I decided to lie. I told the band the gig was going OK and the band was swept off their feet. And also pretty motivated, to put it mildly. One of them knew someone with a van for the equipment, my dad lent me his car for additional passengers. So, two days after my conversation with Mr. Vinyl, we started out for Düsseldorf first thing in the morning. You never knew how long you'd have to wait at the border. Back then there was an inner German border and, by the way, no internet ...

The Philipshalle in Düsseldorf could hold about a million people.
Or so I thought when I entered it on the afternoon of February 19th, 1984 for the first time in my life. Of course I had been to big venues before to see famous bands, but never before had I been in a big venue that was empty. And never before had I been to an empty big venue where The Clash were on stage doing their soundcheck.

Our entourage didn't just consist of the band; about eight or ten of our friends had come along to Düsseldorf to witness the sensation. All of them were going to flail me should something go wrong, and accordingly I felt pretty uneasy. The new Clash members I knew from a few photos, but next to them stood Joe Strummer and Paul Simonon. Those I knew from several thousand photos. We, the band plus friends, stood in the middle of the hall, maybe 10 meters from the stage. And I hoped.

I hoped that those guys whose work turned out to be so precious and important to me in the past years and who had an amount of influence on my young life that my school could only dream of would not disappoint me. And I didn't mean primarily that they should let us play. It was about more than that. It was about the question whether punk, specifically the punk as propagated by The Clash, was real. Whether they really were "different" from all the other bands. Whether you really could talk to them or whether they were arrogant assholes. I was young, but I wasn't clueless. I didn't expect the Redeemer nor better human beings nor the official commando to save the world. But I did expect cool guys. I hoped for cool guys.

Somebody led us behind the stage into a backstage room (the backstage room: myth and legend. Refuge for endless sprees and orgies, goal of all hardcore fans and groupies. So they say. Best imagine backstage rooms of small venues as a loo that hasn't been used in years or as a boxroom. And those are the better ones. Backstage rooms in big venues on the other hand are nothing else than locker rooms, which makes sense, since many big venues are sports halls in real life. And then there are the backstage rooms of open air festivals, those are caravans...).

Nervously we paced our locker room, planned the set list, made nervous jokes. Then came the question I had been dreading: "What happens next?"

Before I could shrug my shoulders a guy appeared who looked like someone who played with The Clash. Kosmo. He asked for me, we exchanged greetings. I handed over our crappy rehearsal room recording and slowly doubt started to spread among the other guys. What was that about? I explained. Obviously they want to hear something from us, I argued.
"But not from this frigging tape!", the others objected. Sure. We had no other.
We didn't have to wait five minutes before Kosmo reappeared. No way could he have received an impression in that short time and I was positive that now we had to pack our things.

"You will be on stage exactly at eight. You have 30 minutes, no encores. Now relax, get a beer and enjoy yourself!"

Had the "Boris Becker fist" been around then (which it wasn't, as, incidentally, neither was the internet), all of us would have performed it then. Instead we showed our delight like normal human beings, fell around each others' necks, laughed, cheered. And all of us were aware that the situation was both absurd and sublime: A completely unknown band from Berlin plays their second gig ever as the opening act of The Clash. And why? Because they asked!

In case you didn't know: Things like this essentially do not happen. Apart from the fact that most famous bands leave the decision about the support to their label or tour promoter, it is also the rule that support bands have to pay for their place in a bigger concert or even a whole tour. That is not necessarily as nasty as it sounds, not only because the support band can count on the marketing effect deriving from the famousness of the main act. A support band actually produces additional costs: technicians have to work extra time, additional settings are necessary on sound and light desks, the stage has to be rebuilt an additional time. Those additional costs are typically passed on to the support band or their label and they can easily sum up to a five digit number when opening for a famous band on a 20 cities tour. Normally. The exception proves the rule.

After The Clash were done with their soundcheck it was our turn to setup our amps and drums and we were able to have a short soundcheck of our own (which again is quite unusual for a support band). The crew was nice and helpful and we actually did relax a little.

At eight o'clock sharp we stood at the edge of the stage, nervous as hell, armed with our guitars.
The lights went out in Düsseldorf's Philipshalle and the audience started a deafening hooting. At that moment I became aware for the first time that my idea had been an extremely crappy one, indeed. Because in my euphoria I had neglected one not so unimportant detail: Nobody in the audience knew we were going to play. Even worse: Nobody in the audience knew there was going to be an opening act in the first place. The crowd was expecting just one thing the moment the lights went out: The Clash.

A few scrawny teenagers teetered on the stage instead. As if that meant anything I shouted "We are Plan B from Berlin!" into the microphone (I didn't dare to go for "Hello Düsseldorf, it's good to be back") and we stumbled into our first song to leave no time for negative reactions.

I cannot remember if we were any good. My guess is we were rather bad, but we were under some sort of puppy license. Booing was just as sparse as applause, the mood was resigned waiting, time for another round (back then there was real beer in the big venues – but no internet …). I remember that at some point I shouted some statements against Helmut Kohl, who was German chancellor back then, into the microphone (hey: punk!) and no-one was interested. I remember how strange it felt to see the other guys playing so far away from me, the stage seemed incredibly huge. I also remember how quickly our fear of this big venue was gone. During the gig you could only see the first few rows from the stage anyway. Behind that everything appeared black.

And I remember my random gaze to the edge of the stage after the second or third song. There they were. Joe and Paul. Watching their support band, twitching their legs a little. I was proud as Punch.

The Clash gig itself was a blur, too impressed were we by what had just happened. Also we had to arrange a place for us to sleep. Fritz, our bass player, came from Dortmund and knew the area. He had some contacts and somehow we ended up in the flats of German band Fehlfarben later that night.

But before that, still on the venue, we wanted to meet The Clash after their gig. Before, there was far to much nervousness all around, but now I didn't intend to miss out on at least shaking Strummer's hand. To thank him. To ask him what he thought of us.

Kosmo entered the backstage room as we were packing up our things. He thanked us (!), took 300 Deutsche Mark out of his pocket (back then there was no Euro and no internet and coaches drawn by chickens travelled the mud-covered roads) and handed them to me. Did this roughly cover our travel expenses, he asked. Yes, of course, it did, but there really was no need and blah blah blah, but he insisted. What a great guy. I was impressed. "Wanna meet the band?", he's asked.

And so suddenly we were all dressed up and nowhere to go in the backstage room of The Clash, who were engaged in animated conversation with those of their fans that had managed to get here.
So the legends about their fan affinity weren't rubbish after all. Strummer was talking to two young girls, discussing their situation at their school (no kidding – the man had an insatiable and genuine interest in other human beings, as I could confirm in later meetings) and slowly we were involved in the conversation.
Eventually Strummer took off to pack up and I saw my chance to say hello to him in private. I thanked him, we chatted. How did he like the band, I wanted to know. His answer was brief: "You're a good leader. But you need to work hard."
You can do it, but you need to practice. Not the answer I had expected. Not an answer I had hoped for. Maybe even an answer he gave unthinkingly, but an important answer for me and the further history of my band all the same. We were a little successful later, and though we never made

much money in the following years, we did tour half the world, had a lot of fun and created a number of good songs, too. And we're back on the road again!

I am aware of how foolish and ridiculous all of this will sound to some. Despite my young age back then I was not looking for "leaders" (nor am I today), but I searched for (and found) artists that weren't disguising themselves and whose lyrics I could trust. I can voice my admiration for a band and for Joe Strummer without fear of embarrassment, simply because it never was embarrassing.

There are many bands out there and even more fans adoring and loving them, following them every step of their way, hanging on their every word, knowing every single interview, every single photograph. I have never been a fan like that because most bands either consciously or unconsciously confirm the social position and status of their fans as just this: Fans. Devotees. Buyers. Consumers. Me, band: here. You, fan: there. The early punk rock, and thus not only but first and foremost The Clash, have proved things can be different, art can be inspiration and motivation for the individual after all, to become more than just the perpetual recipient. They have proved it is possible to become a producer of art yourself.

Because that is what punk means: You can do it, too!

Antonio Bacciocchi, Italy

On 28 february 1984 with my band Not Moving, quite well known in Italy in those times, being one of the most famous "underground/alternative/punk/rock n roll" bands in our country, had the incredible chance to support The Clash, playing at Palalido in Milan. Eddie King one of the Clash crew, called us early in the morning asking for we could be interested to support Joe and Paul that night !!!

Thrilled and excited we did a short rehearsal in the first hour of the afternoon and started to Milan. We played a really short soundcheck (the sound engineer asking themselves (and to us !) "who the **** are these italians ?") and at 21 o clock all the lights turn off, people started screaming and suddenly we appeared on the stage. 12.000 people in the audience fell in a total silence and some seconds after started shouting against us and throwing bottles and any other kind of object on stage. Our (female) singer answered with a **** off all of you all and the battle started. Really funny and exciting. After half an hour of punk rock mixed with surf and psychedelia and 60's garage we left the stage. Paul said to us (after the "good luck" before the start "well done guys", Joe pulled is thumbs up...we were in paradise !!! No picture has been taken with them...it wasn't the time for selfless we care only about playing and chatting with our idols. I met again Joe some month after in Camden Town and talked about our first meeting. Joe has been very gentle and delicious. The only band that matters, really !

Photo 8

Photo 9

Pete Chambers BEM, England

I wasn't at any of those gigs, but I did attend punk night at Mr George Coventry. Half price whiskey then up for work at British Leyland next day.. I recall hearing a bunch of Clash songs on the first night, just loving them, then finding out there were all on the same album a magic moment, I owned it the next day and bought every punk single from then on (well for a year or so). When we talk about these nights, they are often tinged with exaggerated nostalgia, but I recall at the time we felt we were on the threshold of something special (in Coventry's case that was true in a couple of ways of course).

My journalistic career began as I did my first review in the local Alternative Sounds fanzine, yes I did the first review of Bad Manners in Coventry. Sounds all very hip and finger on the pulse, till you find out The Clash were playing at Tiffany's on the same night, then it all falls into perspective. I missed them...
I now run The Coventry Music Museum and write for The Coventry Observer

Phil Wright, England

Rock Against Racism 1978 - Billy Idol was in the crowd! Leopard skin trousers on and a black leather bike jacket, with his girlfriend, at the time.

There is a great book by a local lad called Tony Beesley that details the era

I bought the first single "White Riot" by mail order from an advert in the back of NME, I would have been around 14 years old, it arrived in a cardboard envelope one morning, and I put it on the record player before going to school, I couldn't wait to get back home that night and play it over and over. It was, of course, high speed punk rock, but I really loved the b-side, "1977". I was confused because I had read they were a four piece band, but there were only three people on the picture sleeve, and they all had their backs to the camera, like they were being searched, hands against the wall, and one of them (Mick Jones from memory), had "Sten guns in Knightsbridge" painted on his back, which was a line from "1977". The Clash were different from the Pistols, hard to say why. They sounded exciting, they sounded like teenage rebellion in musical form. I guess a few bands did at the time, but the Clash were a cut above most bands. I guess if I was 10 years older I would be saying the same about The Who, or the Stones.
That was it, I wanted to be in a band, I was lucky enough that the local youth club (where all the local youths hung

around, smoking and playing pool) was run by a bloke who was learning to play guitar, so he arranged for a few of us to have free lessons on some cheap guitars he had bought. Just three or four lessons to learn basic chords, then I bought a chord book, but had to wait until I was 16, in 1978, and working, to be able to buy an electric guitar (me and my mate bought one each, similar to the Gibson Les Paul TV that Mick Jones played, £65 each, although I really wanted a Rickenbacker like Paul Weller, finally got one 40 years later)

Next single was "Remote Control" and again I bought it mail order to get it quickly, it was good, but the b-side was even better, "London's Burning", so much menace and anger in Strummer's voice, still sounds great today. This was the pattern that I had; read about new singles in NME (hardly anything got played on the radio), order them via mail order, hope that the postman delivered them early so I could play them before school, come home at lunchtime and play them again, come home after school and play them again, take them to the youth club at night and play them to my mates (and listen to their new singles).

"Complete Control" was the one that took them to the next level for me, they started releasing these blistering singles that pretty much helped define the punk era; "Clash City Rockers" and "Tommy Gun". There was an urgency about them, like they demanded to be listened to, if that makes sense.

The Clash didn't seem to want fame, they wouldn't do "Top of the Pops", they were famous but they were still sort of "underground". That gave them a ton of credibility with the fans at that time. They were always letting people in to their gigs for free.

Within the blink of an eye, the first wave of punk seemed over, and the Clash came back with the single, and album, "London Calling", which still stands up today. They became a different band then, still rebels but with a more melodic sound (like the brilliant "Spanish Bombs" and "Train in Vain"), they broke in the USA and became a stadium band. One of their last gigs I saw was around 1981 in Sheffield, at the Lyceum, it was packed and they were great, the three front men, lined up like a gang. Played a mix of old and new stuff.

Combat Rock was interesting and it gave us "Rock the Casbah", still one of my fave all time songs.

I was into all those bands at the time, The Jam, Buzzcocks, Damned, Sex Pistols, The Adverts, Generation X, all great, it was a great time to be young and alive. Gigs were cheap and plentiful. I spent all my money on records. The first Clash album cost me £3.50, which sounds so cheap today. That music made me want to play guitar. I can still play loads of those old (and still great) songs!

Phil Curme, England

I heard Career Opportunities on the John Peel show and had never heard anything like it before. Everyone was listening to increasingly pretentious prog rock which said nothing to the average bored teenager in depressed, monochrome Britain. The new music Peel was playing was exciting and spoke to people like me. It is impossible nowadays to articulate how impactful punk was in those early days - it was like a tsunami crashing onto our shores and sweeping away previous conceptions of what rock and roll was all about.

I was at Trent Poly and bought a ticket to see The Clash as soon as I heard they were heading for the Midlands. The original gig was cancelled because Joe Strummer had contracted hepatitis - the spitting thing had got him! It was rescheduled for May 12 1977 - the evening before an important exam I needed to take. I went anyway and dragged my reluctant flatmates along with me. The Buzzcocks supported …. and they were great. Pete Shelly had replaced Howard Devoto and the crowd were sceptical at first …. but not by the end. The Clash came on and Joe shouted "Nottingham's burning" and the place burst into life. I'd never experienced anything like it. Someone on stage made a giant paper plane out of a giant poster of the cover for the forthcoming first album - Joe, Mick and Paul on the steps of Rehearsals Rehearsals in Camden. I caught it and have the poster still.

The first album came out and it felt like the soundtrack to what was going on in my head. I knew every word, every riff and played it until I wore the record out. My copy was one of the first so I got a free EP featuring Capital Radio and an interview with the boys recorded by Tony Parsons on the Circle Line. I got a ticket for their next tour and saw them at the King's Hall, Derby on 2 Nov 1977. I dragged along some mates and I remember one - Rob - being so stoned he couldn't stand up. When the Clash came on he burst into life as though someone had put a 1,000 volts through him! I remember a fight breaking out and the band stopped playing whilst Mick tried to sort it out. After the gig a bloke chucked a load of Complete Control badges into the crowd and I still have a couple of them. Complete Control reinforced my love of dub reggae - (I'm going to see Lee Scratch Perry next month) ....

The NF were making inroads into politics - Martin Webster and John Tyndall .... and Sham 69 were trying to shake-off their racist followers. The ANL concert in Victoria Park was a magnet for disaffected youth and I travelled down in a bus from Nottingham. I remember walking past Nazi thugs mouthing threats behind ranks of policemen. It felt like we were taking back territory from the far right it also felt like mainstream politicians were doing nothing in the face of the

Fascist threat. My abiding memory is Jimmy Pursey coming on during White Riot and thinking "this is him disavowing Sham's skinhead following and nailing his colours to the ANL / RAR mast".

Afterwards - the second album came out. I really liked it but the adrenaline rush of the early years wasn't there. It was almost as if the first album and early gigs went beyond music - there was something much more powerful going on. At the time I felt they had sold out for the U.S. market and whilst I continued to really rate their music they weren't the force in my life that they had been previously. I think in the early days it felt like we were all comrades in arms. When The Clash starting hitting the charts it began to feel like they were public property - just another rock & roll band albeit it one of the best. London Calling was great but more head than heart.

Sandinista … Combat Rock - good in parts but by the time Mick was thrown out they were going into territory that didn't mean much to me - though I accept it took them to a whole new audience. I kept the faith though and bought all the BAD albums, Joe's solo stuff and Paul's Havana 5am album - the latter is hugely underrated. One of the first gigs I took my son to was Joe Strummer and the Mescaleros and the the Good, The Bad and The Queen.

Terry Wilson, United States of America

The Clash show I attended was on October 8th 1981 at Glasgow Apollo.

I still remember that it was a rainy night that night. I went to the show with my mate Johnny . It was my first concert , and i do believe it was his first concert as well.

We both lived in a shitty small town called "Grangemouth" Approximately 26 miles from Glasgow . The town of Falkirk , was 3 miles away , and the only place close that had a train station. The last train back to Falkirk from Glasgow was 11 pm

So we're at the show and I wanted to get as close to the stage as possible, while Johnny was back a bit. Around 10.45 Johnny is tapping me on the shoulder and pointing at his watch while shouting " the last train"!! I said I was staying , and off he went.

The Clash played a really long show and I think it was midnight when the show ended.

I'd missed my train back to Falkirk but all I could think about was how amazing it was to have just seen my favorite band!

I did actually find another way back to Falkirk, thanks to an older guy with a limp (I'm not kidding) who was following me through the rain out on the street that night. I had no idea how I was getting back and this guy had spotted me hanging around the train station.

I saw him watching me and decided to start walking away from him , but he followed me yelling "hey "

Lucky for me it turned out he was trying to help , and took me to another train station that I didn't know about.

In that station , leaving at 3am was a mail train that stopped at Falkirk. I walked up to the train and the guard says " oh here's another one"

The train was packed with Punks all heading back home just as I was. So thanks to this guy I at least made it back to Falkirk .

It was about 3.30am by the time I made it to Falkirk, still pissing down with rain. I started walking the 3 miles home . I got about half way and this truck driver pulled over and shouts " jump in son" This guy gave me a ride home to the end of my street. By this time it's around 4.15 am .

My parents were still up and looked very relieved that I was home safely. I thought my dad was going to be mad at me . Being that I was only 15 at the time. But he did the exact opposite.

My parents were always supportive of my interest in music , and I'm sure they knew that me listening to The Clash and playing along to their music with my guitar in my bedroom (like many of my friends were doing as well) was actually a really good thing.

There was nothing to do in our small town , and almost everyone I knew with myself included all had been in trouble with the cops. I believe the influence of The Clash on my life steered me in a positive path. I ended up moving to London years later and playing in a rock band. I now live in NYC , still dabble in music , and still listen to The Clash.

I like so many other bands , but no one comes close to The Clash .

They will always be , my number one band of all time.

Bill Piekarz, United States of America

I was at the Bonds Casino gig in NYC. It was a magical experience. My friend and drove a 'drive-a-way car' (drove someones car who was shipping it to NJ),
It was a fantastic event, made more pronounced by driving 1000 miles each way and tooling around NYC for a few days. Stayed in a YMCA. The perfect band, at the perfect place, at the perfect time of my life. I still listen to them (and their solo variations) and have artwork, clothes, and most thankfully THEIR ATTITUDE to keep me going! Thank you for this opportunity

David Bright, Canada

How to start? Right now, I am a 55-year old man in Canada who teaches history at a community college in Ontario. Yep, that's as about as boring as it might sound. But do the math. This also means that in 1977 I was a 14-year-old schoolboy in Bath, England, who was in all the usual throes of pubescence/adolescence, etc. And if you were there in the mid-70s, you'd also remember that this was a tribal time in terms of football, clothes and music. The likes of Pink Floyd, Yes, Led Zeppelin, and even shit like Focus reigned supreme, even untouchable. That they were, to my tender ears, also unlistenable did not matter. Like gorillas in the jungle, the dominant males among my peers marked their territory, exerted their will over the young pretenders, and by sheer force exiled all who did not comply.

And then, something changed....

By 1976, I'd been searching for a music that might more suit my own teenage frustrations. I'd latched onto -- in some sequence or another -- the likes of Queen, 10cc, David Bowie, Thin Lizzy and (especially) Bryan Ferry, but they all seemed a little ... what? Well, remote from it meant to be a teen at that time. And then, some time in late '76 or early '77 came my Damascene awakening.

Vague rumours of the Sex Pistols swearing on the Grundy show, word of Richard Hell and the Voidoids from New

York ... and then the Clash, launching 'White Riot' on the world. This was it ... here was the missing link!!!

Except, of course, I lie. Although in the summer of 1977 I did indeed revel to the sounds of Graham Parker, the Stranglers, the Boomtown Rats, the Damned etc., the band I truly latched onto later that year was not the Clash but the Jam. In a repeat of the Beatles *vs.* Stones battle of a decade or so before, it seemed that you had to make your choice. And, for whatever reason, I went with Mr. Weller and Co.

And yet, as the 1970s drew to a close and merged into the early 1980s, I came to appreciate more and more the Clash as THE band that truly meant something. I never lost my love for the Jam, but by the time both bands imploded in the early 1980s, it was a dead heat.
No doubt many others will give you great reasons for why the Clash matter so much. Here, off the top of my head, are just five.

1. Joe Strummer's outro-libs. From the first LP on, Joe would end so many songs with outrageous and (seemingly) spontaneous outbursts to accompany the band's coda. My favourite still, I think, comes in the much maligned 'Remote Control,' when Strummer ends with 'Gonna be a Dalek' and

then in his best mechanical Dalek voice assures us that that 'I obey!' Priceless.

2. 'Complete Control.' Still, to this day, the most complete song that marks the divide between pre- and post-punk. From Jonesy's opening riff -- so simple, so unplayable -- through the *Play for Today* lyrics of the band's conflict with their own record label, to Mick's all-time finest solo (and Joe says so – "You're my guitar hero!"!) to the final helter skelter ending ... can the band possibly bring it all together? Of course they can! Thank you, Topper.

3. All of *London Calling*. Some time in the early 1980s, we were in a pub in Bath at lunchtime and they played the entire LP. I spent some time focusing on my pint and food, but much more on listening to the album. And I was right: there's not a wasted *second* on that album, not a single beat or lick that could be improved upon. Best album ever? Who knows? But still unsurpassable.,

4. *Sandinista!* Mick Jones once said that this triple album wasn't meant to be listened to all at one time, but instead was for the likes of oil-rig workers who could listen to it in bits and pieces. Well, sorry Mick. In 1983, I re-wall-papered my bedroom one afternoon while *Sandinista!* was playing in the background .... and it was perfect. Even Side 6 which,

as we all know, is in fact a bunch of shit. Still, it got me through the afternoon...

5. 'This is England.' From the only Clash LP -- *Cut the Crap* -- for which the demo versions actually excel the final product. The whole exercise was a mistake, no doubt -- Joe and Paul having fired Topper and Mick in the previous months -- but 'This is England' was (and remains) a true testimony to the onslaught of Thatcher. And it gave us perhaps Joe's finest ever line: 'I got my motorcycle jacket, but I'm walking all the time.' Three decades on, we've all got our shiny prizes, yet are still wandering in search of something more.

So that's it. For a while, I thought the world might change as a result of bands like the Clash. It didn't. Thatcher got re-elected time and time again, I fled the country for Canada like a rat, and pop music reverted to its usual banal state. And yet, and yet .... 40 years on, I am who I am today in large part because of Joe, Mick, Paul and Topper. The Clash. The "Only Band That Mattered"? No (I still remain a fan of the Jam). But, and much more important, a band that DID truly matter.

Malcolm Tent, United States of America

It's 1984.

Fort Lauderdale, Florida. The most boring place on Earth... and the Clash are coming to town! Dude, NOBODY of the Clash's stature plays in Florida. Nobody! This is big news! My friends and I (the only punk rockers in our suburban development) get our tickets immediately. True, it's not the 'real' Clash (no Mick Jones), but hey- a fake Clash is better than no Clash.

A few weeks before the show, a controversy develops. The Clash are playing the Sunrise Music Theatre, a venue which has hosted its fair share of rock shows, but specializes in a more upscale performer. The interior walls of the lobby are decorated with pictures of Frank, Sammy, Englebert those kind of people. Upscale performers attract an upscale audience- the kind of people who will happily fork over a premium charge for the 'dinner seats'.

The dinner seats are the best seats in the house. Purchase of a dinner seat includes, as you might have guessed, dinner. Probably Chicken McNuggets, but I'm only guessing because I could NEVER afford one of those seats.

As one could guess, this being a Punk Rock show, the punks weren't too happy with this dinner seat jive. A hue and cry was raised and I have a vague memory of a petition going around (don't take my word 100% on that, though).

However it happened, the band heard about our dilemma and intervened with the venue management to make ALL seats available at the same price. I seem to recall that it was a bit of a struggle, but the Sunrise Music Theatre eventually caved in. A victory for the people brought to you by the Clash!

After all that, I thought show was a bit anticlimactic. I'd already made up my mind that the band probably wasn't going to be that good. Certainly not authentic. Also, I'd read that the Clash were one of the loudest bands in the world and I was ready to be pummeled. They opened with 'London Calling' and my immediate impression was of how UNLOUD and distant the band sounded.

The music didn't batter me like I was hoping to be battered. There were TV sets (or some kind of video screens) all over the stage showing clips of battle scenes and whatnot. There was much tough guy posing from the new kids, Paul was just kind of there, and Joe was wearing white pants, a white jacket, and I think a blue Hawaiian shirt. He was sporting his Mohawk and kept holding his head while he sang, as if he had a headache. He grimaced like he had a headache, too. He occasionally played third guitar and my thought at the time was 'Why?". The sound was murky enough to where his playing was inaudible.

Overall, between my own bias and the poor sound and the weird presentation with all the TV sets and the obvious posing and Joe's apparent pain in the head, I was a bit disappointed by the show. Not disappointed enough to miss a chance to meet the band, though. The people I went to the show with wanted to get backstage.

Not really my scene, but whatever. There was a whole mob of us outside by the backstage door after the concert. We hung out there for a long time and as the evening wore on, the crowd thinned out quite a bit. Finally, after quite a wait, this Rasta dude opened the door and said in a thick Jamaican accent "Do you want to meet the Clash?" We of course said "YEAH" so he said "Come wit' me" and he led us through the labyrinthine backstage area (where mere mortals are not normally allowed) to the dressing room.... and there they were!

It was pretty weird for a young kid like myself to suddenly be face to face with the people who I'd just seen on stage in a big theatre- especially Joe and Paul. I'd been reading about them and looking at their faces on album covers for years and there they were. Just like that. In person and only life- sized.

All of the band members had girls on their arms. Joe had one particularly well known Clash groupie as his entertainment for the night (later I found out that it was through her efforts that the whole dinner seat fiasco was put to rest. Still later I learned that she was a bit more than a mere groupie, but that's another story for another time). The new guys especially seemed to be enjoying their female companionship.

I looked over at Nick Sheppard just in time to hear him make a witty remark to one of his chicks. "Oh, I see they're letting longhairs in tonight", referring to my shoulder length hair. I walked over and asked for an autograph, which made him wince a bit. Good!

Then I found myself face to face with Paul Simonon. He was very polite. I felt a need to talk to him. This is how it went:
ME: So, uhhh, do you like playing punk or reggae better?
PS: Both.
ME: (silence)
PS: (silence)
ME: Oh.
PS: Excuse me, I have to go.

ME: O.K.!

I wonder how many 'conversations' like that poor old Paul has had in his life.

My friend (who I had a band with) gave Joe a copy of our record which he graciously accepted. He actually seemed interested in our little 45. I remember his girl looking at me with contempt. I finished getting my autographs and it was time to go home- or so I thought. One of the people I was with found out that the band was staying at a local Holiday Inn and wanted to resume the party there. We drove around for a while trying to find it (against my will) but had no luck, so the night was finally over.

Many years later I finally heard a recording of the gig and it wasn't half bad. The renditions of the oldies were OK but the new songs showed a lot of promise. In fact, this particular tape kindled within me an intense interest in the latter day Clash. I realize now that they were a good band and had a lot to offer- if they had been allowed to. I often ask myself "What if? What if that band had been allowed into the studio to record Cut The Crap?" Clash history would have a happier ending and that band would have gotten a fair shake.

I listen to that tape of the Clash in Fort Lauderdale quite a bit these days. Now I wish I'd been more open minded about that band's capabilities (I also wish the acoustics had been better at the show). I think I would have enjoyed the gig very much. At least now, more than 20 years later, through the wonder of modern technology, I'm able to.

Paul Frear, England

Wow………………….. where to start ?

 Probably at the end, the here and now, the fact The Clash still influence me (and thousands) to this day in song and spoken word.
Watch any band today with edge and attitude and you'll see The Clash. Watch any musician extolling socialist democracy, you'll see The Clash. Watch any poet with a heart, you'll see Strummer.
I know live in rural Northumberland, the land of finger in the ear folkies and baggy jumpers and yet when I sit quietly strumming my acoustic guitar in the local all barriers and stereotypes collapse when I play I Fought the Law. Not a Sonny Curtis or Bobby Fuller version, but a version from the heart of the Clash. There's nothing better than having a group of folk of all ages and followers of different music genres coming together and firing the lyrics back at you, with the same passion I had at Clash gigs all those years ago. The Clash are forever. Thanks for keeping that flame burning.
One of many never the few.

Geoff Hoover, United States of America

Two Bonds shows for me (Ray Jordan let me in the side door for free for the 2nd show). Plus the Tomorrow Show that they taped during the Bonds run. Also sat in the upper deck behind home plate for Shea.

Randolph Burbach, United States of America

The Clash were a great awakening for me...I saw that music could be a force beyond itself. From the political commentary in the songs to Rock Against Racism, they opened the half-closed eyes of this suburban boy. I was at a show in Detroit, at the Masonic Temple, I think, and hung around after the show. Ted Nugent was there, too, and challenged them to a bit of Russian roulette or something insane like that. They, of course, turned him down and kicked him out. They were great to their fans to an extent I have never experienced.

James Burns, England

We used to look out for the tours in the papers all the time. I remember once before I even started going, I had heard on the radio there had been a riot at a Clash gig @ Newcastle University. What happened is they wouldn't let normal kids in, just students. So they tried to break down the doors. I remember listening to the radio thinking, god, that would have been hell there, it would have been great. I did eventually go and see The Clash. They weren't me best band, but I have never experienced energy like it. It probably is the best thing that has ever happened, just for that one night, 3 hours or whatever. The energy was fantastic, I've seen nothing like it.

It was June 12th 1980, 2 days before my 15th birthday. It was the 16 Tons Tour. The Clash hadn't played Newcastle for 2 years. I remember getting a ticket, there was a lass at our school called Tracy Gibson (they had sold out straight away) so I knocked on her door and said "did yer get me ticket?" She said "yes", and I was delighted because I knew I would get in even though the Mayfair was an over 18's venue. But at the time me sister, our Christine, she worked in the box office & used to come up to the door when I was queueing and say to the bouncers "away, away" and I'd get in.

They started off with Clash City Rockers, the place was just rockin'. The violence was unbelievable. There were like 3,000 people in there and it was heaving. People were just like smackin' each other all over. It was like years ago at football matches a fight would start and a gap would open up and people were just fighting from the beginning to the end. I was at the front & you would get crushed. But I was just a bairn of 14 & I was loving it.

Photo 10

Tony Paknadel, England

In October 1977, the month I turned 20, I was living in Munich.

I'd hitch-hiked there from my parents' home in Rayleigh in Essex, to meet up with my good mate Paul Williams, now sadly deceased*. Under Paul's influence I'd gone there, back-packing and camping, hoping to find work of any description. Paul was the one who'd read Kerouac's On the Road and Orwell's Down and out in Paris and London so had the notion that washing dishes in a foreign country was a cheap and romantic way to see the world!
 We'd ended up both getting jobs as kitchen porters at a large Holiday Inn in the Schwabing district. We stayed in

an apartment belonging to the hotel, in the next block along. Rent was deducted from our wages.

We'd only been there around a month when I saw a gig poster advertising that the Clash were going to be playing locally. Paul and I had both already seen the band once back in the UK in Chelmsford on one of the White Riot tour dates (29th May 1977). That was (and still is) one of the most exciting gigs I'd ever been to, and I've been to hundreds! I'd never seen as band with as much on-stage energy.

How brilliant that we'd be able to see them again! I'd owned the first album since release day and had played it to death from then until I'd left England a few months later. They really were my top band at the time so I was totally thrilled that they were going to be playing locally.

I convinced Paul that it would be necessary for us to both get the entire day off for the gig, and if the hotel couldn't organise the duty rotas to allow this, well fuck it - one or both of us would simply have to call in sick on the day. My plan was to turn up to the venue early in the hope of running into someone – crew member/roadie/anyone/maybe if we were lucky a band member – to try to see if we could turn the whole thing into something more than just a gig and hopefully get close to the band.

Well, the whole day turned into every rock fan's fantasy almost from the moment we got to the venue on the day of the gig in the early afternoon. I don't think we could have been there more than around half an hour or so when a truck pulled up outside the hall.

The first person I saw emerge from the truck was Topper, who came directly over to Paul and me and starting speaking to us as we were literally the ONLY two people there to greet the band. Gradually the other members of the band all emerged, along with a couple of roadies and Bernard "don't call me Bernie!" Rhodes, the band's manager.

It wasn't long before entry was gained into the hall so Paul and I just entered along with everyone else and from that moment on we were really just part of the entourage for the remainder of the day. We chatted to the band whilst the stage gear was set up. We found out that the whole gig was being video-taped. We sat in the dressing room while the film crew taped a short interview with the band. The footage was used in a documentary film by Wolfgang Buld called **Punk in London.**

Joe was impressed by that fact that Paul and I could both speak German and asked us if we knew any choice swearwords that he may be able to use should he deem it appropriate sometime. He wrote some of the words down on the back of his hand, e.g. Arschloch (arsehole), and the phrase for "you're an arsehole '.

It was a thrill to watch the sound check as it was like a private show for just Paul and me, since we were still the only two present who could be classified as mere punters. After the soundcheck it became clear that the next item on the agenda for the band was to find somewhere and something to eat. It was here that the fact that we could speak some German played in our favour as Bernard and the band thought it would be a great idea if we could accompany them to dinner provided we would be willing to act as interpreters of course.

Obviously, this needed less than a Nano-second's deliberation on our part to agree that this was indeed a splendid idea. It turned out that there had been previous difficulties in restaurants for them due to the fact that they had not one word of German between them.

So the seven of us ended up in some restaurant or other – picture it: Bernard Rhodes, Joe Strummer, Mick Jones, Paul Simonon, Topper Headon, Paul Williams and me all sitting around a large rectangular table sharing a meal. I remember hardly anything about the food (come on – it was forty years ago) but I do remember having my head totally done in by Bernard Rhodes as I found him very intellectually challenging to converse with and I felt totally out of my depth. A very interesting guy in fact, but I just didn't really have the experience to appreciate him at the time. Two years ago (2016) I attended a one-man talk that he gave at the British Library in London as part of a season of celebratory events commemorating 40 years since the start of the British Punk Rock movement. He was then aged 76 I think, but he was totally compelling and just as unconventional in his thinking as ever. It was an extremely entertaining evening. I wished Paul could have been with me.

Anyway, to get back to Munich……there was a bit more time-killing between dinner and the start of the gig, some of which was spent backstage (I think this is when the interviews were filmed) and the rest out front at the bar downing German beers.

By the time the band were ready to come on Paul and I were totally stoked. Those of you who saw them around this time may remember that they used to always start their shows with London's Burning. During the final couple minutes before the band struck up, our impatience for them was getting almost unbearable. In an effort to jolly up the band and get them to stop fart-arsing around tuning up and ACTUALLY PLAY SOMETHING I jokingly attempted to start their first song for them, yelling out the first line "London's Burning!" (which Joe always sang on his own) hoping that the band would come in on my cue. I tried twice. Obviously, that didn't work, but if you watch the footage you can clearly hear me do this right at the start (about 20 seconds in, and again at 30 seconds). Backstage again afterwards, then we eventually boarded the band bus and accompanied them to a local night club. The Sugar Shake or Sugar Shack or something like that. I can't remember much about the club other than how steep the prices were. Paul and I were still relatively impoverished and so were gobsmacked at the drink prices! Luckily all the drinks were paid for, we didn't care whether it was the band or management paying.

The day ended with us back on board the band bus, where I sat next to Topper, who I found the most friendly and easy to talk to. I remember we exchanged addresses, and I later sent him a postcard from Crete which turned out to be the next stop on my backpacking travels.

Paul and I got dropped off virtually at our front door. We said our goodbyes and the bus disappeared into the night towards the next gig.

*My friend Paul died aged 61 on the same day as David Bowie passed away, i.e. 10th January 2016. I miss him a lot. Cause of death was idiopathic pulmonary fibrosis.

I don't have much to tell you about the Victoria Park gig other than that I was there.

However, after my return to the UK, the Clash played a straight four night run at The Music Machine in London's Camden Town – July 1978. The support bands were Suicide and The Specials.

I had a friend – Clive - who's rented flat was only a two-minute walk from the venue, so I arranged to take a week off work and stay with my mate Clive. On the day of the first show I went early in the afternoon and hung around the stage door waiting for the band to arrive. The first to show up was Topper, on his motorbike. As he removed his helmet I made sure I was right in his face so that there would be no chance of him not seeing me. I was sure he would remember me as the Munich gig had been less than a year before. He did recognise me, so I took my chance (very nervously in case I was challenged) to enter the venue alongside him as we continued our chat. I followed this method for the remainder of the week and so gained free entry to all four gigs.

On that first day, between soundcheck and gig, I went with Topper across the road from the venue to a Wimpy Bar (burger joint). As we were sitting chatting and eating Topper suddenly jumped up and banged on the inside of the window front as he'd spotted someone outside who's attention he wanted to attract. The 'someone' turned out to be Steve Jones and Paul Cook of the Sex Pistols. The both entered the Wimpy bar and come over to join Topper and me. They ordered no food, but I do remember Steve helping himself to a few chips from my plate. As he did so he said "D'ya mind if I nick a chip Mate?" Any protest on my part (not that I would have protested you understand) would have been entirely wasted as the chips had been half chewed and half swallowed almost before he'd reach the end of his question to me.

Andy Davies, England

I have and still am a lifelong Clash fan. Hearing that first album,was like nothing I'd heard before. The first Clash gig I went to was the 16 tons tour at the Top Rank in Birmingham Feb 1980. They played two nights, i went on the Tuesday which was the first night. I read somewhere The Clash weren't keen on the venue but I think it was ideal, no seating and just huge. I went with several mates and we were all around 15 years old. Mikey dread was supporting. Nothing can prepare you for a Clash gig. The sheer power and presence on stage was incredible. When they came on and went into Clash City Rockers, the place went crazy,programmes,beer went flying through the air. I've seen many of the early punk bands, but The clash that night were on a different level. A 26 song set which chewed you up and spat you out. The Clash were our band and always will be. Me and a couple of mates went the second night hoping to get a ticket and just couldn't get any. We ended up sitting outside the venue with about 30 other Clash fans drinking beer and having a Party while the Clash played inside. A very raw version of what joe did at Glastonbury,minus wigwam and tents.

Joe,Mick,Paul,Topper. To this day I thank you for everything. The only band that mattered.

Cheers Ant for doing this book.

Martin Andrew, England

I have so many stories but for me the 2 that stand out most will always be the first time I heard the Clash and the first time I saw them.

"The First Time I heard the Clash" I was 11 years old. It was 1977 and I was at school with friends. Although I liked music, like many during that era I only really ever listened to glam rock at the time (the Sweet, Glitter Band being my favourites). One of my school friends had got hold off some 7" punk rock singles from his older brother and wanted a few of us to go his house after school to listen to them. When 'White Riot' kicked in on his record player I was completely shell shocked, it was like nothing I had ever heard before. Although we piled through a ton of great tunes that afternoon (999, Stranglers, Sex Pistols, Damned) I kept coming back to the Clash. We must have listened to it a hundred times. Next week we went back and he had managed to get hold off his brothers "the Clash" debut album. I fell in love with it and went out the next day to my local record shop and bought it. I played it end to end every day what seemed forever (well until the next album was released a year or so later). And that was it..my love affair with the Clash had begun and would continue with me until this very day. I have every single piece of vinyl, cassette, CD and digital download and they sound just as good today as they the first time all those many years ago and I can honestly say they changed my life on so many levels.

"The First Time I saw the Clash" was in November 1978 at the Edinburgh Odeon. It was and still is the most amazing concert ever. The energy, passion, commitment and sound just blew me away.I knew & sang along to every song. I was transfixed by Joe Strummer's rasping vocals, thrashing guitar and incredible raw delivery. Every track exploded into life from the opening "Safe European Home" all the way through to the closing "White Riot". They played every song as if it was their last ever time. I wanted it to go on forever though eventually accepted the end as I left the venue dripping in sweat and utterly exhausted. Iwas lucky in that I managed to go and see them on every tour thereafter, right up until the final shows in 1985. They will always be the greatest live rock and roll band on the planet.

Kirk Field, England

Onstage with The Clash!

"There may be a wee bit o' blood, but nothing to worry about, the cocaine will numb it sharpish".

Nurse Gladys expertly inserted the first 10" needle into my left nostril. Up and up it travelled, into recesses even my finger never knew existed, before I felt it piercing the tissue where my nasal cavity became my forehead. A dark red drop fell into the chrome kidney-shaped dish I had been told to hold beneath my chin. SPLAT! Then another. SPLAT! SPLAT! But Nurse Gladys wasn't done. Not until she'd threaded another five needles, each tipped with a numbing nugget of medicinal cocaine into my ever-problematic seventeen year-old sinuses - which clearly needed flushing. So flushed they were. A thoroughly nasty nasal enema which left me bleeding and slightly spaced out.

Nurse Gladys held the door open, *"All done, now go home, tek some Asprin, get yoursel' to bed, and you'll be right as rain in't morning".*

What she didn't say is, *"Now sprint down to the roundabout and you'll just make the Earthquake Records bus, which will take you to Lancaster University to see The Clash on their 'Sixteen Tons Tour'.*

But that's exactly what I did.

Remember at school there was always one kid who had dramatic, lesson-stopping nosebleeds? They'd suddenly erupt without warning, covering the poor sod at the desk in front in claret - prompting screams from the girls and resigned 'here-we-go-again…' glances from the boys. Well on the evening of the 23rd January 1980, on the back seat of the bus, and all the way through Mikey Dread's set, I was that boy. Stood leaning on the stage, in the front row (no pits in those days laddie!), holding a swathe of bloodied bog roll up to my face – which purely coincidentally mirrored the mischievous '*Bankrobber*' inspired capers on stage. So no one appeared concerned, probably thinking it was a homage to Johnny Green and his Porkpie hat and Crombie-coated crew, who prior to show-time, skanked across the stage, faces covered in red neckerchiefs, as the atmosphere and antici……pation rose.

Joe Strummer is above me. So close I could reach out and touch his buckled work boots, which repeatedly shuddered as his left leg twitched in time to the beat…well I could if I had use of my arms. They're currently trapped between my chest and the stage, there's fighting just behind me, (probably skins and punks fighting 'for a good place, under the lighting'), and everyone in front of them is surging forward to get out of the way. I try to push back, but fail. I'm jammed between the stage digging into my chest and a huge Mohican in a studded leather jacket. I can feel the studs in my back. The pressure behind me is too great. I look down. My knuckles are white, my ribs are starting to hurt. It's hot…very hot. Wait - my feet aren't touching the floor, or maybe they've gone numb? It's like I'm floating… I'm being squashed. The music grows distant. I'm in a tunnel. At the centre of the tunnel is a bright light. Someone's walking towards me; he's got dreadlocks. *"BLOODY HELL, GOD IS BLACK!"* I remember thinking. He holds out his hands. Huge muscly arms beckon me. But I can't move. I'm trapped. Then he grabs my shoulders and lifts me directly upwards. I feel hands on my arse and legs, pushing me upwards. I ascend above the seething mass and turn around to see a thousand punks pogoing to *'Garageland'*. I drift passed a sweating Joe Strummer and the bright red sleeveless shirt of Mick Jones steps back from the mic to allow me to float on by, two feet from the floor. My dreadlocked saviour gently places me on a flight case at the side of the stage stamped with the words THE CLASH, on which a pretty blonde girl in a black biker jacket perches. She puts her arm protectively around me, wipes my nose (which I assume must've been bleeding dramatically from the early 'procedure') and raises a bottle of water to my lips.

Now cooler and rehydrated, I come round, and what happened next was the most amazing thing that I'd experienced in my life to that point…

From behind the drums, Topper catches the girls' eye, and in between songs mouths, *"Is he alright?"*

Topper Headon asking if I was alright????!!!!!

She nodded and told me to put my thumb up; which I did and he smiled back…before starting the staccato intro to *Tommy Gun.*

Well, I didn't know if I was on stage or had died and gone to heaven. It felt like both; there I was at the side of the stage, looking across the greatest front line in the history of rock'n'roll: Mick, Joe and Paul taking turns to move forward and deliver vocals, guitar solos, or just one of their iconic trademark stances. A throbbing three-pronged attack which, seen side on, was breathtaking in its elegance, brutal in its power and relentless in its energy.

I had the best seat in the house, to see the best live band in the World…and Toppers girl looking after me!

The show finished and as he departed stage right, Topper came over and handed me a drumstick, before leaving with his girl. A roadie escorted to the front of the stage, from where I jumped down and joined my waiting mates who, on spotting the grin across my face and the drumstick in my hand greeted me with the words, *"You jammy bugger".*

God bless Nurse Gladys!

Cindy Ball, United States of America

Sorry to be so late in responding! I am so busy with my dad who has dementia and requires a lot of my attention these days. I've been trying to write something about it but I find my ability to write anything at all challenging b/c my attention is so wrapped up elsewhere. All I got so far is that my best friend and fellow fan pushed us up front by yelling: out of the way! she's pregnant! (I wasn't) Which worked pretty well. We got so far up front that I was getting bathed in Joe's sweat when he came front of stage (I swore I'd never shower again) and Anita was convinced her future husband, Paul, was making eye contact with her only. We were cowed and respected and admired the courage of those who showed up in full punk gear and haircuts at a packed 80K seat stadium with the sneers and looks of a basically classic rock crowd.

That's it, all I got right now.
FWIW, I wrote a song some years back when I was dismayed by hearing Clash songs and Minstrel Boy on commercials and planned to play it on Joe's front lawn some day (not that I knew where it was!). You know: He who fucks nuns will later join the church. I was clearly inspired by his own lyrics and kind of thought he might actually respect my own song. I'm still a huge fan, I was just disappointed. You may not care for it and I'm certain it

wouldn't make the book but here goes!
Commercial Crucifixion

Your music made the most sense to me
It spoke the scathing truth
And hit me hard in the gut
Of my disaffected youth

You think it means nothing now
Now that you've grown old
But it wasn't yours to sell out
And it wasn't you, you sold.

When you said back then
That you're for real,
It should have raised suspicion
You set us up, you sold us out
It's a commercial crucifixion.

I've seen a lot of ugly things
But nothing made me sicker
Than Jesus waving from the cross
Selling long distance and malt liquor.
When you said back then
That you're for real
It should have raised suspicion
You set us up, you sold us out

It's a commercial crucifixion.

Strange Fruit now sells Starburst
Janis Joplin's hawking cars,
Judas sent his kids to college
While the apostles played guitars.

When you said back then
That you're for real,
It should have raised suspicion
You set us up, you sold us out
It's a commercial crucifixion.
Hey, Joe, London called,
They say you sold out!

Marc Riley, England

"Having a memory like a sieve doesn't bode well when asked to delve into the long gone episodes in ones life. Such as my encounter with The Clash during the legendary shining at Bonds Casino on Times Square New York City.

It was a run of gigs that had been seriously over-sold by the promoter so extra dates were added on. I do remember that the idea was to have a few different British bands opening for them on some of the nights. Thats where I came in to the picture, being as I was at the time, playing guitar and keys for The Fall. It was the 9th June 1981.

We were staying at the Iroquois Hotel on West 44th street which was just a hope away from the venue. Iggy Pop had lived there for a while and the barbers found on the ground floor (?) of the hotel was famous as the stylist who cut James Deans legendary barnet. Well - that's what I was told. Being there for a few days (but playing only one Clash show) we went down a couple of other nights to take in the carnage outside Bonds. There were thousands of people being herded around by the Police - some on horseback.

On the night we played my recollections are sketchy. I recall Mark E Smith telling me that Joe Strummer approached him before the soundcheck with the words "I bet you hate me don't you"....tho I can't remember what Mark had said he'd replied. To be fair Mark didn't have a good word to say about most people - lol... but ironically I know that when I first joined The Fall, Mark had a page torn from the NME on the wall of his flat which was an advert for the single White Riot...with the lyrics on it. So he had at least at one point in time been a fan.

The Fall put in a good shift that night and went down well. Perhaps too well. Before we'd finished the Clash's roadies took to the stage and pulled the plugs on us. Literally. My memory tells me the audience showed their disapproval.

Back at the hotel there was more drama. The Gang of Four (another band who I think were to to open for The Clash at Bonds) had fallen out with their Bassist David Allen - and he quit the band. We caught up with the GO4 a few weeks later in San Francisco where they did a storing set - with Buster Cherry Jones on bass."

Thats all there is in my woeful memory bank Anthony. I hope there's enough there.

Cheers… and well done on the Charity aspect of this project.

Christopher Downey, United States of America

Memories of the Clash Concerts – October 1982

Since August 16th and October 17th 1982 I have seen the Clash in concert in three different cities. I have seen some great performers and concerts over the last six years. The list includes Elvis Costello, Iggy Pop, the Ramons, Blonde, the Jam, Squezze, David Johansen, and DEVO to name a few, however, these three Clash shows were the most intense and memorable concerts I ever saw.

The first show was in Detroit at the Grand Theater on August 16th. I went to the Show with Hale and Hunter Driggs. We got there early and I took pictures of the crowd outside of the show. We crashed at Hales Uncle Fred's house after the show. The next morning we drove to Toledo to drop Hunter off (he was not going to Akron to see the show that night).

Hale and I left Toledo for Akron in his car. He drove on a sunny summer day. It was a great day for the three hour drive, not many clouds in the sky with very little traffic. We were on I-80 listening to a tape of Give'em enough rope, about eighty miles from Akron when a maroon Lincoln Town Car passed us. I was not paying attention when Hale said "look at that car…the guy sitting in the middle seat in the back." I looked and saw the guy sitting in the middle had a mohawk hair cut. I responded, "They are probably going to the show too." Hale looked at me and said, "Of course they are going to show, that is fucking Joe Strummer in the back!" "Are you sure?" "Yea, why do you think he is sitting in the middle?" "We are in rural Ohio some of these country folks might not appreciate The Clash." At this point they began to speed up. I told Hale to catch them; they were driving about 90 mph. I found a piece of paper and a marker and wrote "The Clash" on the paper. We were in the left lane and pulled up next to them. Paul Simonon was in the front passenger seat, Joe Strummer was in the back but I don't know who the other three people were.

As we pulled up next to them they were driving way over the speed limit, Hale was honking the horn and I rolled down my window and leaned out with the paper with the Clash written on it. I began yelling "The Clash, the only band that matters!" Paul Simonon was laughing and pointing at us and then waved. As they speeded up we pulled up behind them and were still trying to get their attention. Joe Strummer turned around and waved to us. I had no film for my camera, luckily Hale had his and we took a picture of the car. We followed them as far as we could, however we were low on gas and had to stop. They continued on to Akron.

The show in Akron was great. I took a lot of pictures.

On October 17th I saw the Clash for the third time, this time at the Kent State Memorial Gym. I took my camera but for this show I did not take it in, I left it in the trunk of the car. I wanted to get closer and not worry about taking pictures. I went to the show with David Walland and a friend of his. David kept saying we are going back stage after the show. I never believed him. I said, "How?" He said, "After the show we are just going to hang out by the backstage entrance and they will let us in." After the show ended we did just as David said…we went backstage. There were only a handful of people. At the door was a big black bouncer. He looked at us and said, "What are you here for?" David spoke up and said, "We are here to hang out with the Clash." The bouncer said, "Wait here" and walked inside for a few minutes. He came out and said, "Alright you can go back." Holy Shit! I couldn't believe it was that easy! David just smiled and said "I told you." We walked in. All the members of the band were there. The room was not big and not many people. At this point I realized I left my camera in the car. I went back to the bouncer and told him of my problem. He told me to hurry and get it. I ran as fast as I could the whole time thinking I didn't have much time and I didn't want to waste it.

The temperature was in the low forties and when I got back I saw Joe Strummer sitting quietly by himself at a folding table that had a bouquet of fresh flowers on it. He was wearing dark sunglasses and a black shirt with a button on the label. I went over and asked to photograph him. He smiled and nodded. I raised my camera to take a picture. At that point a panic look ran across my face. Coming from the cold temperature to the warm caused the camera lens to fog up. Joe looked at me and said, "What's the matter mate?" I told him about the situation and he said, "sit down, give it a minute." Un-fucking believable! I am sitting next to Joe Strummer about to engage in one of the most memorable conversations in my life. I

t began with me telling him how much I loved the Clash music. I told him "you have changed the direction of music around the world. I went on to say how the Clash stands for social and political reform and delivers the message with passion and idealism like no other band. He thanked me and asked if I liked the show. I told him it was intense, "It was the third time I had seen the band on this tour and each time you played in a way that blended power and excitement with garage, thrash, funk, rap, and rhythm & blues with reggae. All types of musical styles in one." I went on to tell him that they played one of my favorite songs at this show, "Spanish Bombs." I said Joe "you are the Ernst Hemmingway of punk music. Spanish Bombs is a three minute version of his book "For Whom the Bell Tolls." Think about it, Something about England, The Call Up, Rebel Waltz and Tommy Gun are written like a Hemmingway short novel. He looked at me with a smile and said "let's hope I don't end up like him!"

I asked why they survived while other bands like the Sex Pistols or the Damned didn't. He said. "We have used negative situations and tried to stirrup the people listening. The Clash has a clear relevant political message. Basically, redirect your frustration and anger and try to change the status quo. Those other bands were confused, mixing various political ideologies and some just concerned about the money." I looked at him and said "you mean…looking for a real good space under the lighting." He just smirked. I wasn't sure if it was because he thought it was funny or he believed I understood his point.

I then asked him what he listens to. He responded "I like English Beat, Bo Diddley, MC5, reggae and funk music. He then asked me what I listened to. I talked about all my favorite bands and the great concerts I have seen. He listened very politely and didn't say much. He appeared drained from the show.

For the next few minutes we made small talk about America, Ohio and where the next concert was and the tour in general. When I got up to leave I shook his hand again and thanked him for his time. I told him that as long as I live I will always remember this night. He nodded and said, "Come back stage next time we come to this area or at another gig." As I walked away he began talking to another person. I turned and raised my camera to take one more picture of him and said "Joe, the Clash the only band that matters." He looked up and stuck his tongue out and made a face. At that moment I snapped the picture. I waved and smiled he just nodded.

I walked over to Paul Simonon and Terry Chimes and introduced myself. I said to Paul, "I have seen the Clash three times on this tour and I don't know if you would remember but when we were driving from Detroit to Akron back in August we drove by you on the highway." Paul smiled. He looked at me with an expression that said you got to be kidding. I continued. "You were in the front seat in a Lincoln town car and Joe was in the backseat in the middle. I was hanging out of the window yelling." He became very animated and said he remembered. "We did not know what was going on we were driving along and all of a sudden this car pulls up and you are yelling at us out the window. We realized that you knew who we were and were Clash Fans." He went on to say it was an eventful road trip to Akron because they were pulled over by the police for speeding.

I also asked him it was true that they released Sandinista as a triple album to say Fuck you to Bruce Springsteen's double album "The River?" Paul said, "We did what we thought was right. If they didn't like it they could piss-off." At that point two girls asked him to have there picture taken with him. Mick Jones was very entertaining. He was over by the food having something to eat. I went up and introduced myself to him. I said, "Great show." He said, "Thanks," and asked if I was hungry. There were trays of deli food. I thanked him but declined. He acted comical. I asked to take a photo he agreed and smiled. I took the photo and said "let me take one more." He then made a face where one eye was half closed.

I asked Mick "can you accomplish anything through rock & roll with a political theme?" He said "We try to be realistic; there is a difference between optimism and realism. Who knows, maybe it won't change anything, but I still believe in it and still believe its something worth the effort."

It was about that time when the bouncer began to herd everyone out of the room. I said good bye to Mick and headed for the door. As I got to the door I turned and looked around one more time. I new this would be something that may never happen again.

Photo 11

Photo 12

Photo 13

Photo 14

Robert J. Binney, United States of America

In 1982, it was as if the Clash didn't want anyone to become fans. The Shea Stadium show is held out as some pinnacle – but like the climber who makes it to the top of Everest but can't make it back down to camp, by the time they got to Queens the band may have been out of oxygen and didn't have anywhere near enough rope. To be fair, I wasn't there that day – but I'd been at JFK Stadium in Philadelphia two weeks earlier.

The Who claimed this was their farewell tour – and they were going out in style. The marquee that day included Santana and local faves the Hooters, in addition to the headliners and the only band that mattered. My ticket – from a scalper – was $15!

I'd become a fan a few years earlier when I saw a picture of Pete Townshend wearing a ripped Clash shirt onstage during their '79 or '80 tour. At the time, being a Who fan was transgressive enough – but these underground guys? <u>Punk rockers</u>? The sense of dread – of *danger* – that the Clash presented to my milquetoast suburban community was something that could not be ignored. Meanwhile – as my teenage band was wrestling with Creedence Covers and trying to insert a drum solo into "Sunshine of Your Love" – *Rolling Stone* was raving about *Sandinista!*

I couldn't justify the price of a three-record set on neighborhood leaf-raking wages, but a post-Christmas trip to the Princeton Record Exchange landed a nice used copy of *London Calling* – which, nearly 40 years later, remains my all-time favorite record of all-time.

In general, crowds in Philadelphia don't behave well (see: booing Santa, throwing batteries, "Eagles Court"), and they were not going to disappoint that day. It was uncharacteristically warm, and the opening acts went on early – the Hooters were done by noon. In other words, an early start on a lot of beer, a lot of sunshine, and over 100,000 rock fans shoved into a crumbling arena. The fuse was lit for any form of combat rock: when the lines for the men's room got too long, fans walked to the top of the stadium and pissed over the side into the parking lot; to get better views of the stage, several concertgoers climbed the lighting stacks. And that was before the Clash took the stage.

Santana's set was lackluster, and their sound mix was all wrong (a now-dated comment by my friend: "It sounds like someone is playing Space Invaders on the board!"). The crowd was drunk and ornery and tired of bands that weren't the Who. So who do they get? Some jackass with a mohawk in camo pants and combat boots, and an attitude that one-upped Philly's classic I-don't-give-a-fuck stance.

The band ripped through "London Calling" and "Rock the Casbah" – many knew the first, and the second had heavy radio play – but that was enough for most. But the Clash weren't going to stop there. They didn't want the paltry second-hand woolgathering given to a mere opening act – they wanted <u>attention</u>. Which they weren't going to get. Of course, that was all Joe needed.

The crowd may have turned against the band first, fueling their ire – or the band may have come out ready to rumble, which put off the 100,000 drunks in the stands. Was Joe legitimately angry we threw frisbees on stage or was it an act? Who knows? Who cares? (For what it's worth, Daltrey threw them back into the crowd – dude has an arm!)

It didn't help that they didn't sound great. The Who's PA system was state-of-the-art for the time – but the Clash didn't benefit from that. Whether it was mixed poorly, or the Clash just wasn't sonically prepared for that environment, doesn't matter; Philly was done with the Clash.

The more they were booed, the angrier they got; the angrier they got, the more they were booed. It was an awesome spectacle– exactly what my 15-year-old self believed a rock show *should* be.

They were both terrible and fantastic; what should have been a triumphant passing of the torch became self-immolating. It's always fun to play the game of "What one band do you regret not seeing?", and so many people I know wish they'd seen the Clash (for me, it's Talking Heads). I know I'm one of the lucky ones – sure, it wasn't the Times Square gigs, it wasn't even "their" show. But if there's one band to see with their backs against the wall, who will come out swinging and not afraid to take on a room (OK, a football stadium) full of belligerent drunks – who else would there be? Who else could there be?

Stephen Rioux, Canada

Four thousand eight hundred kilometres. Or if you prefer, three thousand miles. That is the approximate distance across the Atlantic Ocean from London England to Fredericton New Brunswick in Canada, where I lived for most of my youth. And while many of this charming city's historical buildings, landmarks and street names reveal a British heritage, I dare say any similarities between Fredericton and London end right there. That was especially so back in 1977 when punk was breaking wide open.

Fredericton was and remains a relatively conservative town, having an idyllic almost Pleasantville-like quality. That is to say, if you were to deviate from accepted norms or stand out from the crowd you risked instant ostracization.

The music of Fleetwood Mac, the Steve Miller Band, the Eagles, Bob Seger, Styx, Supertramp plus a handful of other artists – today's Classic Rock acts - was all the rage at that time. I don't recall hearing anyone speaking about The Clash, or the Sex Pistols, or The Damned. But somehow those archetypal punk bands managed to infiltrate my musical consciousness, from which they have never departed. That's especially so when it comes to The Clash.

Punk arrived at absolutely the right time for me. It proved to be an amazing emotional outlet. It was transformative, not unlike what Mick and Joe sang in "Clampdown" in that punk showed how *"anger can be power."* There was almost an overwhelming energy to the music. It was a massive kick in the ass of all that was mundane. And when it came to The Clash I found their music instantly mesmerizing, while their lyrics felt as though they were speaking to me directly. London was indeed calling to the faraway towns. No wonder I consider them to be my favorite group of all time.

I recall ever so vividly where I was on August 16th, 1977 when over the radio came the news that Elvis Presley had died at age 42. This was just over four months from the release of The Clash's self-titled debut album on April 8th, 1977. It was as if the *"King of Rock & Roll"* was making way for *"The Only Band that Matters."* And of course much has been made about the iconic London Calling album cover being of similar design to Elvis Presley's self-titled debut from 1956. Elvis represented the beginning of rock'n'roll, while The Clash was to be its future. That was the message I received.

Unlike the United States where their eponymous debut album didn't see a domestic release until 1979 and in a modified version, here in Canada it was released in all its original glory in1977. It was a raw, back to basics album with songs about social and political issues that truly mattered to ordinary people. From the pulsating drums that opened "Janie Jones", the first track on side one, until the abrupt ending of "Garageland" that closed out side two, the album is truly a frenzied ride. I would call it a most enjoyable short, sharp, shock. Standout tracks for me were "I'm So Bored with the U.S.A.", "White Riot", and "Police & Thieves". It left me longing for more!

Hence, I would read as much as I possibly could about the U.K. punk scene. In particular I subscribed to Trouser Press magazine, which was published monthly and often focused on both the U.S. and U.K. scenes. And when it was possible to find a copy I would read the U.K. music weekly's such as NME, Sounds and Melody Maker. However, living in Fredericton meant it felt as though all of this was occurring in an entirely different universe. I would therefore be left to my own imagination.

But it wasn't long before news came of a second album by The Clash. *Give 'Em Enough Rope* arrived in stores on November 10th, 1978. While perhaps a bit more tuneful and polished, thanks in part to Sandy Pearlman's production, it was in my opinion no less electrifying. In fact, the rapid fire drum roll and blistering guitar chords that open "Tommy Gun" still thrill me to no end! Personal favourites are the aforementioned "Tommy Gun", "Safe European Home", and "Guns on the Roof". I believe that the music on this record has held up incredibly well over the years.

Shortly after the album's release came the announcement that The Clash would finally be coming to North America on what was to be their *Pearl Harbour Tour*. They would make their continental debut on January 31st, 1979 at the Commodore Ballroom in Vancouver, British Columbia, Canada. Bo Diddley and local act The Dishrags opened.

Then on Tuesday February 20th they made their first ever appearance in Toronto at the Rex Danforth Theatre with Bo Diddley once again opening. Unfortunately, it's almost 1400-kilometres from Fredericton to Toronto. Having no money, no transportation and no ticket I was simply left to read about it.

The Clash returned to Toronto later that same year when they brought their *Take the Fifth Tour* to the O'Keefe Centre on Wednesday September 26th. They were supported by The Undertones and local group the B-Girls. Their set list for this tour included a few new tunes that would soon see the light of day on their next album *London Calling*, which would be released on December 14th, 1979 in the U.K. However, it wasn't released until two weeks later in North America.

Their O'Keefe Centre gig has become something of legend in Toronto. That is primarily due to the fact of some rambunctious fans having ripped out a few seats at this rather posh theatre. In reality there were only about 20 seats damaged, which prompted Cosmo Vinyl to sarcastically declare on the local television program The New Music, that there were probably just *"20 rock 'n' roll fans in North America."* Nevertheless, that is the one Canadian concert that I would have dearly loved to attend. But alas I was still in Fredericton and my circumstances remained unchanged. Therefore, I was yet again left to read all about it! That was becoming customary!

As much as I had already come to love The Clash, the release of their third album *London Calling* took that to an entirely different dimension. Hence, nearly 39 years later it remains my most treasured record album. In fact, it's the one that I would take with me to my grave. For me this double slab of vinyl is near perfection. It's sort of a cultural hodgepodge in that it crosses over multiple musical genres. While it's a punk record it's also infused with rock, rockabilly, R&B, ska, reggae, and it's even a little bit jazzy at times. On top that it revealed a social and political consciousness. And while the title track "London Calling", and perhaps a few others, may have stood out slightly for me, I think it's fair to say that every song on this album is an absolute gem. I never tire of listening to it!

I once visited World's End Estate, the high-rise public housing development in London where Joe lived during the recording of *London Calling*. It's located at the western end of the Kings Road where it meets Edith Grove. On its south side is the Thames River. During the recording sessions Joe would ride the Route 19 bus between World's End and Highbury New Park, where Wessex Sound Studio was located. In fact, in the opening verse to "Rudie Can't Fail" Joe sings; *"On the route of the nineteen bus."*

It does seem appropriate that he would be residing at World's End Estate given this is where he wrote the post-apocalyptic title track to the *London Calling* album. I went there to see what if anything might have been his inspiration. Certainly with it being located immediately adjacent to the Thames you understand the fear expressed in the lyric, *"London is drowning / And I live by the river."* Furthermore, the Thames Barrier, which was built to prevent flooding in Central London, was only under construction at that time. In addition, when Joe was writing the song lyrics the Three Mile Island nuclear disaster (i.e.

"a nuclear error") near Harrisburg Pennsylvania had just occurred on March 28th, 1979. Plus, there was the Cold War's enduring threat of nuclear confrontation, which if it ever did happen might result in enough atmospheric smoke to shade the Earth from the Sun, thus causing a "nuclear winter", destroying agriculture and plunging global temperatures. It appears that even climate change may have been on Joe's mind back then. Although I find it difficult to decipher the meaning of his lyrics in terms of it being related to a nuclear incident only or was he also concerned over a changing climate. Regardless, being there gave me a better appreciation of Joe's extremely imaginative and perhaps even brilliant mind.

After 1979 The Clash wouldn't perform in Canada again until 1982. So I would have to wait a bit longer if I was ever to see them perform live in this country. However, on Friday April 25th, 1980 The Clash appeared on the television program Fridays, which was the short-lived west coast version of Saturday Night Live. It was to be their first ever live, nation-wide television appearance in the U.S. There was just no way I was going to miss out on watching that!

The Clash would perform "London Calling", "Train in Vain", "The Guns of Brixton" and "Clampdown". I recall that Joe's leg was really pumping, even though he looked a bit tired. In fact, he had written a message on his white guitar that said "*I may take a holiday.*" And by the time they played their final number, which was "Clampdown", Joe was bouncing all over the stage. Simply put, it absolutely blew my mind! I thought it was truly fantastic and I was hooked forever from that point onward.

And incredibly just eight months later, on December 12th, 1980, the triple album *Sandinista!* would be released. I remember my initial disappointment upon listening to it for the first time. It seemed so far removed from what had come before it. I thought perhaps there might be enough good songs to fill a single LP. But a triple LP! Really? However, *Sandinista!* has proven to be an album that I have come to enjoy immensely. In fact, I listen to it with some regularity these days. It really was an album ahead of its time. In essence it was world music, which almost foreshadowed what Joe Strummer would do with his band the Mescaleros at the end of the 1990s.

That said, there were some instantly catchy songs on the album such as "Somebody Got Murdered", "Police On My Back", "Up in Heaven (Not Only Here)", as well as "Washington Bullets" to name a few. However, I believe there was much more to this record than initially met the eye. My overall impression is that perhaps the album was attempting to make a bold political statement concerning the direction the world was headed. It was a bit of a newspaper in that regard.

By the time of *Sandinista's* release, Margaret Thatcher had been Prime Minister of the United Kingdom for more than a year, while Ronald Reagan had just been elected and was soon to be inaugurated President of the United States. And of course the Cold War was still on with relations having been further strained in 1979 following the so-called invasion of Afghanistan by the Soviet Union.

Hence, some of the album's songs were themed around the ongoing East-West tensions such as "Ivan Meets G.I. Joe" or the aftermath of the Vietnam War with "Charlie Don't Surf". Others like "One More Time" touched upon poverty and race. As well there was other subject matters raised. But arguably the most important aspect was the album title itself, *Sandinista!* What message was it attempting to convey?

While I remembered hearing that name mentioned in the news occasionally, I didn't actually know much about it at the time. So I decided to look into it further where upon I discovered how the Sandinista National Liberation Front - Frente Sandinista de Liberación Nacional (FSLN) - or simply the Sandinistas, an armed opposition group, had successfully ousted Nicaragua's U.S. backed president Anastasio Somoza in 1979, thus ending the Somoza dynasty. The Sandinista's then established a revolutionary government in the country, which would subsequently become the target of the Reagan Administration, who set out to topple them though their support of the contra rebels, which also led to the Iran-Contra Affair.

The other interesting facet was the catalogue number for the U.K. album release, which was FSLN1. Again in reference to the Sandinistas. Taking it even further, in the official video for "The Call Up" both Mick and Paul wore authentic FSLN scarfs. Hence, one is left to conclude that via the album title (and its catalogue number) The Clash were actually acknowledging their support for the Sandinistas.

Then there was "Washington Bullets", which offered up something of a history lesson, particularly in terms of the relationship between the United States and Latin America. No other song by The Clash would open up my eyes more widely to the world's geo-political affairs than "Washington Bullets". It's fair to say that it contributed to the shaping of my personal politics. To this day I continue to be moved by this particular verse in that song; *"As every cell in Chile will tell/The cries of the tortured men/Remember Allende and the days before/Before the army came/Please remember Victor Jara, in the Santiago stadium/Es verdad, those Washington bullets again."*

Indeed, those words will always remind me of Salvador Allende and Victor Jara, both of whom died in the U.S. backed coup d'état in Chile, which occurred on September

11th 1973. Arguably the toppling of the Allende government changed the course of world history as it made way for a capitalist revolution that is better known today as neoliberalism. Correspondingly, it gave rise to the brutal and repressive dictatorship of General Augusto Pinochet as well as the neoliberal experiment that saw the Chilean economy restructured at the hands of the Chicago Boys. This was to be dubbed by economist Milton Freidman as the "Miracle of Chile."

Thatcher and Reagan are generally credited with having officially launched the neoliberal free market era, the evolution of which we are living today. There is a lyric in "Charlie Don't Surf" that I believe really speaks to that evolution and our failure to curb it. That is *"The reign of the super powers must be over/So many armies can't free the earth."* That didn't occur. Hence, it only seems appropriate to declare *Sandinista!* as the era's landmark album. It's almost as if it was announcing to the world that neoliberalism had arrived. That is, people everywhere, beware! But I digress.

Then along came 1982 and the month of May! On May 14th, 1982 The Clash would see their *Combat Rock* album released. And low and behold it was in May of 1982 that I moved from Fredericton to Toronto! I was now one giant step closer to seeing them perform live! Unfortunately, by that time they were beginning to disintegrate. Joe had famously disappeared in Paris during the spring of 1982, only reappearing on May 18th. Then Topper Headon was sacked on May 21st. Fortunately, they weren't finished yet, as Terry Chimes (i.e. Tory Crimes), the band's original drummer, was brought in to replace Topper for the upcoming *Casbah Club Tour* that was to begin on May 29th. That tour did not have a Toronto date unfortunately.

Meanwhile, the *Combat Rock* album would continue with similar themes to that of *Sandinista*, in particular post-Vietnam War America, while also adding a few new ones such as religious fanaticism as expressed in their massive hit "Rock the Casbah". Politically, the record was perhaps a bit less overt though. In that sense another similarity to *Sandinista!* was the U.K. album's catalogue number, which was FMLN2. In this case FMLN was in reference to Farabundo Martí National Liberation Front.

The FMLN was an umbrella organization formed in El Salvador in 1980 from five guerilla groups. They became engaged in an armed struggle against the country's military dictatorship that had come to power via a coup d'état in 1979 and who was being supported by it's mighty northern neighbour. As a result, El Salvador would be locked in a bloody civil war that ran from 1980 until 1992. Perhaps the most famous occurrence during the period of violence that immediately followed the coup was the assassination of

Archbishop Father Óscar Romero, an outspoken critic of the regime.

What I found to be really quite brilliant was how The Clash were able to make bold political statements simply through their album's catalogue number, which meant they did so without actually having to say anything specific about it. Ingenious really.

Then on August 9th, 1982 the *Combat Rock Tour* would begin with its first stop being the Red Rock Amphitheatre in Morrison, Colorado. This time their tour was scheduled to make a stop in Toronto at the Canadian National Exhibition Stadium on Sunday September 5th and yes I had a ticket! It was indeed a day to worship…The Clash!

The stage at Exhibition Stadium was set up for the Grandstand only (i.e. the covered north-side seating) as was typical for most concerts. There would be close to 20,000 in attendance. This would seem to be a long way from the band's debut performance at Sheffield's Black Swan on July 4th, 1976 or their first ever London gig at the Screen on the Green on August 29th, 1976! A lot had certainly changed over the course of just six years. You talk about "career opportunities"!

The opening act was the marvelous Black Uhuru who brought with them the incomparable Jamaican rhythm section of Sly and Robbie. They put on a tremendous performance and were extremely well received by the lively crowd. Personally, I was thrilled that they were the opening act as I had been into their music for a couple of years by then. In fact, it was The Clash who really turned me on to reggae music.

Beyond Bob Marley & the Wailers plus a few others like Jimmy Cliff, I hadn't spent a great deal of time exploring other reggae artists. However, that began to change upon hearing The Clash version of Junior Murvin's "Police and Thieves", which was included on their debut album. But especially so following the release of *London Calling* with songs like "Guns of Brixton" and "Revolution Rock". At that point I began to immerse myself in it, quickly developing a passion for its off beat rhythms.

With Black Uhuru's gear now out of the way and the stage reset it was finally time for The Clash to make their appearance. They did so against a backdrop of camouflage, and immediately they dove straight into my all time favourite song, "London Calling"! Fantastic! That was like an instant shot of adrenaline. In fact, the entire concert felt that way to me. The raw energy and excitement they generated was truly contagious with virtually everyone in attendance being totally enthralled by their performance.

They played 23 or 24 songs including two encores and they did so with such passion and intensity. What's more, as if they were a group of arsonists lighting a torch, the final two songs of the second encore were "I'm So Bored with the U.S.A." and "White Riot", which meant when they finally exited the stage for good it was as if they had left a house on fire. And nobody in the audience wanted it to be extinguished. But alas the crowd was to be left buzzing and wishing for more. For me it was certainly worth having to wait all those years to see them live. They did not disappoint. In fact, it would be days before I came down from my adrenaline high.

I soon began to wonder what The Clash would do next. Where would they go from *Combat Rock*? I suppose like most of their fans I couldn't have imagined that it would be to fall apart. But they did, and by all accounts it had been coming for some time.

As their loyal fans know well, the final concert with Mick Jones in The Clash line up was at the three-day US festival on May 28, 1983, which was held at Glen Helen Park in San Bernardino California before a quarter of a million people. As well Pete Howard was now on drums replacing Terry Chimes who had recently departed.

Their performance at the festival was certainly not without controversy. And once they finally took the stage - two hours late - before a banner that read "The Clash Not for Sale" Joe stood at the microphone in what appeared to be a foul mood. Before playing even a single note he would say with a snarl, *"Alright then. Here we are, in the capital of the decadent U.S. of A. This here set of music is now dedicated to making sure that those people in the crowd who have children, there is something left here for them later in the centuries."* Was this Joe prophesizing the future of humanity? Or what was it?

He would follow that up a few songs later with what appeared to be an anti-capitalist rant. He vented, *"I know the human race is supposed to get down on its knees in front of all this new technology and kiss the microchip circuits. It don't impress me over that much. You make, you buy, you die. That's the motto of America. You get born to buy it. And I tell you, those people out in East L.A. ain't gonna stay there forever. And if there's anything going to be there in the future it's got to be from all parts of everything not just one white way down the middle of the road. So if anybody out there ever grows up…for fuck's sake!"* I took that as being a slap down on the rabid consumerism and greedy materialism being generated though the newly emerging requirement for maximizing short term corporate profits (i.e. infinite growth). Joe may well have been a visionary!

Whether or not Joe's words were contrived, I don't believe they were, he was definitely onto something way back then. Certainly his demeanor would suggest that he was passionate about it. I do think he understood the path humanity had embarked upon under Thatcher and Reagan was not one that would be sustainable. We see that now, given the dreadful state – a collapsing biosphere - the world has evolved into today.

Flash forward to Glastonbury in 1997 and you discover Joe Strummer being at the forefront of carbon offsetting as a means of tackling climate change. It was backstage at Glastonbury where Joe decided to plant his own forest in order to offset the carbon emissions generated from the manufacture of his CDs, thus becoming the world's first carbon neutral artist. That idea gave way to the environmental "charity" known as Future Forest (later rebranded the Carbon Neutral Company (TCNC) they would have their fair share of controversy). In 2003, following Joe's death, Future Forest oversaw the planting of a Joe Strummer Memorial Forest (i.e. Rebel's Wood) in Orbost on the Isle of Skye with the trees having been purchased by Joe's family, friends and fans.

That aside, by September of 1983 word came down that Mick Jones had officially been sacked. Nevertheless, Joe and Paul would carry on under The Clash banner (i.e. The Clash Mark II or MKII), enlisting guitarists Nick Sheppard and Vince White as well as bringing back Pete Howard on drums. In the Orwellian year of 1984 the new lineup set out on their *Out of Control Tour* playing Toronto's Maple

Gardens on Monday April 30th with local reggae band Messenjah opening. Once again I had a ticket!

The attendance that night was modest, with the Gardens being at about 50% of its concert capacity (i.e. about 9000 people). But that didn't prevent them from playing with the passion and fiery intensity you'd have expected from The Clash. But it did seem as though Joe had a bit of a chip on his shoulder, as if he was trying to prove himself to all the naysayers.

I vividly recall Joe introducing the band and when it came time to introduce himself he sarcastically quipped, *"My name is Pierre Trudeau, are you ready for war?"* Of course Pierre Trudeau was Canada's Prime Minister at the time. But in the end I thought they put on a great show, which left me quite anxious to hear what they might just put down on vinyl in the way of a new album.

In November 1985 I discovered what that would be when they released *Cut the Crap*. My reaction to it then remains the same today. What happened? The music on that album bore little similarity to that of the original lineup nor to the one I saw during the *Out of Control Tour*. I found it extremely difficult to listen to, especially given all the ghastly synthesizers and drum machines. Wow! In my opinion, which has also been expressed by many others, *Cut the Crap* was more or less just that, crap. But as we're now well aware, Bernie Rhodes, the bands manager, was not an innocent party to all of this. Regardless, this proved to be the final nail in The Clash coffin.

The Clash MKII officially called it a day at the start of 1986. But unlike the Soviet nuclear reactor explosion at Chernobyl near Kiev in April of that year they went out with a whimper, not a bang. As good as The Clash MKII were live, it's fair to say that The Clash as we truly knew them ended on May 28th 1983 at the US Festival. At least that's how I prefer to remember them.

In the years that followed their demise I didn't really jump onboard Mick's Big Audio Dynamite (BAD). Other than purchasing Joe's solo album *Earthquake Weather*, which I thought contained some good material, I preferred listening to the original Clash albums instead. However, by the late 1990's when Joe decided to emerge from his wilderness years, bringing with him a new band called the Mescaleros, that all changed. They sounded fresh, new and exciting. Their music was diverse containing elements of traditional music from all across the globe. It was as if they had put it all together in a blender and made it their own. It was *Sandinista!* taken to the next level. It was certainly not a stretch to call this world music.

Unfortunately, I never had the opportunity to see Joe and the Mescaleros live. Sadly, he passed away before I ever had a chance. In fact, on November 15th 2002 I found myself in London at a conference. That was the very day Joe played a benefit concert for striking firefighters at Acton Town Hall, which saw Mick Jones join him on stage. It was to be the first time they played together in public in almost two decades and I wasn't able to be there! Damn! Here I was back to simply reading about it once again!

Joe Strummer died the very next month, on December 22nd 2002, which hit me, as it did many others, like a ton of bricks. It seemed surreal and I was stunned by it. I remember going to the Joe Strummer & The Mescaleros' website and seeing a picture there of Joe sitting in a field, which compelled me to send an email enquiring about the photo. It wasn't long before I received a reply from a fellow named Anthony Davie who ran the band's official website.

That would be the first but not the last time we crossed paths.

I don't recall exactly when but it was around the turn of this century that I went on one of those organized rock 'n' roll tours of London. While it was fantastic I found it to be very short on punk history. I longed to see more, particularly with respect to The Clash who I always felt had this incredible mystique about them. Hence, I began to research and therefore devise my own punk tour. As a result, I made numerous trips to London throughout the first decade of this century in order to explore London town's rich punk rock history. I walked all over the London neighborhoods where The Clash, The 101ers, the Sex Pistols and others lived, hung out, drank, rehearsed, gigged, recorded and were even jailed, plus much, much more. Fortunately, I was able to do so before many of these historic sites became caught up in the gentrification of London's neighbourhoods. Sadly, so many buildings and landmarks that were so closely associated with punk have now been lost or dramatically altered.

I did a similar rock and punk tour in New York City with a particular focus on The Clash. I even stayed at the Iroquois Hotel where most of the band lived during their recording of *Combat Rock*. Such tours always proved to be wonderful experiences and truly great fun!

Furthermore, along the way I was fortunate enough to meet a few individuals with links to The Clash such as Alex Michon who designed and made their stage clothing, as well the roadie Steve "Roadent" Connelly. Plus, on May 31st 2007 I attended the Carbon-Silicon gig at Bush Hall, which was the short-lived band formed by Mick Jones and Tony James of Generation X fame. I saw many familiar faces there such as Ray Gange, the star of The Clash film, *Rude Boy*. Mick certainly looked to be loving it.

Then at some point around 2005 or so I reconnected with Anthony "Ant" Davie who had since written a book on his personal experiences with Joe Strummer & The Mescaleros titled *Vision of a Homeland: The History of Joe Strummer & the Mescaleros*. I just happened to be purchasing a copy of his book directly from him online. ne thing led to another and Ant suggested we try putting something together to celebrate Joe Strummer's music. After all he had the connections to well established musicians that were willing to participate. o after a couple of failed attempts, it all finally came to fruition in 2009 when the band Los Mondo Bongo was born.

Los Mondo Bongo consisted of Pablo Cook and Steve "Smiley" Barnard from the Mescaleros plus Mike Peters (The Alarm), Derek Forbes (Simple Minds), and Steve Harris (Gary Numan's band). Also involved would be Ray Gange, the aforementioned star of the *Rude Boy* film, as well as Andy Donaldson, roadie and former Joe Strummer guitar technician. Ant organized five shows in the U.K. starting at the legendary Cavern Club in Liverpool while I organized six more in Canada.

As I would soon discover perhaps the greatest challenge of all was getting people to understand who Los Mondo Bongo actually was. The name didn't mean anything to most people. So I incessantly hounded the media hoping that someone would be willing to write a story on them. And eventually they did, which meant that all but the first show in Montreal was sold out or nearly sold out. The audiences were electric and the band was overflowing with energy. I had the time of my life on that tour.

But the highlight for me was seeing them play Toronto's legendary Horseshoe Tavern, a club that even The Rolling Stones had played. Their gig at the Horseshoe was to be on Sunday March 15th. That just happened to coincide with Canadian Music Week, which Los Mondo Bongo was not originally a part of. But after a bit of finagling that all change and shortly thereafter an article appeared in the Toronto Sun. They told their readers that during Canadian Music Week there would be 500 artists playing in 45 different venues but if they were only able to see just 10 performances then Los Mondo Bongo would be number three on their list. Ticket sales then took off. And what an amazing night that turned out to be! Yet another total adrenaline high!

About the Horseshoe Tavern show, Steve McLean of Chart Attack Magazine wrote, *"I saw bands for four straight nights during Canadian Music Week, and I'll be seeing a ton more over the next six days and nights of the South by Southwest Music Festival in Austin, Texas. But it will take a lot to impress me as much as these musicians did on Sunday night."* In fact, virtually every Canadian city that the band played the reviews were to be glowingly positive. As for me, I felt as though I had done my part and therefore I continue to cherish the memories of that amazing time.

I suspect that anyone having read this far now appreciates the importance that I place upon The Clash. Their music, and in particular their lyrics have remained a big part of my life. When I look at the world today, which I view as being in an absolute mess and perhaps existentially so, I always think back to what The Clash were singing about all those years ago. In many ways they forewarned what was to come. In that respect there really hasn't been any other band quite like them to my knowledge. Hence, as far as I'm concerned they truly were the *"Only Band That Matters".*

With that, it's time to signoff and to take my dogs Daisy and Strummer for a walk.

Frank Moriarty, United States of America

Author of "Modern Listener Guide: Jimi Hendrix"

On the afternoon of September 22, 1979, I was in a state of high excitement. At last, The Clash were in Philadelphia, scheduled to play the ornate confines of the Walnut Street Theater on the band's "Take the Fifth" tour. In just a few hours I would be one of the hundreds of people to fill the intimate theater, seeing a band that had skyrocketed to the upper echelons of my appreciation.

I'd landed a UK import copy of *The Clash* months before the realigned US version hit the shelves, tipped off to the band by Patti Smith. I loved everything about that first album, just wishing the potential power of the band was more evident, as had been the case with Chris Thomas' wall-of-Steve-Jones production on *Never Mind the Bollocks*. And then came *Give 'em Enough Rope*. The alliance of The Clash with Sandy Pearlman may have been an uneasy one in the studio, but there was no arguing with the results – from the first massive whack of Topper's snare to kick off the album it was clear the power and fury of The Clash were lurking in these grooves in full force.

I'd managed to snag a large promotional poster reproducing the cover of ...*Rope*, and was fixated with the idea of possibly getting one of the group to sign it before their show. So, ink marker and poster tube in hand, I set out that warm September day, leaving my apartment in central Philadelphia to travel just a few blocks. My destination was the Benjamin Franklin Hotel, a historic building that had opened in 1923. Its proximity to the Walnut Street Theater made it a likely temporary residence for The Clash while in the city for that night's concert with The Undertones opening.

I walked through the doors of the hotel and into the elegant, old world lobby, crossing the expansive checkerboard pattern floor while searching to see if I saw anyone with the band, or even one of the band members. In a matter of seconds, I realized there wasn't just one member of The Clash in sight – there were all four. Lounging on the lobby furniture, The Clash had set up camp near the elevators and were happily chatting with a small group of Philadelphia fans.

I made my way to the gathering and extracted my poster and marker, starting with Paul and Topper, then moving on to Mick. Joe, who was pretty much my guitar hero by that time, was last. He not only signed the poster, but helpfully drew arrows on the artwork to indicate which buzzards represented which band members.

My autograph mission complete – if only there'd been digital cameras in days of yore! – I settled into a quite relaxing conversation with Mick Jones. Eventually he asked me if I played in a band. No, I responded – I told him how I'd seen Jimi Hendrix when I was 13, and had since seen so many brilliant guitarists that the idea of playing myself was intimidating. "I've always wanted to, though," I concluded.

Mick looked at me for a second.

"Why don't you, then? I'm no better than you are," he said.

The mental light bulb switched on – and I got after it, better late than never. It just took the encouragement of someone

I admired to make it happen. I was off to Eighth Street Music in Philadelphia within days, buying my trusty '78 Fender – and I suppose you can guess why I picked a black Telecaster. Like Strummer's Tele, this guitar was indestructible, serving me well over the months and years as my band Informed Sources played with everybody from Black Flag and X to Bad Brains and the Replacements. It took on a battered vintage sheen the old-fashioned way, complete with my blood on the Informed Sources sticker between the pickups.

But how were The Clash in concert that September night? Everything I'd hoped for, blazing through 20 songs ranging from first LP highlights to sneak previews of *London Calling* material. The night ended with a sweat-drenched Strummer on stage alone, the PA cut off, shouting out an apology for not being able to play longer. No apology was necessary – they'd done their job.

As has often been documented, the fact that I'd easily reached the full band earlier that day was nothing unusual – nor did that access change. Two years later I was at the Bonds International Casino riot and a couple of the earliest shows in their New York City run. I'd happened to get a nice photo at the band's headquarters at the Grammercy Park Hotel of Joe and his "Sweet Gabriella." I thought Joe might want a copy so, before heading up for my next Bonds show, I had a print made for him.

Back in New York, I walked into the Grammercy lobby and immediately saw long-time crew member The Baker standing near the front desk.

"Hey, I've got this photo I think Joe would like to have," I said.

"Right!" The Baker replied, heading for the elevator. "I'll go get him!"

Two minutes later Strummer emerged, suggesting we go down the hall of the lobby for a chat.
At that time The Clash were one of the biggest and most influential bands in the world. Imagine something like that happening in our modern era of superstar isolation.

The day Joe Strummer died I took my portable CD player – loaded with *Give 'em Enough Rope* – and ran my headphones hard as I walked though the doors of the Benjamin Franklin Hotel for the first time since my initial meeting with the band that long-ago day. The building had since been converted to private residences, but the lobby looked exactly as I 'd remembered it.

Months later I went to The Clash exhibit at the Rock & Roll Hall of Fame in Ohio. I went straight up to the fifth floor the moment the museum opened, while everyone else was busy looking at the lower floors. The display was mine alone for a full hour. There was a powerful resonation to be in this space with the aura of The Clash all around me. Late in my solitary visit I was kneeling, reading Joe's handwritten lyrics to "Tommy Gun." Impossibly, that same song suddenly materialized at full volume on the video screen behind me. I saw Joe's face reflected in the glass over the lyrics as the song played.

Joe was always a really good guy to me, and we got to know each other enough to where he always remembered my name when we met.

I can still hear him croak it out in that unmistakable voice: "Hey, Moriarty!"

Photo 15

Phil Lovering, England

In 1977 I was 16 years old and recently left school I was unemployed and living in a small seaside town. I was into punk rock and went to see The Clash at Bristol Colston hall with The Slits, Buzzcocks and Subway Sect. The next week I bought White Riot 7" and then "Remote Control" and the "White Riot" album soon followed, the next time I went to see The Clash was later on that year in Bristol, Exhibition Centre which was a huge warehouse venue at Bristol Harbourside, there was a big gang fight at the centre after between Millwall, Bristol Rovers and Bristol City football supporters with punks, so I missed the bus back to Clevedon and met some St pauls punks who took me to a Jamaican blues club for the night away from the agro, so I met some new friends due to The Clash concert.

Then I formed a band (The X Certs) and the next time I saw The Clash was in 1978 at the Anti Nazi league festival in Stockwell park in London, my band (The X Certs) were also playing at the rally on the back of a lorry.

I enjoyed the clash because it was fast and furios minimal angry punk which represented the way so many young people in UK were feeling at that time because of unemployment, war in Northern Ireland, The national Front stirring it up and the left wing stirring it up.

I saw them play at The Locarno in Bristol a couple of times in 1978-1979, they introduced us all to an unknown band at the time who had no records at all and only ever played in Coventry, that was The Coventry Specials, who changed the name to "The Specials", they were supporting The

Clash on that tour. It shows that The Clash had good taste in music and were prepared to try to accommodate new acts on their tour. In fact after I split up with my band "The X Certs", they too were offered a support slot for The Clash in a big venue in Cardiff. That was in 1979, I went along to the gig as a roadie/stage hand for The X Certs and I was a little bit disillusioned by The Clash then. All the music had changed to pop reggae or just freeform jamming by the sound of it. They had some guy called Mikey Dread on the stage toasting away on the mike with Mick Jones the guitar player skanking around the stage trying to look cool, and not really playing the guitar. For me, it was not The Clash that I had grown up with and quite frankly their punk pose stance did not last very long did it? No, I was disillusioned and felt let down by someone I was looking up too. They were not punk anymore and just turned into pop stars

Alan Cross, Canada

Growing up on the Canadian prairies in Manitoba meant I never had a chance to cross paths with The Clash. All I had was my copies of London Calling and Sandinista and whatever I could find in the pages of magazines like Rolling Stone and Circus. Never being able to see the Clash live at their peak was always a regret. So when years later I had a chance to meet Joe Strummer in person, I wasn't about to miss out.

It was Saturday, October 30, 1999. Joe had rolled into town a few days before a gig with his band, The Mescaleros, to do a little press. At the time, my radio station, 102.1 the Edge in Toronto, had a storefront studio on Yonge Street where anyone could come in to see radio being made. The studio was especially popular when an artist came by for an interview or performance.

By the time Joe arrived at around 1pm for his interview, he was in a foul mood. He was suffering from a cold and was terribly congested. Because he had also brought his beat-up acoustic guitar to perform a few songs solo, he didn't want to disappoint anything with a croaky voice. He sat in the interview chair, warming up his voice and trying to work the phlegm out. But it was too noisy in the studio. Joe couldn't hear himself or properly tune his guitar. You could see he was getting frustrated.

Suddenly, Joe jumped up and bolted for the door. We were mortified. Was Joe bailing on us?

A couple of us ran outside onto Yonge Street in hopes of hauling him back inside. But Joe hadn't gone anywhere. He was leaning up against a fire hydrant on the other side of a very busy sidewalk, playing his guitar and warming up his voice singing "Janie Jones" from the first Clash album. He was busking.

I stood back and watched. One guy and his girlfriend walked past Joe with a glass. About ten feet down the sidewalk, the guy stopped, turned around and stared back at Joe.

He then turned to his girlfriend. "Nah, that's not Joe Strummer. Looks and sounds like him, though."

Alan Cross is an award winning Canadian broadcaster, consultant and music writer

102.1 The Edge. The call letters for that station are actually CFNY-FM and it was CFNY-FM who presented The Clash at the O'Keefe Centre in 1979....which was before Alan's time. CFNY was merely rebranded as 102.1 The Edge

Mark Sanders, Canada

Give 'Em Enough Rope was released in Canada at the end of 1978 and by the time I bought the LP I had missed their show at the Rex on the Danforth… so I was pleased as punch to see them returning to Toronto very soon for a gig at the O'Keefe Centre. My buddy Grant bought 2 tickets and we were set to go. The day before the show I became bed ridden with the worst stomach flu so Grant was desperate to find someone to tag along. Eventually he took our friend Marjorie who had never heard of the Clash and only wanted to go because there was an all girl band (the

B-Girls) opening up. That show received a ton of attention because of a feature done on our local TV show called the New Music about the Clash, the Punks and the damage caused at the venue. Suddenly it hit home, while my friends were watching a life changing punk rock show, I was in my pyjamas watching Upstairs Downstairs with my mum.

Years later I was playing in a band called Directions East. We sounded a bit like a cross between U2 and Simple Minds. In 1984 we had just finished an EP that was to have Canadian distribution through a major label. Around that time, the Clash were touring and promising local bands would open for them. Our manager Carl, who was one of the better Canadian managers at the time, reached out to the promoters. Eventually it was down to us and a reggae band called Messenjah (as I remember) We were told by the promoters the gig would be ours if … WE PAID THEM $10,000.00. We passed.

We didn't instantaneously pass, we actually had a meeting about it. Without a record to sell, it would have been $10,000.00 to stroke our egos. I was massively relieved as I thought we were a bit too "new wave" for a "Clash" audience and we would have been most certainly booed off the stage. Messenjah opened and they were certainly the right band for that opening spot.

Alessandro Zangarini & Giuseppe Rivela, Italy

Once upon a time, it was the first years of 90s, Giuseppe (an italian old Clash fan, from Turin) started to collect Clash bootlegs. His way was: "I send one live to you and you will make the same thing". At the beginning, all the thing was in Italy. Then it came Internet and the trade turned into "international".

One day, Ant Davie contacted him, and they reached an agreement. Beppe sent some bootlegs to him, Ant sent some pics about Joe & Mescaleros, because in that period he was following the band, all around U.K.

Since then, it started a mutual friendship that's still alive nowadays.

About me and Beppe, we met in the middle of the nineties, when I was the singer for Triggers, a punk-rock band, Clash, Jam, SLF oriented.

I was a great Clash fan too, and this common ground, between me and him made easy to become close friends.One day, I heard him play Rudie can't Fail tune on his bass : well, the Writing was on the Wall.

In 1999, Joe came back to the World with his Mescaleros. A new record (since his last '89 solo album), tour...we couldn't wait!

He went to play in Bologna, September 4th, a Festival with a lot of bands, Offspring e Sick of it All, to mention some. A good live that probably made the band to return in Italy after two months. On December 4th, they came in Milan, Rolling Stone. It was a great gig and for me and Giuseppe, a crucial moment for both of our lives.

After the show, we waited for him, with another dozen of people, Clash addicted and...Yes! He showed up: autographs, pics, talks, everything you had been dreaming for a whole life.

He was there, he was THERE FOR US.
Giuseppe was carrying with him his personal Clash bootleg list and showed it to Joe.
Joe looked at him, serious, no smile, straight in the eye.
We thought Beppe was going to be a dead man when Joe asked him: "Where did you get this informations?".

But he wasn't angry, he was only curious, so curious. Then Giuseppe explained to him his passion, all over the years, only one live for another live, with other people all around the world. That meant no profit, to move every step he was making.
So Joe asked Giuseppe to send him some good gigs – "With Topper!", he specified – and above all the first Pistols

gig, when they opened for 101ers...Could you imagine this? Amazing!

Everything ended with Bye and thanks but...no address was given to anyone...
But Giuseppe was a man of great hopes and send the stuff to Ant, knowing the he could reach Joe in some way with Mescaleros. And it was.

July 2000, Mescaleros came back to Italy, near Venice (Jesolo)to play for another festival.

Beppe came there, alone, and he reached the band, after the show, in the big tent where they were. He came in and Joe immediately recognized him, and gave him a great welcome.

On that occasion, Beppe could get Joe address and e mail too. It started a good friendship between the two men. Over the years, when Joe mentioned Giuseppe he called him "The King of Collectors", 'cause he was very impressed about the list he saw that day, in Milan. After that, Ant invited Beppe to follow some Joe gigs, in U.K. and Ireland. Obviously great moments.

What about me and Giuseppe? Triggers ended his story in 1998, after that, in 2000, we talked about a Clash Tribute Band. At that time, in Italy, it wasn't anyone who played

Clash stuff only. We called Gigio and Antonello, once with Triggers, to play guitar and drums.

About the name, a sort of mixture between two Clash anthems, Radio Clash and Guns of Brixton. Radio Brixton started to rehearse and, after a couple of months, had their first gig, outskirts Turin, their town. Ant Davie did his best as M.C. , we were happy about everything. That night, we knew that our aim was true, we was in the right direction to give a good tribute to Joe & Clash.

Ant Davie has been a great mate for us : he managed for us to play in London,in 2002. On July 10th we played in Fulham by a pub called King's Head. And the following day, to see Joe gig at Shepherd's Bush Empire. We met Joe again, lots of pics he was kind with everyone. If you think that on December 22nd he left us...so sad, heartbreaking. Radio Brixton, after Joe's death, kept on playing their gigs and, since 2003,every year at the Italian Joe's Tribute. Along the years, many Joe's mates showed there: Smiley, Pablo, Richard Norris, Chris Salewicz, Johnny Green, Robin Crocker, Pat Gilbert, Ray Gange and others. Good Old Ant... in 2007 he managed to make us play at Strummercamp. Radio Brixton ended in 2009, lot of passion to move them, during those years.We are still mates and Giuseppe and I wrote this kind of story,hope you enjoy.

Viva Joe Strummer!

Photo 16

<u>Grant Cermack, Canada</u>

Ah yes the Clash O'Keefe Centre gig. I was around 16. My friend and partner in punk Mark Sanders was sick so his ticket ended up with Marjorie McGeachy. She was one of the girls we hung out with in high school and exclusively an Aerosmith fan. We were pretty chummy so she ended up going with me. There we were, two Scarborough teenagers dropped into this crazy Clash "Take the fifth tour." I was a big Clash fan and thrilled to be there. Scarborough was all about lumber jackets, Kodiak work boots and 70's rock music. The O'Keefe was ablaze with early punk fans and an energy I can still feel to this day. I'll always remember this guy who was wearing 2 tone everything. Half his spikey hair was bright purple and the other was lime green. His suit jacket green and purple, opposite to his hair. And so it went with his shirt, pants, shoes and even socks. It doesn't sound so crazy now but back then it was radical. Kind of a punk rock Joker. I can still see him in my mind. People were pogoing on the lovely O'Keefe Centre seats and they kept collapsing. That scene was immortalized in the opening segment of City TV's New Music. The clip is out there somewhere. I did find this one while searching.

Jonathan Ganley, New Zealand

The back of the back of the BACK!

The Clash, pictured here playing at the Logan Campbell Centre in Auckland, New Zealand on February 6 1982. The Clash were at their peak that night and they gave everything to an audience that was hungry for roots rock rebellion.I
 recently heard a bootleg tape of the show, and so many memories came back as the Ennio Morricone introductory music swelled up and the crowd roared as the band appeared. Here's Joe Strummer's opening words, just before they launched into 'London Calling' and the whole place went crazy.

"All right, all right! It's quite a shock, it's quite a shock for us to see this here, like back home! We've just come from Japan where they sit way at the back of the back of the BACK!"

Photo 17

Photo 18

Nick Smash, Canada

It was seeing the band live at The Rex Theatre on Danforth Avenue, Toronto February 1979, with their backdrop of sewn together flags of nations from around the world, which seemed to say that there were different possibilities, but perhaps it was also a plea for unity; after all their homeland was on the verge of tearing itself apart.

The Clash were the last big punk 'stars', and by process of elimination were now voted to bring punk into the next stage. And what would they do? The band were already aiming higher than the Pistols - they didn't want to destroy...well they did, but they also wanted to build something that was better, both sonically and with a passion for fashion, which replaced the brain dead, dull and tired music industry and the bland radio stations across North America.

As we froze in the cold winter of 1978/79, it was our first chance to see punks' biggest stars at an old Greek cinema just over there along The Danforth. There was no fanfare when the tickets went on sale, Q-107 were promoting the gig, which didn't make sense as the station probably never played The Clash. Tickets were sold in the usual way...we went up to a shopping mall in North Toronto at 5AM and stood in a queue of...er...3.

We had front row tickets. Row A, seats 15 and 16.

There was a small mob of poseurs in front of The Rex...this bunch looked different though from the usual fans who went to the Edge, The Turning Point, or Larry's Hideaway around that time. They had quiffs, upturned collars and looked more like rockabillies than punks and they had better clothes than us in our ripped up DIY charity shop gear. The lobby was jammed full of people...a B Girl here, a Viletone there. Posters were up on the walls trying to promote The Clash's just released second album, 'Give 'Em Enough Rope' to punks who probably had import copies already. But of course, we Canadians were the first in North America allowed to hear the band's music as their first album wasn't even released in the States.

But what was it about these stories, images and myths that seemed so relevant to us living 3,000 miles away from where they happened in real life, not only to these bands but to a whole generation of bored and alienated teenagers? To us it was a vibrant, alive music with attitude that actually had something important to say to us in the back woods of Toronto. It was the pure-having-fun-being-dumb of the arty New York scene mixed with the more aggressive English scene that gave Toronto the best of both worlds. It was the antidote to the fading peace and love music that rock had turned into by the mid 70's, all big hair, flares and Fleetwood Mac's soap opera. It's just that 'Career

Opportunities' and 'Blitzkrieg Bop' seemed to say so much more than, 'More Than A Feeling'.

You didn't want to rush into the hall right away as there seemed to be too much happening out in the lobby...hanging out with friends exchanging furtive glances at each other checking out what everybody else was wearing, and who was hanging with who. Maybe the little Toronto punk scene had splintered, but on this night everybody came together in a makeshift old cinema in Toronto's east end to witness one of the best rock n roll bands ever.

Walking into the hall was like stepping into the world under the Westway or into The Hammersmith Palais. It was the tunes being spun by DJ Scratchy that added an extra element of atmosphere. He was mixing together some roots reggae with some old rockabilly, recent ska out of England and some 60's rock. It transported the crowd into Clash world and Clash time. This was the full experience. The band wanted to prove a point. Expectation was high.

True to the spirit of The Clash and the manifesto they continually preached during their tours in England, they always championed unknown groups to support them, and Toronto was no exception. While their short North American tour (dubbed The Pearl Harbour Tour) took in many American cities dragging Lee Dorsey or Bo Diddley, as supports, the honour for their debut Toronto gig went to True Confessions featuring singer Ruby T. Little known True Confessions played their set and filed off the stage with not much reaction from the partisan Clash crowd.

Slight problem of course was that the theatre had seats, and big burly hippie bouncers down the front were trying to keep the unruly punks back from the front of the stage. Joe rescued the 2 bouncers from a certain death. You can hear this on a bootleg live tape of the show as a frantic Strummer was trying to pull these guys onto the stage after the first number, 'I'm So Bored Of The USA'..."*You can stand over there! Stand over there side stage and just help anybody who gets crushed down the front alright?*" He wrote about it in the NME 2 weeks later. Scared the hippies off! We did that, we did! The crowd surged forward and the band kicked into 'Guns On The Roof'. The front rows became a scrum of belligerent punks trying to pogo while being mashed together, pushing and shoving.

There was a batch of new songs from 'Give 'Em Enough Rope' inserted into their set, but the sound was so awful you were forgiven for thinking they were doing different versions. Still there was no doubt Joe was giving it 110%, Topper more, and Mick and Paul just looked... well, they just looked the part.

My brother and I tried our best to take photos but have you ever used a manual camera in the pit of a show by The Clash in 1979? Forget about changing the film. What we got was a series of energetic images which were a bit rough and blurred around the edges perhaps, but they capture the explosive fire of the best live band I had ever seen.

Reprinted with permission from his book *'Alone and Gone - The Story of Toronto's Post Punk Underground.'*
https://aloneandgone.wordpress.com/

Ralph Heibutzki, United States of America

INTRO: AH, 1-2, 1-2-3-4...
Nobody grabbed me harder than the Clash.

As a teenager, I liked them long before I even *heard* them: I fell in love with those stark black and white press shots of those heavily-buckled, multi-zippered leather jackets and pants, topped off by spiked wristbands, studded boots, and simple, but solid shades of black, white and red.

Seeing those snaps in *TIME* magazine, of all places, made me exult: "If this sounds half as good as it looks...we've got a deal!"

So I duly snapped up *The Clash*'s import edition, and *Give 'Em Enough Rope*, in quick succession, and fell in love, all over again – twice as hard, and twice as fast.

Growing up in a conservative Southwest Michigan resort town – one that hadn't, and *still* hasn't, sent a Democrat to Congress since 1932 – I could definitely relate to Clash City's complaints of boredom ("City Of The Dead"), alienated youth ("Remote Control"), and repressive society ("Clampdown"). Check, check, and double-check!

INTRO

Alas, I was a shade too tender to catch the original Clash in action.

But once they'd parted ways with Topper Headon – and then, most daringly, and improbably, Mick Jones – my social circle suggested that The Only Band That Mattered sorely needed a tuneup.

Now, alone among my peers, the crazy quilt, quirky feel of *Sandinista!* posed no problems for me.

To this day, it's one of the albums that made me want to be a musician – yet the prevailing argument ("The Clash have lost their way") became easier to make on hearing *Combat Rock*.

The global dabblings that once felt so daring and inspired now sounded soggy and self-indulgent. Once again, I wanted to hear what had brought me to the dance, starting with those declamatory, ringing chords, via "Clash City Rockers":

BAH-BUM-BUM, BAH-BUM-BUM, BAH-BUM-BUM, BAH-BUM-BUM!

My only chance came on Thursday, May 10, 1984, at my future alma mater, at Michigan State University Auditorium (East Lansing, MI), where I joined a carload of friends, anxious to hear how this leaner 'n' meaner Clash might pull its own weight in the ever-glossier, ever-slicked-up '80s.

I don't remember anyone among our four-person group debating if the Clash's remaining founders – singer Joe Strummer, and bassist Paul Simonon – had the right to continue.

If anything, Mick Jones's absence offered a greater incentive to buy a ticket, as my late compadre, Tony Salazar – who taught me how to play bass, then guitar – summed up, in his own account, now posted on my website: "I can't overstate how divided I felt when founder-guitarist Mick Jones was dumped, but as a Clash loyalist, I *had* to see them."

MAIN RIFF

Jones or no Jones, Topper or no Topper, on this much, we all agreed, as our car rolled up near the MSU Auditorium: the old riskiness and uncertainty seemed well and truly back in the equation.

Reports filtering from Detroit, where the Clash had played a two-night stand at the Fox Theater (May 5-6), sounded encouraging – but what would *this* particular show bring? That answer took some time in arriving. Our tickets touted an eight o'clock start time, but that's not how it works, as any savvy showgoer knows.

First, came the inevitably ill-received opening act – who they were, I don't recall, but they lasted roughly 20 minutes, chased offstage by the Clash-hungry crowd.

Then came a string of reggae and hip-hop remixes – including a version of "The Magnificent Seven," crackling with gunshot-style effects, echos, and trick fadeouts – that I haven't heard, before, nor since.

Finally, just as the hour crept towards ten o'clock, and we couldn't shift in our seats any longer, a single white spotlight fell over the mixing board – and we heard the gonzo intro, courtesy of Kosmo Vinyl:

"Hip-hoppers...pill poppers...punk rockers...
flat toppers...showstoppers...and nooow...we haaave, for you..."

The roar of the crowd filled in the remaining blanks, as Strummer and company wasted no time bashing out the familiar opening one-two punch of "London Calling," and "Safe European Home."

I leaped right to attention, with my fists in the air, amid those clanging martial guitars.

Suddenly, I forgot the banalities I'd seen trotted out in the pre-gig press release: "Sound the alarm, as the casbah comes bringing combat rock to the MSU Auditorium."

Forget "The Star-Spangled Banner"! *This* sound felt like the real stuff – the rebel national anthem, as I noted years later, in a spoken word piece of the same name.

VERSE ONE

Still, as I've always taken pains to tell people, the band played a wider variety of material than its critics acknowledged – a quality that separated the Clash from many other lumpen punk acts back then,.

What stands out in my memory is how the lesser-known material fared, like "Know Your Rights." A song that sounded stiff and tentative on *Combat Rock* roared back to life onstage, raised from the dead of 24-track trickery by the guitar raunch of Nick Sheppard and Vince White.

They proved equally adept at dishing out subtle washes of color, when the song demanded it – notably, on "Straight On Hell," one that Tony singled out as "far more haunting than its recorded counterpart."

Nick's guitar leads provided a consistent highlight, as well as his gutsy vocal delivery of "Police On My Back." That moment suggested, given time, Strummer might a find vocal foil worthy of his departed partner, and restore a major element of the old Clash sound.

VERSE TWO

Peter Howard's drumming, we agreed, also offered the right blend of thunder, and finesse. Still, even Pete's deft touch couldn't redeem "Rock The Casbah," which – to our ears – suffered greatly without that bright, bouncy piano riff to drive it along.

Then again, it *was* the big hit, right? We hadn't come just to hear *that*, even if the band felt obliged to play it.

Paul stepped right up to the fore with "Guns Of Brixton," on which he played guitar, along with a haunting harmonica intro that breathed new life into his longtime vocal showcase.

Naturally, the band ventured into its share of spookier, dubbier turf, which it explored on lengthy versions of "Armagideon Time," and "Junco Partner" – the only other *Sandinista!* touchstone aired that night, but one that came as another welcome surprise to hear, all the same.

VERSE THREE

The night's set also featured four new songs: "Are You Ready For War?", "Sex Mad War," "Three Card Trick," and "In The Pouring, Pouring Rain." The MSU Auditorium's rickety acoustics made Strummer's lyrics hard to make out, although they all sounded promising, well and truly in the Clash groove.

Of those four, "Pouring Rain" impressed the most, giving Strummer a much- needed chance to catch his breath, and wring out every last ounce of emotion from a song that meant a great deal to him. Or so we felt, at the time, anyway.

"Are You Ready" and "Three Card Trick" cameo across equally well – with all the fire you'd come to expect – while "Sex Mad War" sounded a tad undercooked, to put it mildly. "Ah, well, it's only a new song," we agreed. "They've got time to get it down on vinyl."

Still, we came away, all fired up, and ready to join the Clash cause of setting the world's social ills right. On this night, at least, there seemed plenty of life left after Mick Jones.

CODA

Of course, this being Clash City, the show couldn't pass without its share of chaos, as I discovered, after taking a bathroom break in mid-gig.

I heard a furious commotion in the lobby, and emerged, just in time to see a towering guy, with an equally massive Mohawk, chasing the outline of a second guy, whose form I couldn't see.

"What the hell happened just now?" I asked.

One of my friends informed me that someone had just run off, carrying a stack of T-shirts under his arms, leaving someone – from the road crew, or more likely, the merch table – in hot pursuit.

History does not record who won.

For those who don't already know, this gig also went down in Clash lore as "Night Of The Missing Money."

A blurb in *CREEM*'s August '84 issue put the amount at $1,700, though the news didn't pass without a customary jibe: "Don't worry, Joe, we're sure it's going to some acceptably revolutionary cause."

I remember asking my newly-minted cohorts on the MSU Programming Board about it.

Apparently, somebody left the cash unattended – in a briefcase, with a combination lock – in a hallway, backstage. Somebody else then spotted that particular briefcase, and walked off with it, into the night.

Rumor had it that the briefcase contained the proceeds from that night's show, and that the *CREEM* blurb was meant to save face – though I've always been skeptical of that claim.

I asked Nick about it, years later, but he didn't remember, either.

Alas, no tape or CD bootleg of that night has ever surfaced, though I'm not ready to give up yet – if the Sex Pistols' final soundcheck can pop up, 40 years after the fact, there's ample time for my show to appear on somebody's CDR/tape list.

I *did* wind up with an equally interesting artifact, a couple years after I transferred to MSU in the fall of 1984.

I happened to be discussing the show with a journalism classmate, who then mentioned working the show that night, as an usher – and proceeded to give me the white, sleeveless T-shirt that he'd worn, no questions asked, and no money sought.

I wore it proudly, off and on, for the better part of decades. When it no longer fit well, I sold it on eBay, for $30.

OUTRO

Back on the car trip to Grand Rapids, my friends and I debated the usual topics: which of those new tunes might make a cracking new single, and who'd pulled off the better guitar parts, Nick, or Vince?

We felt invigorated by this blast of power and aggression that we'd just witnessed, one that promised to wipe the floor with all this top 40 blandness that our ears just couldn't stand anymore – starting with all that sickly synth-pop slush that Strummer spent so much time denouncing on this tour.

"If they can get *this* sound on a record," we agreed, "they'll prove all the naysayers wrong,"

Make no mistake, we felt – this band could throw down with anybody. Our heroes still had the stuff.

Our commitment continued beyond that night, such as in the fall of '84, when I rang up *CREEM*'s Detroit headquarters to debate some of the negative assertions that I saw in Bill Holdship's feature about the band ("They Want To Spoil The Party, So They'll Stay).

Lo and behold, Holdship came to the phone, and we had a civil debate – almost an hour and a half, as I recall – about the contents.

History does not record who won.

Not even the raspberries blown toward *Cut The Crap* – viewed largely as a dismal punk by numbers exercise at the time, but a bit more kindly now – could change the excitement I felt that night, when nothing seemed out of bounds, nor out of reach.

That's how the Clash made its fans feel, then and now, which remains – in my view – their greatest legacy, once you get past the music, and the echo of those guitars and drums. It's the sound I hear in my head today, and one that thrills me still.

REBEL NATIONAL ANTHEM NUMBER ONE
Whenever somebody claims,
"This can't be done," or, "It's always been this way,"
My mind harks back to that 40-odd-city US Clash tour of '84

& the greeting that kicked off every show:

"Good evening, hiphoppers, punk rockers, pill poppers, showstoppers, flattoppers, beboppers, young ladies... If you want to be out of control...now...is...the time!"

So, therefore: I pledge allegiance
To the shadow government of rock 'n' roll
& the no-nonsense R&B shakedown,
& the jive after five, for which it stands:

& the beats that hit us right between the eyes
& rearranged every one of our ever-lovin' five senses
& turned us on to something more than secondhand truth,
to wit;

#1: Freedom is more vital than a job.
#2: The blander the hit parade is getting
...the rawer the music must become, in response.
#3: We have the right to free speech...
...and we're not dumb enough to actually stop trying it!
So, therefore, per Joe Strummer & company:
I pledge allegiance to the shadow government of rock 'n' roll:
& the rebel national anthem for which it stands:

One nation under a groove or the sideways stomp
Of rival tribal double-barreled punk rock.
Like everything else, you pays your money & takes your choice,

...but I'm an unapologetic old-fashioned guitar romantic:
We the people, I think, can do a better self-management job
than all those crooked cops, bosses & corporations
Always trying to beat us back into line
(like so many dominoes): Therefore, once again,
I pledge allegiance to the shadow government of rock 'n' roll,
So: "If you want to be out of control...now is the time!"

JOE STRUMMER LIVE: REBEL RECOLLECTIONS (TAKES 1-2-3)

by **Anthony Salazar (1966-2005), United States of America**

REBEL RECOLLECTIONS (TAKE ONE)

I've been lucky enough to see Joe Strummer live at four phases of his career and have strong impressions of each one.

Although I missed the classic Clash when the COMBAT ROCK (1982) tour took them to Grand Rapids, Michigan, I vowed to see them next time. Unfortunately, that wouldn't be till two years later, when the Clash Mark II played on May 10, 1984, in East Lansing, at Michigan State University.

I can't overstate how divided I felt when founder-guitarist Mick Jones was dumped, but as Clash loyalist, I had to see them. Although I missed Mick and the songs that he put his stamp on ("Stay Free," "Train In Vain," and the newly-ironic "Should I Stay Or Should I Go?"), lead singer, spokes-bloke Joe Strummer carried himself well.
From bootleg audio and videotapes, I expected the first song of the night to be "London Calling," and indeed it was, which felt so formal that I thought I was standing for the national anthem.

However, Joe and the band -- founding bassist Paul Simonon, new guitarists Nick Sheppard, and Vince White, and not-as-new-as-them, but drummer par excellance Peter Howard -- pushed out some of the best, if not always the best-known songs in their repertoire, with gusto.
It may have been the moment, but I was pleasantly surprised by how well COMBAT ROCK's songs fared. "Know Your Rights" -- stiff on the album -- was actually convincing, and the moody, mournful "Straight To Hell" sounded far more haunting than its recorded counterpart.

The new songs that they played, "Are You Ready For War?", and "In The Pouring, Pouring Rain," showed promise. The new Clash carried themselves capably. Maybe there was something to this.

Alas, it was not to be, and a Clash fan, I had to suffer another kick in the teeth when the band fizzled out in early 1986, including fossilized versions of those new songs on their flagrantly-named final album, CUT THE CRAP (1985).

Ralph Heibutzki, a/k/a Chairman Ralph, is a musician, spoken word artist, and author of *Unfinished Business: The Life & Times of Danny Gatton* (2003), and co-author, with Mark Andersen: We Are The Clash - The Last Stand of a Band That Mattered (2018). We Are The Clash For more information, visit: www.chairmanralph.com

Jonathan Parry, England

The Clash were everything to me and I still believe they are a big part of me and inform the way I feel about the world.

But. The greatest thing that happened regarding the Clash is that, aged 14 at a concert at De Montfort Hall Leicester, Joe Strummer held up my shoe (which I had lost in the crowd).

I have recently located a recording of this very moment from January 1980.

Sadly, as I was now at the back of the hall (one unshod foot too vunerable for the crowd at the front) i could not communicate with my hero.

Ian Templeton, England

I spent the latter years of my teens and the bulk of my twenties wishing I was five years older. If my parents had only had the foresight to conceive me in 1961 (and move to the Capital) I would have been able to see all the early punk shows, including, of course, the first Clash gig up in Sheffield. In all likelihood I would probably have met and befriended Jones and Simonon well before and most likely been an ever present at the bulk of the 101ers shows in squattville. I don't think it's inconceivable to suggest I might even have been **in** the band. Bloody parents !!

Once exposed, circa 1980, I did my best to make up for lost time. After dabbling with some lesser outfits and amassing some starter vinyl I set about learning all things 'Clash'. This culminated in me seeing the band on the Casbah tour at the Bristol Locarno on August 3rd, 1982. It was the second night in Bristol and transpired to be Mick Jones' last ever UK show. Topper had already gone and there was some sort of tension/on stage aggro (I can't really remember), Police On My Back does stick in my mind, Jones' guitar hook piercing and magnificent. Keith Allen was the 'edgy' comedic compare and I felt small and slightly scared in among the seasoned 'punks', but I entered the dancefloor fray and got stuck in.

The deal was sealed and from then on I vowed to never miss another hometown show.

They returned once! It was in January 1984 and I was on the front row. Mick had gone and Joe was sporting a savage trim. Paul was still cool and I grabbed his boot during the encore. Why would anyone do that? I remember the stage was a wall of TVs and that a large fella jumped down onto the speaker stack from the Colston Hall balcony and hugged Strummer.

Regardless of the general negativity in the music press I couldn't get enough and when I got wind they were playing in Denmark at the Roskilde Festival the following year, off I went with a school friend and my younger brother. We inter-railed via Holland and Germany and the friend's dad (who happened to live somewhere within half an hour of the festival site – how lucky was that!) collected us and took us to his home. It's still the only foreign festival I've ever been to. I think the Cure probably also played and maybe The Psychedelic Furs? The Clash headlined the Saturday and I remember being impressed by Pressure

Drop and an extended mix version of The Magnificent Seven I'd never heard before that was played over the sound system once the performance was done.

A month or so later and it was all over. What was I to do? I didn't fancy becoming a New Romantic and the whole emerging Goth scene just struck me as slightly silly. The situation seemed bleak, but I needn't have worried. One by one all the players re-emerged and as they pursued their varied paths they took me with them and lots of great nights followed.

First out the traps was Mick with his new 'technology heavy' band, Big Audio Dynamite. I saw them a whole bunch of times, mainly in London and with various different line-ups and name changes. Always different but always excellent.

I saw Joe fronting the Pogues, went to a couple of solo shows and a number of Mescaleros gigs. The highlight though, was meeting Joe on the steps of the sadly recently closed Bristol Bierkeller in 1988. He was in town for his Class War show with Latino Rockabilly War. Just around the corner from my office I was dressed in my work clothes (I'm cringing thinking how uncool I was), but Joe fresh back from a toothpaste mission to Boots greeted us, signed my copy of Permanent Record (released the same day I recall) and said he was looking forward to the gig. The show was brilliant and one of the hottest, sweatiest nights of my life.

The joy of shaking an exuberant Mick Jones' hand at the Bristol Fleece & Firkin as he walked the floor prior to a sparsely populated Carbon/Silicon gig in the early 2000s still makes me smile thinking about it. Paul's brief reincarnation within Havana 3am was another great night at the Fleece circa 1991 especially The Guns of Brixton rendition.

Nick Sheppard popped up in Head and they were amazing. Numerous great nights, mainly in Bristol spanned their three albums in the late 80s.

Not everything went to plan. I thought better of travelling to the Palace Theatre in Bridgwater on November 17th, 2002 to see the Mescaleros – they'll be back in Bristol before long …. The unused The Good, The Bad & The Queen guest pass in January 2007 (you fool) and only a couple of years back whilst parked next to Keith Allen at Morrison's in Nailsworth I was too shy to ask him about his stint on the Casbah Tour or his subsequent West Country escapades with Joe. It was my youngest who spotted him, "look Dad, it's the baddie from Robin Hood".

Brit Pop, The Smiths/Morrissey, Dylan, Teenage Fanclub, REM, The Fall, Stone Roses, AC/DC, Sonic Youth, Wreckless Eric, Portishead, Green on Red/Chuck Prophet, The Stones, Sleaford Mods, Undertones, Grunge, The Beatles, Brilliant Corners, Pavement, Charlatans, Julian

Cope, Manic Street Preachers, Pixies, Foo Fighters, The View, The Kinks, Ash, Madchester, Buffalo Tom, Billy Bragg, Husker Du, Stiff Little Fingers, Kelley Stoltz, Beastie Boys, Arctic Monkeys, Velvet Underground/Lou Reed, Idles, Ramones, Trampolene, The LAs, Violent Femmes, Super Furry Animals, Kings of Leon, Housemartins/Paul Heaton, Libertines, PIL, Dinosaur Jr and numerous others have all played their part in my musical journey, but The Clash underpin everything. Whether it was a direct association or a simple reference in the music press, one thing led to another and thirty eight years later I have a house full of

vinyl, books, paraphernalia and CDs and a wealth of belting memories.

My eldest loves music and recently told me he wished he was older and had seen all the great bands I'd seen over the years. Funny huh !!

Up The Gas.

David Zensky, United States of America

This is my Clash story: from the first time I heard them as a teenager through today when I perform in my Clash tribute band Mockingbird Hill with some really great band mates. I'm old enough to have seen the London Calling tour - forever etched in my brain — and most of the Sandinista shows at Bonds. It is no understatement to say that the band has played an important role in my life - musically, politically and emotionally. I think all the time (like every day) about what Joe would be doing and singing about if he were here today to confront Trump, the rise of nationalism in Europe and worldwide, and the agony and demonization of refugees.

I am pretty sure the year was 1978, and even more sure the song was Safe European Home. That was my initiation. Rope had just been released in the U.S. and this cut got some airplay. Against a prior steady diet of Zep, Yes, ELP, and Pink Floyd (I was 16, cut me some slack), Safe European Home sounded like a cannon shot, booming, urgent and alarming. Power chords, searing arpeggios, authentic vocals and a reggae outro - It was like nothing I had ever heard before, and it expanded my musical taste forever. I bought the album and was hooked.

Of course I soon thereafter bought The Clash, and then on its release London Calling. Wow. The album left me and countless others speechless. Clampdown! Death or Glory! I'm Not Down! It taught me a lot about diverse musical influences, and even more about how quickly a band could progress. Rolling Stone Album of the year!

Feb 1980: My very first live clash show - Capitol Theatre, Passaic NJ. I had been to 100+ concerts at this point in my life, from Arenas, to mid-size venues, to clubs. I had already seen Springsteen and knew about the power of live music. But the Clash circa 1980 took it to a new level. 4th row center seats. How do you describe something that is equal parts chaos, exuberance and majesty? There is a very grainy video of this show from the in-house system; some of you may have seen it.

The first time I met the band was sometime around this show. A friend of mine found out that they were rehearsing at some studio in the garment district in NYC. A bunch of us took the train into New York and waited outside. We could hear the muffled music from an upstairs window. Too afraid to go in we just waited outside. Hours passed. Eventually our heroes materialized through the front door - guitars and bass still strapped to their back, sans case. They chatted us up for a few moments and then took off, walking right up 8th avenue into Times Square. Yes, just walking up the street, dressed mostly like urchins, with guitars slung across their backs.

Sandinista: Everything about this album impressed me. The lyrical sweep and its political content, the studio experimentation, the attention to what was new and from the street, and the fact that they priced a triple album so low (to make it affordable to most) such that they would make nothing on it until more than 100,000 units were sold. Up until now I had read and thought about their lyrics, but lyrics were always secondary to the beat. After Sandinista the message and the music were equally powerful and important in my mind. Songs like "Washington Bullets", "Rebel Waltz", "The Leader" and "Somebody Got Murdered" made me think about history, government, abuse of power and humanity in a new light. They opened my eyes politically, and I loved them for it.

From 1980 to 1984 I was away at College in Upstate NY. Returned to NYC for several of the Bonds shows in 1981. Lots has been written about that already. So special. Later, after "Combat Rock" was released, they played in the gym at our college! Yes, they came to Binghamton NY and did a two hour show! Before the show they autographed my buddy's combat van (a minivan finished in camouflage paint) with cans of spray paint. After they show we hung with them (Ray Jordan always made sure the kids got in to see them) and got our first pics and handshakes. Joe was earnest, Paul was friendly, Mick a bit hazy. We had previously nicknamed one of my best friends Russkie Bear (before Ivan meets GI Joe was released I should say); backstage Joe asked him if he was a Russian bear. Other shows I saw in 1982 included two in Philly and one up in Toronto and the Canadian National Exhibition. At the end of that show crazed fans (me included) tore the camouflage "combat" netting away from the front of he stage

In 1983 `when I started an alternative music magazine at College, I named it "Crookedbeat" (with the "db" Inc the middle in bold). We put The Alarm (heavily influenced by the Clash) on the cover of our first issue, around the time Mick and Joe parted ways. I saw Joe's new Clash a few times. Excellent live, but not the same thing.

Rude Boy: When Rude Boy was released we were all thrilled. The scenes of early rehearsals and early UK shows provided more excitement and Adrenalin than anything, including substances of choice. From the first year it was released and the next several, my friends and I had a "Combat Rock" party every summer in which we all convened at someone's house for the weekend, enjoyed each others' company, partied heavily, and then sat down for a communal viewing of Rude Boy. One summer we had the party in Buffalo, once in Binghamton, and once in Boston. We usually had a sign-in board at the entrance, where you had to sign in with a clash lyric of choice. Mine usually was from "Gates of the West".

Today I am a well-paid lawyer. I sometimes think about the scene at the bar in Rude Boy between Joe and Ray where Ray says he wants to be rich and Joe says "I've seen that road and it leads nowhere". In my case it has led somewhere, I have a beautiful wife and two great kids (16 and 19) who know all about the Clash and why they were the Only Band that Matters. When I am not busy lawyering, the past 4 years or so I've been rehearsing and gigging with some really excellent musicians (and awesome human beings) in a band we named Mockingbird Hill (right, from Spanish Bombs). I usually play a black Les Paul, Custom to try to get Mick's look and sound. In June we headlined at a club in Westchester called Garcia's and did a 1.5 hour set that included all the best Clash cuts, a few Ramone's songs, and an acoustic version version of Redemption Song a la Joe's take on the song. Long live Joe, long live the Clash.

Photo 19

Photo 20

Photo 21

Rich Baybusky, United States of America

I was indeed at a bunch of these Clash gigs,including Palladium 1980,Bonds shows and both Shea shows,as well as Philly gig opening for the The Who. I was also at a bunch more as well including the Pier shows and Asbury Park .

I actually first heard the Clash during a WNEW FM bdcast of one of the two Palladium shows,their first shows in NYC in Sept 79.

Although I was into the Pistols and Elvis C,Ramones Patti Smith right from the get go,it took slightly longer for the Clash,can't remember why that was but once we heard that live show,it was game on.

I can tell you one interesting story about the Clash at Bond's shows. Here in NYC it was well known that a rival club called the Ritz were more or less responsible for what happened with the fire marshalls. When the band was booking these shows,the Ritz was dying to host them. The Ritz was pretty awful most of the time,always oversold and packed with an extremely surly staff. The Clash,realized,I'm sure that club would be way too small for them by this time,however the Ritz was not appeased.

I was at the very first night of the Bond's shows and it was NOT dangerous or oversold,not really. The place was huge and there was plenty of room towards the back,if you needed a break from being in the crowd.Fantastic gig!

Anyhoo,when the shit hit the fan,the band were forced to cancel that one night,believe it was night 3. So we went down to the Gramercy Park hotel,in the village because we found out the band was there. Sure enough they were as was John and Keith from PIL. We hung around and talked to Keith Levine,who was sitting around waiting for John who never showed,at least not while we were still there. Finally members of the Clash started to appear,it turns out it was Topper's birthday or something they were gonna head out super late. Paul and Topper both left,believe Paul had quite a hot babe with him when he left. I went into the bar to get a drink and sat down at a table with my friend and who walks in but a completely sloshed Joe Strummer. I walked over and said hello and he actually sat down at the table with us. He seemed very upset indeed,he was saying that he thought the fans hated the band now because of this huge mess created by the Ritz.He loved NYC and was deeply upset about this. We assured him we were huge fans and we weren't mad at the band at all,as we knew the score. He liked that and started to talk about how much he loved the city and they were going to fix this no matter what it took. He then went on to talk about some hot babe he was chasing for the evening and that he had to go to this party but he couldn't find his girlfriend. We talked for maybe

10 or 15 mins and then he was gone into the night . He was just an extremely nice guy and we really felt bad that he felt so guilty about the mess,which they really had nothing to do with. I'll go on to see a few more Bond's gigs as well as many others.

Was always so sad about Topper,I like to think had they continued ,he might have gotten himself back together and rejoined them but it wasn't to be.

As for the split with Mick,well,that took me some time to get over.I never saw ,what I called the "bogus" Clash,as it didn't seem important to me to do so,the band w/o Mick wasn't the Clash and I was super pissed at Joe's behaviour. Joe was having a hard time with the size the Clash had grown too and he didn't handle it well. Plus I'm reasonably sure Mick was a giant pain in the ass.At the time I didn't care and when BAD appeared I was right on them,saw lots of their NYC shows,including the landmark shows at Irving Plaza ,which for me ,was the highpoint of BAD live.

Sadly I won't see Joe again till 1999 at Irving Plaza and it was wonderful! Loved him and the Mescaleros. Great gig. I actually would have seen,his 1989 Palladium show but had other tickets to see D Harry. If I had known he wouldn't play in NYC for 10 years after that show,would have handled that differently. Oh well,it's all ancient history now.

One other thing that really stood out for me,was their Asbury Park shows in 1982,very soon after Topper left.We were all quite worried about Topper's absence,he was such a great drummer,like seeing The Who w/o Keith. But Terry was great and I think lesser fans didn't even notice. The night we went was extremely foggy and the atmosphere at that gig was really special. It somehow really added to the show and Joe made several comments about the fog off the stage that night. The show really cemented how solid we thought the Clash were and we would see them many more times very quickly in 1982,we had no idea it would be the last times we would ever see them. I always say,we went to Shea to say goodbye to The Who and what we really turned out to be doing is saying goodbye to The Clash. The Who still continue in a very watered down version to this day! BTW,The Clash were very well received by the crowds at Shea,I remember thinking perhaps this whole passing the torch thing was going to work,sigh. Guess that's all I have to say for now. Hard to sum up what the Clash meant to us,although we thought the whole fashion thing of punk was not all that interesting,tons of the music that came out of that movement I still love to this day. Punk was nothing but rock and roll reinvigorated,the label "punk" meant little here in the US. If it's a crime to say I love both the Beatles and The Clash,well guilty, I think they did too!

I'll say one more short thing. My friend Gene went to almost every single show of the The Clash at Bonds! Think he missed one of the matinee shows,as his boss insisted he work. He lived on mescaline and bananas ,it was Gene who actually taped most of the surviving audience tapes of those gigs. I still listen to these shows all the time,it was like seeing a whole tour in one venue! Good times indeed.

Perhaps it's time to release a Bond's show officially,perhaps you guys could put in the word!

Last thing,we could sure use a new Clash and a new Joe Strummer for these current times. I think Joe would have been extremely upset about the current world situation,esp here in the US with that lump of poo Trump as ,gulp,president. But the great thing about Joe was,it was never over and now the battle would be on,miss him so much.

I forgot to tell you maybe the coolest thing,I did with the band,they never knew about.

In Feb 1981 Elvis and the Attractions appeared on The Tomorrow Show with Tom Synder here in NYC. I was working across the street in the mailroom of some insurance company. It was taped at the NBC building in Rockefeller Building, where SNL has been for decades, among all the other shows. Anyway, we were all the way down front in the aud,all the way over to one side, where lots of staff were hanging out. When Elvis finished and we were leaving, we started talking to the guy in the suit ,who was watching the taping along with us. Don't know his name or anything but as we were finishing up and heading out I said to him ,he should have the Clash on. He looked at me,I could tell, he had no clue. I said something like, they just announced like eight shows(don't remember the original number of gigs before the problems began, offhand) in the city and instantly sold them out. He got interested,I said check them out their great. Well, you know what happened. So I went to NBC building after they announced the show and asked if there were going to be tickets available. They told me,that show is super hot and after the tickets they hold for NBC tour groups were gone ,only NBC staffers are going to be allowed in. I was so pissed,I begged them to let me talk to that guy on the Synder staff but was more or less laughed out. So I got screwed! I helped make that happen with an off hand question ,then got shut out of the taping. Now it's just a fun story but I was so pissed back then. Anyway, I did go back a few more times and saw the absolutely great Jam appearance on the show,sadly the best version of Funeral Pyre ever got mostly cut from the bdcast but man,it was great. I also saw The Ramones,who were annoyed that Tom was on vacation and were openly rude to the substitute host. They then snuck out the back to avoid their fans,the only band I saw do that there. Such is life. Again,good luck with everything and I hope to read the whole book one day. I'm thrilled to be part of it.

Graham Southard, England

We went up to Birmingham Barbarella's on a Sunday for a one off gig being filmed for the Rude boy.

The Police and Thieves was used in the film. You can see my head at the front and my now wife Lydia.. It was a great gig and the Specials were support. One of there first if not the first as the Specials, Terry Hall still had a pony tail!

After we missed the train home so ended up going back to the Post House hotel with group. We got in the back with Mick and his girlfriend Johnny Green and Topper up front.

We had a few drinks and crashed out in Toppers room and Johnny . Where Topper proceeded to show us his Bruce Lee skills by jumping on the bed flying through the air and putting his foot through the wall, and demonstrating the use of nunchucks by taking out the ceiling lamp shades. In the morning we covered the hole over with one of the pictures in the room.

The shades went in the bin.

We got the train back to London in the morning and back to work Tuesday. We have lots we could talk about the group and Johnny and Robin and Baker. They treated us like family.

What more can I say. The only band that matured!

Photo 22

Jeff Frelich, United States of America

The Clash – Roots, Rock, Reggae

The Clash was, and continues to be, a major influence on my life.

Before discovering "the only band that matters," I was a big Who fan. I saw The Who when I was only 12 years old on the "Quadrophenia" tour in 1973. Lynyrd Skynyrd opened and it was the first concert I ever attended. I still don't know how my parents let me go, but thankfully they did.

I loved The Who all the way through high school. They were always my favorite band. My friends and I were stuck in the past, though, as we lived in the Midwest and simply didn't know any better. Who, Stones, Zeppelin - among others - is what we listened to. And believe me, we listened at full volume. We loved Dust but didn't realize their drummer would go on to play with Richard Hell and then the Ramones. If we did, we for sure would have gotten into Punk much earlier, but as it was, the early years of the punk revolution sadly passed us by.

I used to subscribe to Creem magazine and remember seeing articles on the punk bands but never acting on any of them. There was also tons of negative publicity, which I'm sure influenced me tremendously. But in March of 1979 I finally decided to go to a local record store and check out the band they were raving about and whose live shows were incredible – The Clash. That was before social media, of course, and I remember seeing a picture where Jonesy was in mid-flight like Pete Townshend and I was very intrigued. I also thought the name was extremely cool. The Clash.

So I went to the store and as luck would have it a huge Clash fan, Jim Roehm, worked there. We hit it off and I went home with the import of "The Clash."

Man, it was so raw and so unlike anything I had ever heard. I was just blown away. It was angry and rocking and catchy – I played it non-stop and just fell in love with it. Not sure if I bought "Give 'Em Enough Rope" at the same time or a few weeks later. I loved that one, too. Lots of critics didn't, I know, because of the polished sound, but the songs were all fantastic - and powerful. Roehm then got me the lyrics to the debut (I had spent countless hours trying to decipher them). I also purchased all of their singles and by the time the "Cost of Living EP" came out a couple of months later, I was all caught up and was the biggest Clash fan around. I also started getting into the Pistols, Buzzcocks, Ramones, Wire, and others - everything I had missed the previous couple of years.

In the fall of '79 I was away at college when Roehm called and told me The Clash would be in Chicago on their "Take The Fifth" tour. I was 18 years old and more than ready. There was no way I was going to miss this. I drove 420 miles with four buddies and was psyched beyond words. It was a Friday, September 14, 1979. We got in town around noon and after checking into our hotel I remember we drove by the venue, the Aragon Ballroom, and to our dismay saw a line already forming! So we hopped out, got in line and waited for close to seven hours.

The doors finally opened and we sprinted in and got great seats about 70 feet back or so, directly in the middle. On the bill with them was Bo Diddley and the Undertones as well as DJ Barry Myers.

I remember the support bands were cool, but I was there for The Clash. Around 10:30 pm a giant backdrop of assorted Nation's flags dropped behind the band and brought them so much closer. We all then stood up on our chairs. The atmosphere was absolutely perfect and charged with electricity. Jonesy started things off by saying "this is Chicago, 'ome of the Blues, right?" He then played a slow, bluesy riff (I later realized it was "Jimmy Jazz" which had yet to be released). Joe sauntered across the front of the stage with just an awesome presence. I remember his feet were together and he shuffled slowly across the stage; toes to the left then heels to the left, toes then heels, toes then heels, etc.

I will never forget what happened next - as the song wound down, bright lights hit and all of a sudden a big cacophony of sound exploded and they went right into "USA" and it was insanity. Jonesy was all over the place, Paul was so cool, and Strummer - you couldn't take your eyes off of him. He was just so intense. They played for about 75 minutes, I knew all the songs (except the few from the soon-to-be released "London Calling") and the band exceeded any and all expectations. It was the greatest show I ever saw in my life.

It's funny, too, how I remember certain things, all these years later. During "English Civil War," Joe didn't always sing "marching right over our heads," but instead just looked up in a possessed kind of way when it was time to sing those lyrics. And during "Jail Guitar Doors," Jonesy didn't drop the F-bomb after the verse about Keith and the Stones.

A few months later Roehm somehow got me a cassette of the show. Apparently it was recorded for the King Biscuit Flour Hour. Even though it omitted a couple of songs I was still knocked out. And to fill up the end of the tape, someone (I still don't know who) added some reggae tunes. Two tracks from Linton Kwesi Johnson as well as one each from Leroy Smart, Big Youth and Tapper Zukie. I still was rockin the punk bands but I started getting into this cool reggae sound that The Clash (and especially Paul Simonon) loved so much. I also purchased the original versions of "Police & Thieves" and "Pressure Drop" and slowly started to get into the world of reggae.

Roehm then told me The Clash would be in Detroit the following March so it was road trip time again. We stopped in Chicago on the way and saw The Jam play twice. They were fantastic. We then went to Detroit and I think we went to a place called Bamboo Records and somehow Roehm got the band's itinerary. We met them at the airport as they came off the plane. I'll never forget it. The Clash. Right there. Wow.

They played at a roller rink that evening with Mikey Dread and Lee Dorsey. It was the final gig of the tour, a benefit for Jackie Wilson. It was really crowded (I was pressed up against the stage and could barely move) so it wasn't the same incredible vibe as the Chicago show, but it was still awesome. And afterwards we partied at their hotel with them and their entourage until 6 am. It was an unforgettable time.

My memory is hazy after all these years but when "Sandinista" came out I wasn't sure about them performing it live, but then I saw them play "Magnificent Seven" on the "Tomorrow Show" with Tom Snyder and at that moment I knew I had to go see them again. I didn't have any tickets but it's when they added all the shows at Bonds in New York. So I took a chance and hopped on a plane. Luckily, Joe got me in every night. I can't remember how. Or maybe I talked to Kosmo. Regardless, it was seven nights in a row, with a matinee on Saturday. Two shows on the same day! It was insane. But I had youth on my side. I remember seeing Billy Idol in the dressing room one night, too.

After that experience, my brother and I saw them in Austin and Dallas the next year, and partied with them after the shows again. (I went to school in Austin because on the back of the "London Calling" album there was a pic of them playing at the Armadillo World Headquarters in Austin. Seriously, that's why I chose the school!). I went out to dinner with Jonesy after interviewing him in Austin one day. We went to some Deli and listened to some reggae I had in my car. I was also there during the filming of the "Casbah" video. Great memories. The next year some friends and I drove to Chicago and saw them at the Aragon Ballroom again. They were still great but nothing ever equaled the first time I witnessed them. Then in 1984, I finally saw them in my hometown of St. Louis, but it was after Jonesy left and it wasn't nearly the same.

Like I wrote at the outset, The Clash has been a major influence on my life. In fact, they changed my life. Like many others I bought an instrument (a bass guitar) and started a band. I turned all my friends on to them and one is still a lead singer all of these years later, in Burlington, VT, of a great punk band called "Blowtorch." Because of The Clash I got into reggae and by the time they officially disbanded I was totally immersed in the crooked beat. I decided to follow that route and have never looked back. I'm a reggae DJ on KDHX www.kdhx.org since 1992 (the show is called "Positive Vibrations"). I've promoted shows since the following year (1993) and I also have a record label I started in 2003, Skank Records, through which I've released ten of the best reggae cds you'll ever hear available from www.skankrecords.com. And to think it all started because of my love of The Clash. They turned me from Jeff Frelich into Professor Skank. Thank you, fellas.

Photo 23

Photo 24

Photo 25

Photo 26

Photo 27

Photo 28

Photo 29

Sébastien Roblain, France

I'm too young to had the chance to see the Clash on stage, but I spent a lot of time gathering the testimony of those who had seen them. But I remember as if it was yesterday the first time I had the chance to see them moving... We are at the very end of the 80's. I used to pick up my music in my discotheque's sister who had turned 18y in 1977. Between the first U2, Joe Jackson, Bauhaus and Siouxie etc, I listened and already enjoyed some pieces of the Clash. But at the time I was a the Cure's fan. One day, returning from high school I bought the VHS tape of "Cure in orange" and back home began to watch it. But instead of being packed, I was very much disappointed. I found that live soft, static, boring. So, the same evening, I went back to the store to exchange my VHS and in front of this wall of video tapes, I came across the one called "Video Clash". and I thought "why not". I went home with this VHS under my arm and the first few seconds of the video of "Tommy Gun" I was struck down. Those guys, had the sound, the anger, the clothes, the attitude, everything ! That's how I became a Clash fan. I started, listen to all the albums, looked for live boots, started to learn the guitar, changed the way I dress, my entire world changed. The years have passed and I do not listen to their music anymore, but I keep an eternal respect to these four musicians, to have opened my ears, forced me to think for myself, and so much more. Music may not be able to change the world, but it can change every individual and I like this idea.

Andy Unger, Scotland

The Punk Rock Sound from a Safe New Town Home.

The new town of Cumbernauld is a sprawling overspill "Satellite City" - initially seen as a "solution" to the overcrowding and slums of Glasgow. But despite all the brand new concrete and pebble dash housing we had a safe and happy upbringing there as young kids - growing up in our new town home felt safe, unlike the mean streets of the city most of us regarded as our original "home"... That is until adolescence (and good timing) gave us the ultimate music to vent our anger at the boredom of a town that offered nothing when you're 14 years old: Punk Rock. Musically our generation had grown up through primary and high school with the Glam Rock sounds of favourites like Bolan, Bowie, Glitter, Slade, Sweet, maybe Mott, or Roxy Music, and although we likely caught one or two of them live they always seemed so distant, so ethereal, so... popstar. By the tail end of '76 we started hearing about this new music; "Punk Rock" which was causing mayhem in London. And it was kids, just like us, disillusioned and bored with the fame, money and the clothes of these pop stars that were beginning the new wave, one that was available to all. No musical ability needed... or at least that what the papers said.

By the time we hit the summer of '77 we were all about tight jeans, everyone had their own customised "punk rock t-shirt" emblazoned with rips chains, safety pins and band names. And - if you were brave enough - a short "punk" haircut. I was the first in my class at school to get the chop, while all my buddies were still sporting long hair n' flares - and at that point I didn't know if I was brave, or stupid. Both?

Like many other kids living outside the big cities, we probably missed loads of punk gigs touring the UK through the spring and summer of 1977. The first punk gig I attended, with my best mate Billy, was the Clash in the

Glasgow Apollo December 1977. Support bands were Model Mania, The Zones, the Drones (Bone Idol!); who were all great, but nothing, nothing compared to the phenomenal firepower of The Clash. In the live setting the songs seemed more fully realised than they had been on the first self-titled LP. The Clash were awesome! Loud, tight, and full of an energy that I hadn't realised was possible from a live band. Strummers leg pumping in like a full speed pneumatic piston, half the strings on his Fender Tele broken by the end of the set, the spit dripping from his mic. Even their clothes were great (this was the "zips-on-everything" phase)! With the back drops of Notting Hill rioters, and Nazi bombers all adding impact to the theatre of 100% full effect punk rock concert.

1978 began a strange start to the year, with the Sex Pistols split, and the Clash City Rockers single not really hitting the mark - certainly in comparison to the adrenaline rush of The Clash's 1977 vinyl output. Was punk over, so soon? So when we heard White Man (In Hammersmith Palais) our faith was restored, our favourite punk band were truly of legendary status. Everything was once again alright with the world, and everyone was playing that single on repeat. Both sides!

Fast forward to summer 1978, and the anticipation of The Clash coming on tour once again was palpable everywhere. Our gang of new town punks were so excited that they were returning to the Apollo - it was the hottest ticket in town, and me and my mate Dee grabbed a couple of seats in the mid stalls.

On the day of the gig - probably around 1pm - me n' Dee set off. It was a sunny summer's day, summer holidays and off school as we walked through the semi-rural setting of Cumbernauld. One side mother nature, the other concrete jungle - heading into town. Dee had to hide his punk clothes in his bin shed from his dad, who was an ex-paratrooper, and hated anything to do with punk! We caught up with other mates and made our way into the big city.

Myself and Dee were also big fans of the sole support act Suicide, as John Peel had been playing loads of tracks from their first Red Star LP, and the remixed Cheree, which was out on 12", which was quite a rarity for a "punk" act.

By the summer of '78 our gang had become quite seasoned at meeting the bands, sometimes blagging guest list, and most certainly trying to make it into Glasgow for soundchecks during the day of the gigs. Now, at some point earlier I had sold my original 7" of white Man (with the green sleeve), probably to pay for my ticket to the gig, but managed to buy another copy on the day, with a very nice yellow sleeve. On the afternoon of Tuesday 4th

July we struck lucky, and met Strummer, Jones, and Simonon, all on their way to soundcheck. I was lucky enough to get my record signed, Jonesy mentioned that he didn't know it was available with a yellow sleeve (nice!). Strummer, on the other hand seemed a bit out of it, we though drunk (Special Brew for breakfast), or stoned maybe? Definitely wobbly. I managed to get a scrawled JoE on my single, my mate Billy didn't fare so well, all he he got was a line of ballpoint as the pen slid off the sleeve. By the time of the gig we were surprised that Strummer had managed to make a full recovery. Must have had a good doctor on tour - or maybe lots of honey tea!

By the night of the main event it was pretty clear that there was not only a heavy police presence, but also some kind of vendetta from the bouncers in the Apollo. Was the venue due to shut down, and they wanted to get a few last kicks and punches into the punks? Maybe they just hated punks, and punk gigs, period, who knows?

Inside the hall the atmosphere was also heavy, oppressive, a mix of anticipation and something else... dread? Support act Suicide bore the brunt of The Clash fans' negative energy. Myself and Dee kept looking at each other, loving what we were hearing, but definitely too scared to show much of our appreciation of Rev & Vega. The hordes bayed their hatred of the electronic duo as they melted our ears with their brutal New York electronica, and the even more intense performance art from Alan Vega taunting the audience. It was as if The Clash fans were hating the "new" of this electronic duo, in the same way that all the long hairs had hated the punk rock only 12 months earlier. If it wasn't a four piece guitar/ bass/ drums line-up then it seemed too much to comprehend for some of the audience. You could feel the hatred in the air, you could almost have cut it with a knife (or an axe? Never saw the legendary weapon getting thrown, but that's not to say it didn't happen). Most definitely the most intense live music performance I have experienced in my life. And a difficult act to follow. To their credit it showed some amazing foresight by The Clash, booking such a groundbreaking act - albeit a decision that was not accepted by many in the audience that night.

By the time The Clash came onstage the shine had really gone off the whole night for me. It felt wrong. Had I seen the future, and realised that The Clash of that era were just part of the same mainstream rock music machine that produced all the other rock stars? Was it the violence that was in the air? Was it all these kids that hadn't been into punk last week, or last year - the neds with the punk t-shirts? The Clash certainly seemed not as together as they had been just six months before. The atmosphere was electric, for all the wrong reasons.

They carried on in spite of the negativity, flashes of

brilliance tempered by the frustration at the violence in the air. We all played the game - getting excited and disappointed in equal measures by The Last Gang in Town, all of us touched by the stress and fear of the situation that felt one small step away from a complete riot or bloodbath at any point. Or were we just going through the motions?

Was punk dead by that point? Probably. The music press seemed to think so - "New Wave" and the safety of the more melodic post-punk acts like Blondie and Elvis Costello and "Power Pop" were being pimped as the new frontier. The original spirit of punk passed away when the Pistols, the Damned, and - it seemed - so many first generation bands split up or gave up. The Clash certainly sounded great, albeit extremely polished, on Give 'Em Enough Rope, but on July 4th 1978 something was not as it had been the previous year. You get a sense of the violence, anger and frustration during the live clips featured in Rude Boy.

The subsequent post-gig riot that followed, as fans rampaged outside the Apollo, down Renfield Street, then Union Street - with shop windows getting smashed and looted seemed fitting somehow. The fighting, violence and the police presence only underlined the negativity of the preceding few hours. What started off as a hot summers day full of excitement and anticipation, ended in smashed glass and disillusionment. No White Riot, just Police and Thieves.

Epilogue: I managed to catch The Clash live a couple of times after this performance, and I'm pleased to report that they delivered the goods. They moved away from rock star to real innovation. Their ability to take on all styles from reggae, funk, dub, to dance floor and invite some of the most diverse support and accompanying acts showed a real drive to create a new experience with every LP and live performance. They could have played it safe and released endless versions of "Give 'Em Enough Rope" and satisfied a small number of their original audience. That they didn't, that they stretched themselves, that they branched out, is testament to their greatness, their fearlessness. That is their legacy.

Photo 30

Scott Parker, United States of America

I was a lost 13 year-old boy, struggling to find an identity, when London Calling was released. For many it was just a record. To me it was so much more. It changed everything and sent me on a path I continue down to this day.
I don't recall how I came across the album or its creators. It was through London Calling I found the first band that was truly mine. It wasn't a band my older sister, a cousin or a neighbor turned me on to. The Clash was and still is MY BAND. Two years later I saw them at The Hollywood Palladium on the Club Casbah Tour. It was a perfect storm. To this day I remember Mick, Joe, Paul and Terry being larger than life. That night set the standard by which all other rock n roll bands would be measured.
After college I embarked on a career in the music industry including stints with Island Records, Arista Records, Sony Music, founded two independent labels and spent thirteen years at the helm of the Foo Fighters' recording studio, Studio 606. It was during my time with one of the independent labels, Ace & Eights Recordings; I had the pleasure of working on a track with Joe Strummer.
We were putting together an album to benefit the legal defense fund for The West Memphis 3. I can't recall who connected us with Joe. I hope I gave them proper credit and thanks. Joe was interested in contributing a track, but

there was a bit of a snag. He didn't have a band together at the time and didn't think he could pull something together in time. About a week later I ran into the Long Beach Dub All Stars' manager and hit him up for a track. He reminded me that the All Stars didn't really have a singer. Usually featuring a different singer on each track. I asked him if he thought his guys would be interested in doing a track with Joe Strummer. He laughed until he realized I was serious. He committed the band on the spot! Everyone agreed Jimmy Cliff's The Harder They Come was the obvious choice for a record to benefit three adolescent boys wrongly imprisoned for murder. For the sake of time and money the decision was made to have the Long Beach Dub All Star record the track with Tipper Irie in Los Angeles and send the track to London for Joe to lay down his vocal.

One morning shortly after the tracks had been sent to London, my kitchen phone rang. The English accent on the other end said, "This is Joe. Is Scott available?" I replied, "Speaking". Without hesitation the voice launched straight into how much he like the tracks, but had a couple questions. It was early; I hadn't had any coffee yet, so I was a bit slow to make the connection. The voice continued, asking which of the 3 tracks he was to sing to. Then it hit me! JOE STUMMER was the voice on the other end of the phone! Trying to keep it together, I told him the drive had been sent straight from the studio in Los Angeles and I had not heard what was on it. I told him I would call the producer and asked if he could call back in an hour. He asked me to give him a call back when I had it sorted out and preceded to give me his HOME PHONE NUMBER! I think I kept it cool until I hung up. But man, as soon as I did I was instantly transformed into a squealing schoolgirl in the throws of her first encounter with The Fab Four! Needless to say the track was epic, remains the highlight of my career and The West Memphis 3 were later released from prison thanks in part to Joe and all the others who contributed their time and talents to the Free The West Memphis 3 benefit album.

There you have it. Proof you never know who's on the other end of the line. So, answer each call with Humility, Gratitude, and Optimism!

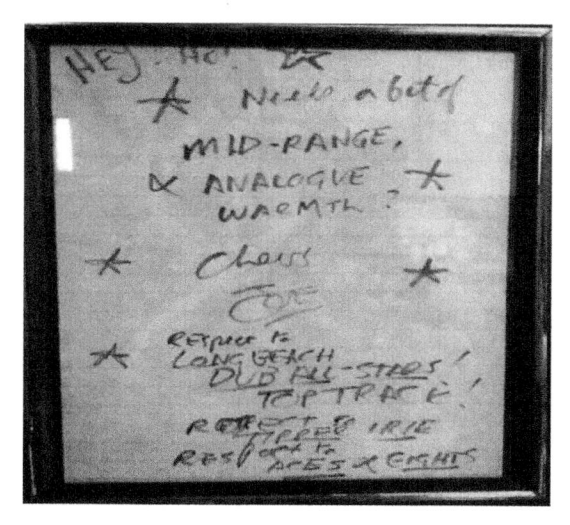

Photo 31

Marguerite Van Cook, United States of America

The Innocents 1978: Sarah Hall, Fiona Barry, Greg Van Cook, Suzy Hogarth and me.
In from the cold.

We were so broke we never paid tuppence for a box of matches, nor did The Clash it seemed. Joe, Mick, Paul or Topper would appear hopefully through the heavy swing-doors of our dimly lit rehearsal room, with unlit cigarettes in hand looking for fire. Magically, after we had all mimed searched for what we already knew were non-existent matches, Greg would always find a box hidden in his guitar case. He enjoyed the moment of reveal. After Mick and the others got a light, they'd stay and smoke in the hall. Not that everyone didn't smoke in the rehearsal rooms, but they'd hangout upstairs for a breather and we felt lucky that they were there. This was how I first got to know them. Sarah Hall was their old friend, she had been in The Flowers of Romance and knew them all for ages. When we started The Innocents, Paul had lent Sarah his bass and so he was interested in how she was getting on with it.

Once back in their basement room, their songs filtered up to us on the ground floor. One day, they were practicing "Julie's been working for the drug squad," and every time they ended the song, Greg started playing it over. After a few times of this, they came upstairs to find out who was making so bold. When they saw that we were the culprits, Paul and Mick laughed and asked what was up. Paul told us that they were going on tour the following Wednesday, this being Friday. Sarah point- blank asked, "Can we come?" Paul smiled and took a quick poll with Mick and Joe, and said if it was up to them we could come, but they'd have to check with their then manager Caroline Coon and let us know if it was alright. Sarah heard back that night; we were welcome to open for them and The Slits, although Mick explained apologetically that they could only pay us fifty pounds a night. We thought that was more than generous. No one had any money.

I remember Dave Goodman saying, "You have to go, Marguerite!"---and he prompted The Adverts manager Michael Dempsey to help, who kindly proposed to add another 50 pounds a night to our kitty. As it turned out, our new managers Lenny and Barry offered to get us on the road. We missed the Edinburgh gig on the 16th November, but we set out excitedly for the Middleborough gig in a cramped white van with our equipment and clothes in the back, just as a terrible snowstorm began. The management's driver Mark had decided to drop LSD, which even if terrifying was appropriate given the surreal nature of the journey. We drove through a whiteout landscape, on zero visibility motorways and roads. We slid around on black ice, afraid that we might crash, but just as fearful that we'd be late. The time for the sound check came and went, then the doors-opening time and it became clear we might not make it. Driving in blizzard conditions was risking our lives, but the idea that we would miss the gig was unthinkable. Finally, we pulled in to the parking lot and with massive relief walked into the hall. We had caught them up. We were part of it now.

We had missed our opening slot, but as we came in from the dark blue of the freezing snow, we entered a bright hall where the stage lights blazed bright white and warm and a small but enthusiastic crowd pressed the stage. We were just in time to catch The Clash playing "Safe European Home." The Slits were in the audience with us and we were all dancing and hugging. Everyone that was there was bound in by the storm. We were unified by the music and the weather. The Clash seemed particularly close to the punks who made it there that night. The songs that I heard them do in rehearsal were now played at full volume. Joe was doing his trademark heel stamp which brought him to a frenzy. I loved how melodic Mick Jones' guitar was and how he sang "Stay Free," especially that night. The set just got stronger as they played.

We, The Innocents, went on to play every night of the tour into the first week of January. We'd load in our equipment and sound check first, which meant we were always there to see The Clash sound check. Baker and Johnny Green were always kind to us and made sure we got good sound. I watched The Clash from the side of the stage most nights, I came to know all their songs and I saw them get tighter and even more dynamic as the tour went on.

A few times along the route, the towns held meetings to decide whether to ban the tour. I think we enjoyed the havoc that punk caused, despite the stress. It was hard work opening for The Clash. In the beginning we had to fight to get the half-full audiences' interest. People were coming to see The Clash and it was still so new that they weren't even sure about them. Some came with long hair and bell bottoms ready to judge. For the most part, when they came to the next gig they had cut their hair and ripped up their shirts. I saw the crowds grow and turn from the curious into the committed.

We were learning to play as the tour went on. Greg was picking up the music slack and I was running around the stage, yelling to the back of the hall, trying through force of will to get the audience to come to the front and get excited. It was a good sign if the audience spat at you, and though it did get a bit much sometimes, I took it as gobs of honor. Sarah and I did kick a few lads who grabbed our ankles and tried to pull us off stage. This action seemed to go well, so we did it more often. One night, some boys in the balcony started to chant "Get your tits out" and pretty soon the whole place was shouting along. For a minute, I couldn't think what to do, but then Greg said in Brooklyn style to tell them "Eat shit motherfucker," which I did to the same rhythm as their chant, as I mimicked Joe's body movements. Very soon they were all happily cursing with me in rhythm.

In Newcastle, I was almost crushed getting into the Polytechnic. The crowd was huge and the Poly almost caused a riot by excluding the town kids. Eventually the college relented, but the audience was angry, that they had almost been turned away, hurt really. The Clash were known for their fairness and this was wrong by all accounts. The stage crew was very nervous about how the gig was going to go, about potential mayhem. I wasn't worried though, because my dad was a Geordie. As soon as I had the mike in hand, I called out, "Haway the Lads!" and the Geordies all melted for me and we all had one of the best gigs. The Clash were especially good that night, they rose to meet the energy of the room.

How could you not love The Clash of 1978?

Michele Lupi, Italy

From: a Clash veteran. To: all the young punks of the world.

The night of July 11, 1982 was a hot night, indeed hot, in every sense: in Italy, at the Stadio Comunale in Turin, they would play the Rolling Stones. At the Santiago Bernabeu stadium in Madrid the final of the World Cup between Italy and Germany would be played. And in London, in Brixton, at the Fair Deal Cub (later to become Brixton Academy) the Clash would play for the second consecutive evening. The Clash, in those days, were on tour to promote Combat Rock, their fifth album: Joe Strummer had a Mohican style haircut and often went around with his Doc Martens hanging from his neck (held together with strings), Paul Simonon went around dressed as a para-military with a red beret on his head (as in the video of "Rock the Casbah") Topper Headon had been fired for addiction to heroin and Mick Jones, with his shrill voice, had now definitively freed himself from his "Keeeef" look and had by now aligned himself with the idea that the Clash - aesthetically - were a group of "guerrillas in permanent service", as later said by photographer Pennie Smith. In addition, the original Terry Chimes had been hired on drums instead of Topper Headon.

On the morning of July 11th I woke up in London, but I don't remember where exactly: I still had all my Clash fan gear: a pair of black 8-hole Doc Martens with yellow stitching to reinforce the sole, a pair of white pants sewn on with the lapels and patch pockets on the outside of the thigh, a white T-shirt bought I can't remember where (ah, I could get it back today!).) with the inscription "Hate & War" and a series of English soldiers running and - in addition - a crumpled copy of the newspaper Sounds that had on the cover just a color photo of Joe Strummer.

That morning I found myself so dressed up walking on King's Road, at the height of World's End. I was with two friends, Leonardo and Niccolò, plus my girlfriend at the time, Chiara, and none of the four of us had any money. With our noses stuck to the shop windows of the Robot store, which sold the original creepers shoes that Paul Simonon wore years earlier, we should have decided whether to stop in a pub that night to follow Italy against Germany in the World Cup final or whether to go to the subway to Brixton to see the Clash concert.

There was an objective fact: we didn't have enough money to eat at noon and buy the ticket for the concert, which cost £4.

The advantage of opting for the World Cup final is that if we had stopped in the evening in any pub with a television, we would have spent nothing to watch the game. A maximum of 50 p. of half a pint of lager.

I, as far as I was concerned, had already decided: I would go to see the Clash, even alone. I was 16 years old, that summer I was in London to learn English, if it was for me I would leave immediately on tour with my favorite band leaving everyone. My other two friends weren't willing to give up: they wanted to see the final of Italy. What if they won? Did we want to miss a celebration like this? Honestly, I didn't care: football had never really interested me, and I only wanted one thing: to see Joe Strummer. The question of money was not a joke at the time, but the most important thing was to buy a ticket for the evening. So I spent my four pounds, plus the pre-sale rights. And I only had a few coins left to get into Wimpy's and buy a simple hamburger. I had it split in two, with an idea. I would have had half for lunch and the other half - cold - for dinner. I had a small backpack, I could have put the white and red cardboard box inside. The other two decided instead to go and see the World Cup final in a pub, while Chiara had already seen the concert the night before and twice in a row seemed too many. So all of them kept the money I had spent on the ticket.

We continued to travel around London without a precise destination, until after lunchtime, when we decided to go to Brixton with the subway to place ourselves outside the club, the Fair Deal, and look for the backstage road door, from which the band would enter. We found it on the narrow side street, to the right of the club's facade: if I remember correctly, it's still called Astoria Walk today.

My two friends came with me, with the idea of leaving me then alone to go and see the game in a pub in the area. Around 3 p.m., at the end of the narrow street, the snout of a Ford Granada station wagon, of a bright red color, appeared. He walked the road slowly, until he stopped in front of the backstage door: first came down Black Ray, the giant security man, followed by Joe Strummer in a blue sleeveless shirt with mother-of-pearl buttons open on his chest, the Doc Martens on his shoulder (which in the following years I also saw Patti Smith doing) and a copy of a tabloid newspaper in his hands (could it have been The Sun?), then Mick Jones, Paul Simonon and Terry Chimes. We were waiting for them, plus a small group of Japanese fans (not many, three or four) who were very hard at work. Joe Strummer, as he used to do, beckoned to the Japanese fans to come in, while Chiara - the only one with a camera with her - was taking pictures (one of which you can find here). The Japanese were quick to get in, and I don't really remember why we were prevented from following them. It was a tradition: the Clash always let their fans in with them in the backstage of the concerts. I don't know why it didn't happen that time.

In my backpack I kept some original black and white prints that Pennie Smith, the band's "original" photographer, had made in Thailand.

A few days earlier we had discovered - I don't remember how - that Pennie had her studio inside the former Osterly train station, on the way to Heathrow. We went to browse: Pennie ran a very nice old bookshop protected by the National Trust and on the ground, among the used books, she kept a large cardboard box full of prints of her original Clash photographs around the world, including those of the tour in the States, which then formed the material for the publication of her beautiful book Before & After. I know I'm giving a grief to a few collectors here, but those beautiful photos, in the shop, Pennie Smith sold them at the beauty of 1 pound each. Still today it seems incredible to me, but also an extremely generous gesture by a great photographer like Pennie (and still today no one takes me out of the head that the designer Hedi Slimane, first from Saint Laurent and today in force from Celine, was inspired by her for her photos very engraved in black and white). In the end, then, I found myself alone: I entered just before 8 pm. from the main entrance, finding myself

in the middle of a bunch of pretty rough skinheads. The venue was quite baroque, as if it were an Italian villa lit up by red, purple and brightly coloured lights. The most exciting moment for me - I was in the front row, leaning against the stage and stretching an arm I could grab Strummer's microphone shaft, it was when the lights went down and the classic intro of their concerts started, taken as usual from the soundtrack of Sergio Leone's spaghetti western movies. They started with London Calling, the theatre exploded with energy, Italy won the World Cup with Germany, Joe Strummer announced it in a break between one song and another, I was happy, sweaty, young and spent the night around London, full of adrenaline.

Photo 32

George Stroumboulopoulos, Canada

We all know people who like listening to music as they go about the day. They get in the car, stream something to their stereo, and zone out. I'm not like that. I can't listen to music passively. It is not background to me. It never has been. The reason is simple: punk rock.

When I was young, somewhere between five and ten years old, I'd tag along with my mother to family get-togethers. My family are Eastern European immigrants. They knew how to party. So much so that my mother didn't feel comfortable having me in the room with the grown-ups. She thought the whole scene was a little too adult for me, so she came up with a plan: distraction. Put the boy in the kitchen, give him a radio. I don't need to remind you how banal most radio was/is/was -- a seemingly safe choice for my mom. She had no idea I was going to stumble on a radio station that would be a perfect fit for my brain chemistry. The DJs were unencumbered, talking about records, sex, drugs, and government. The music was fresh and reckless, different from anything I had ever heard. It was the late seventies. Suddenly, amidst the Zeppelin, Maiden, and Marley, the DJ spun "White Riot." If the station had cocked the hammer of my rebellious spirit, The Clash pulled the trigger.

Rebel music. It may have sounded simple, but it wasn't plain.

The band wailed over the airwaves. They were picking a fight, and imploring us to pick a side. From that point on, music needed to matter to inspire me. I have forgotten a lot of things from my childhood but I will always remember that day.

Same with July 26th, 2001.

By this time, my love of music – fuelled by the forces behind it – had helped me land a job at the music video channel, MuchMusic. I was the host of an interview show called The NewMusic, and was lucky enough to sit across from a lot of great artists. July 26th was different. That was the day Joe Strummer was coming over.

The interview was set up by my friend Tonni at Epitaph/ANTI. She was representing the new album and knew what The Clash meant to me.

The interview was set to take place in a church courtyard up the road from the station. I was hanging with my crew, not processing what was about to happen, when the black car pulled up. Tonni gets out, then the man who belted out "I want to riot" all those years ago on the radio stepped out. He was low to the ground. He didn't stroll, he marched. I said under my breath… Holy Shit. Joe Fucking Strummer. Wearing a white T-shirt, black jeans, black jacket, black hair, black glasses, he extended his hand. "Hiya doin' mate, I'm Joe." I paused, almost frozen before snapping back into the moment.

Our conversation started straight away. Joe was honest, open, vulnerable, strong, and incredibly focused. His respect for punk. His gratitude for the fans and the life it gave him, and most importantly, that he was ready for more! The fight was as crucial as ever, and he expected you to be a part of it. He was wise, but not burdened by it. As the conversation came to an end, we started talking about the in-store that he was set to play in the city. His band was meeting him there, but his drummer wasn't. The drummer hopped off the tour to play with another artist. I commented, "That's cool; he's going to play with his friend." Joe looked at me purposefully, with no hint of a glint in his eye and said, "Fuck that, he should be here with us. We're his brothers and we've got work to do!". With that, a handshake, a smile and the march back to the car. A punk rock warlord heading to his stage.

George Stroumboulopoulos is a well-known Canadian interviewer.

Mark Andersen, United States of America

Mark Andersen is co-author, with Ralph Heibutzki, We Are The Clash - The Last Stand of a Band That Mattered.

Take No Heroes

The hour was late. November 8th, 1989 was bleeding into the new day in the ragged basement dressing room of the 9:30 Club in downtown Washington DC. Joe Strummer's lean frame was doubled over, swaying in a metal folding chair, dripping with sweat.

The singer had just come off stage from an oddly dispirited performance with his backing band, the Latino Rockabilly War, on a tour supporting his equally disappointing solo record *Earthquake Weather*. Even "City Of The Dead," a beloved Clash gem that railed against shallow half-lives had seemed pretty lifeless. "His heart isn't in it," I had thought, "he's just going through the motions." If so, Strummer had expended extraordinary exertion in the process.

With Strummer so obviously spent, it almost didn't seem right to be here now. I had worked hard to get this interview for a local fanzine, *WDC Period*, however, and also harbored my own unspoken agenda, so I pressed forward.

The sweat-drenched man before me was more than simply an "interview subject." Punks weren't supposed to have heroes, yet Joe Strummer was surely that for me, dating back to spring 1977 when I was a desperate, punk-obsessed teenager growing up on a farm and ranch on the prairies of Montana.

I had ridden my punk rebellion—fed foremost by The Clash—out of the rural working class into college activism and academic success. My acceptance into an elite East Coast graduate school in 1983 offered a trajectory into the lower ranks of the American ruling class.

My journey had taken a sharp left turn, however. Strummer's return to punk roots in The Clash's final version had helped inspire me to abandon my upwardly mobile path to dive into the turbulent DC punk underground, co-founding an activist collective, Positive Force DC, and living in its punk commune. Only 3 months before this night I had taken the biggest step of all, going to work in the inner city, amidst an exploding "drug war" that made DC "the murder capital of America."

The Joe Strummer I now met, however, was a far cry from the righteous punk rock warrior I knew from my youth. What I found was a human being, humbled and hurting, no longer up for the fight.

Before my startled eyes, Strummer dismissed not only the final version of The Clash, but punk itself: "Punk rock was of its time. We didn't really realize in 1984 that an idea drowns like a fish out of water, out of its time. We thought, 'Let's do an experiment to find that out...' We didn't know we would find that out, but I think I found that out, that punk was of its time, and it couldn't go again."

Strummer seemed to welcome this passing, in part for the weight taken from his shoulders: "Now we have rap and other things that are heavy, heavy like 'Fuck Tha Police' and all that. As far as I'm concerned, I've just got to drift off somewhere and try not to annoy people. That's how I see my role: try to write something good, try to record it good, maybe play it around on stages sometimes, maybe not. Maybe do film sound... I just try to keep useful. I don't see myself as having any influence left, or any message left, really."

Asked if he hoped his music could still inspire change, Strummer was guarded: "Well, that would be nice, but... Life is a funny ride. You go up and you go down. I think both experiences are interesting."

Strummer dodged when pressed on how The Clash connected to his work now: "I can't think of an answer to your question. All I know is: I write a song--why I don't know. And when I get up on the stage and sing it--why I don't know. There is no answer. Why does the sun rise? Why do we get up in the morning? Why do we drive the automobile down the right hand side of the road? Why don't we just do a U turn and drive it up the other side of the road? I don't know why…"

Strummer only seemed to come alive discussing the cozy grunge of the 9:30 Club, whose legal occupancy was 199: "I prefer playing in a club like this than some huge amphitheater with cheering fans. We're not supposed to say that, we're supposed to be trying to get up there, but I don't know… I started out playing in places like this. It ain't luxury, but it has some soul, like it was made for people, not cattle."

In a way, even that emotion seemed to reflect his sadly diminished ambitions, however. A sense of profound melancholy was impossible to miss. In "Clash City Rockers" Strummer had sang "You got to have a purpose/Or this place is gonna knock you out sooner or later." I knew this to be true, had embraced the idea, found my purpose: *changing the world*, in some sense, however silly or pretentious that might sound. Yet here, to my face, my inspiration was disavowing the mission he more than anyone else had set me upon.

I have rarely felt so thoroughly deflated. I felt kind of stupid giving him a copy of the new Positive Force benefit compilation, **State of The Union**, at the end of our conversation. Strummer took it, graciously commenting on the poignancy of the cover photo—homeless men hovering over a steam grate on a frigidly cold day with the US Capitol looming up behind—but the moment felt hollow. I came away with respect for his humility and frankness, but deeply shaken.

"Trust the art, not the artist" it had been wisely said of Bob Dylan. But surely not Joe Strummer? In DC's fervent and burgeoning punk scene, our vow was to 'live the life I sing about in my song." A bracing exemplar of that credo was the band Fugazi, one of those on the record I gave Strummer bleakly assuming it would never be played.

I wrestled with the value of what I had on tape, and decided to not even write it up for *WDC Period*, out of a perhaps maudlin wish to not speak ill of Strummer in public. I moved on sadly, as if missing an absent friend, but with a perhaps hardened determination not to be deterred from my mission.

Strummer soon seemed to live up to his new aim "not to annoy people" and largely disappeared from the stage, from recording, from music as far as I could tell. It would be ten years before we shared the same room again, on June 29, 1999--and a lot had changed.

The punk rock Strummer dismissed as over and done had exploded to the top of the US charts, beginning with Nirvana's "Smells Like Teen Spirit.' As if echoing this movement, the 9:30 Club was no longer a downtown dive shoehorned in among derelict office buildings. Transplanted to a former black gospel radio hall, 9:30 was now one of the world's finest performance rooms, if inevitably losing some of its intimate charm as its legal occupancy exploded fivefold.

As 9:30's ascendance suggested, DC's embattled inner city was now witnessing the rise of gentrification. Meanwhile, the local punk scene had become celebrated worldwide for its relentless creativity, social justice commitment and anti-commercial zeal. The brilliant, unbowed Fugazi—described as "America's Clash" by none other than *Sounds*--led the way. The band's deep, ongoing collaboration with the Positive Force activist group had become one of the more successful marriages of politics and art in rock history.

And Joe Strummer had returned to the 9:30 Club stage, with a new backing band, The Mescaleros. Still stinging from my last encounter, this time I went grudgingly, more of out of duty than excitement. Even the new band's name—evoking alcohol and psychedelics--put me off.

Imagine my surprise when Strummer opened the night with an unheard song, "Diggin the New," that he offered, in part, as a tribute to Fugazi. The song was arresting, the words ringing with purpose, and the music compelling. Strummer had put on a few pounds, but more importantly, he seemed to believe his songs again, both old and new, and they lifted me, as The Clash once had.

The night was not a fluke. The Mescaleros record was an ace, as sparkling and vital as *Earthquake Weather* had seemed muffled and confused. Strummer's interviews showcased a revived rabble-rouser, with the singer repeatedly paying tribute to the newer bands, especially Fugazi, who he described as "the true spirit of punk."

It was an astonishing and heartening turnabout. I even included a couple of Strummer's newer quotes in *Dance Of Days*, the narrative history of the DC punk scene that I co-wrote with my friend Mark Jenkins. As fate would have it, Strummer was to return to 9:30 Club on October 4, 2001, a day after I returned from a chaotic post-9/11 US book tour, having driven 8000 miles in three weeks solo.

I returned exhausted but excited to see Strummer once again, this time, I hoped, in the company of a young woman that I fancied. But when she seemed to spurn my invitation, I was bereft. In a fit of over-the-top pique all-too-typical of the lovesick, I decided if I couldn't go with her, I didn't want to go. But knowing the show to be sold out, I took the tickets to give away to some lucky soul outside the show.

As I turned to leave, I was startled to encounter Joe Strummer. I had been to many a show at the new 9:30, but--save for Fugazi's Ian MacKaye—never had I seen the headliner turn up to chat with the crowd milling outside. As Strummer engaged with the same humility and graciousness he showed me in 1989, I found myself smiling.

In that moment, I deeply regretted having given away my tickets. "Oh well," I thought, turning to walk away, "I'll catch him next time."

Of course, there was no next time. It's hard to believe Strummer's sudden, untimely death is now almost two decades ago, just as hard as it is to believe that I will turn 60 years old next year. However, the woman who didn't join me for the Strummer show that night is now my wife, our daughter and son 5 and 8 years old respectively.

The regret I felt for skipping the last show is now replaced by a certain satisfaction. The last memory I have of Strummer is not of the performer, but the person, at home amidst the people, just one of the crowd. I try to carry that spirit with me always, especially in my on-going work in DC's inner city, now entering its 30th year.

For me, the lesson is plain: Joe Strummer was one of us. He never claimed--nor wished--to be above that shared station. More than some trendy punk pose, this populist instinct was simply who he was. Far from claiming perfection, he owned his fallible humanity. From 1977 on, he spoke it, if only I had ears to hear. Even my personal anthem "City Of The Dead"—whose seemingly half-hearted rendition that night in 1989 left me feeling so low--copped to that reality: "But sometimes we hide inside/all courage gone and paralyzed."

Strummer sometimes experienced the depths of darkness, but he also could rise towards the light. And so must we all, each in our own way. *Take no heroes*, the Redskins cautioned, *only inspiration*. It was a line Strummer might well have written and surely believed.

Some of us can be a bit slow on the uptake, however. When working on a new book, *We Are The Clash,* a Strummer quote from 1984 jumped out at me, ringing with renewed clarity and lasting relevance. Strummer told *Creem* magazine's Bill Holdship he wanted fans to "get out from under our shadow, be your own person. I'm proud to inspire people and from then on, they should take it from there."

Message received, brother, will do.

Chris Salewicz, England

CLASH FOOTBALL

In 1979 The Clash wrote and recorded London Calling, the double album that was their finest artistic statement. Not released in the United States until January 1980, it would be hailed ten years later by Rolling Stone as 'the album of the decade.'

But when they started work on their masterpiece, The Clash were at a low point: having dismissed their original manager, Bernie Rhodes, and his temporary successor, the group had no-one to fall back onto but themselves. And it was football, as much as their supremely able songwriting abilities, that pulled them into the mental form necessary for writing and then recording the album. Getting themselves in shape to write the London Calling songs, each afternoon The Clash played long soccer games on the recreation ground in front of Vanilla, their rehearsal studio in Pimlico in central London.

'I just think we really found ourselves at that time and it was a lot to do with the football,' said Clash founder and guitarist Mick Jones. 'Because it made us play together as one.'

'We'd just play loads of football until we couldn't manage another single kick,' Joe Strummer told me the next year.

'And then we'd start playing and writing music. It was our way of warming up.'

Each day at around 4pm Vanilla's front door would hear the knocking of local kids arriving home from school: 'Can you come out to play?' 'They were typical London working-class kids, aged between about nine and thirteen, from the local council estate,' said Andrew Leslie, who managed Vanilla. 'They'd seen The Clash playing against each other, and joined in and it became a regular thing. I think they were vaguely aware they were in a group – and they could boast about it at school.

'It was a good time for the group to take a break: they would have started working at about 1pm. They'd play against each other with the kids, two on one team, two on another.'

'Topper particularly liked a good kickaround, probably the best player,' Andrew Leslie said of the group's diminutive drummer, Topper Headon's body perpetually fit from emulating the karate prowess of his idol Bruce Lee. Mick Jones was flashy, remembered the group's tour manager Johnny Green, but his skills didn't quite match his ambition; Joe Strummer was ceaselessly determined, but lacking in true ability; and bass-player Paul Simonon was equally endlessly keen.

Before he discovered rock'n'roll Mick Jones had immersed himself in football culture. At a similar age to those kids who'd come knocking on the Vanilla door, he would join other pre-adolescent fans every Saturday morning outside the rows of hotels around London's Russell Square; it was there that out-of-town football teams would stay in the capital before an away match.

The players' autographs secured, he would then travel across town to a match, either at Chelsea or Queens Park Rangers. 'You could climb in over the fence from the railway line at Chelsea. Once I got stuck, snagging my leg on the barbed wire, and nearly got caught.

'First I was a footballers' autograph hunter. Then you cross that age-line and rock'n'roll was before me - I became a big music fan and wanted to be in a band.

'But collecting footballers' autographs stood me in good stead. Because some of the footballers were really high-and-mighty – I don't want to mention any names, but I could. How they treated you was a good lesson as to how not to treat others when you found yourself in the high-and-mighty position.'

In fact, The Clash's magnanimous treatment of their fans became part of their legend. And Mick Jones's abiding love of both football and music – shared by other Clash members, especially Joe Strummer – personifies how football or rock'n'roll were the traditional escape routes for young men from the drab ennui of everyday UK life in that age.

It was during the London Calling era that Joe Strummer lived with his girlfriend Gaby Salter and her mother in a housing estate not far from Chelsea's Stamford Bridge ground; the property was just back from the Thames: the lyrics of the London Calling song itself state, 'I live by the river.' When the Blues were playing at home, he would go to their matches most Saturday afternoons.

Accompanying him would be 12-year-old Josie Ohendjan, who later became the nanny for Joe's two daughters, Gaby's 16-year-old brother Nicky, Nicky's schoolfriend Black John, and Crispin Chetwynd, a family friend. Meeting at Gaby's mum's home, they would smoke a spliff, and - buying a bag of chips en route - head off on the ten minute walk to the ground. There, having paid a couple of pounds, they would stand in the Shed.

Joe Strummer was a Chelsea fan: he would read all he could about the team. Yet these were dark days for the west London side, stuck down in the second division. According to Josie Ohendjan, however, Joe Strummer 'loved the tribalism of it, the movement of it, coming together under the colours. Joe lived nearby and was a fan, and really liked that aspect of being a supporter.' What Strummer didn't care for was 'the aggression and racism.' This was a couple of seasons before Paul Canoville became Chelsea's first black player, often greeted by his own fans with bananas thrown onto the pitch and chants of 'We don't want the nigger.' Hardcore Chelsea fans were notorious for containing elements of the National Front, the extreme right-wing faction: black players with other teams coming to the Bridge received similar treatment.

The visual identity of the man who wrote (White Man In) Hammersmith Palais didn't cause Joe Strummer any problems at the games, however. 'At Stamford Bridge Joe would be recognized,' said Josie Ohendjan. 'We were punks and stood out amongst the skinheads but he wasn't hassled.' Sex Pistols drummer Paul Cook was also a regular at Stamford Bridge, as were Suggs and Chas Smash from then new band Madness – all three of whom continue to this day to go to matches at the Chelsea ground.

But after a game against West Ham in September 1980, Joe and his crew were chased by Hammers fans, who brandished Stanley knives and flick-knives. 'We had to run as far as the fish and chip shop opposite where Joe was living,' said Josie Ohendjan. 'It was frightening. All of us, including Joe, decided to stop going for a while after that.' Another London team, however, would prove an inspiration on London Calling. The material written at Vanilla for the album was recorded at Wessex Studios in Highbury, north London, in August and September 1979. Highbury was also the home of Arsenal, and the record's producer, Guy Stevens, a legendarily eccentric maverick in the UK music business, was an obsessive fan of the club.

Discovering that some of the Arsenal ground staff were Clash lovers and conspiring with them, Stevens was able to establish a daily ritual that he felt could only heighten the magic he was attempting to inject into the group's new record. The mini-cab summoned to take him each morning to Wessex would make a slight detour, stopping at the Arsenal ground: there, Stevens would briefly exit the vehicle to enter the Highbury centre circle, where he would kneel and pay penance to his mental image of the team's attacking midfielder Liam Brady. Then he would continue on his way to Wessex.

After London Calling at last had hit the shops, Joe Strummer returned to the Chelsea ground to watch a match. Leaving Stamford Bridge that Saturday afternoon, Joe glanced in a local branch of the Our Price Records chain, where he discovered something even more troubling than West Ham's knife-wielding skinhead fans. To his horror he saw that a copy of the recently released London Calling was on sale for £7.99 – The Clash had decreed it should sell for no more than £5, the cost of a single album.

Furious, Joe Strummer berated the shop's manager until the price was reduced to the ordained amount.

Then he rejoined the massed ranks of fans leaving the Chelsea ground.

Chris Salewicz is the author of Redemption Song: The Definitive Biography of Joe Strummer.

Tony Beesley, England

Tony Beesley is the author of (amongst many others) the 'Our Generation' trilogy ('Our Generation' 2009, 'Out of Control' 2010 and 'This is Our Generation Calling' 2010).

The Clash represented hope! As a young & impressionable punk obsessed teenager during 1978 & 79, I tried to accommodate as much of the new music around as I could. There were a positive number of bands I embraced & loved, buying their records & studying their look & statements of intent within music weekly interviews. But, The Clash were different. Whereas many of the other so-called punk bands toed the party line of nihilistic 'don't care' indifference; speaking of fashionably anti-establishment ethics & looking after number one, making a fleeting impression beyond my wide-eyed teenage curiosity – as much as I enjoyed the majority of them – The Clash were a completely different proposition. They offered a future, spoke of change & of multi-cultural influences & musical heritage. They were fiercely anti-racist & not afraid to state as such. Despite their initial Year Zero manifesto, their musical influences incorporated an array of diverse styles from reggae & ska to rhythm & blues, American 60s garage punk, the Ramones & sixties beat. Their music took on even more diverse musical styles as time went on. They cared about their fans too. I loved The Clash with a passion & still do to this day!

I was, relatively, a late-comer, due to my fragile disposition of age. All through punk's chaotic media-saturated year of hate, 1977, I would hear of this band called The Clash, but, so far, I had never actually heard them. My very first sight of how they looked, visually, was by pure chance in an Art lesson of all places, coincidental or not? It was the *Sunday Times* punk special supplement issue & it was poking its colourful & strangely captivating pages out of a pile of magazines there for one purpose – Paper Mache or some other art class intended use! The very second I saw those images of The Clash within that issue, I was hooked: those arrogant, though carefully studied, poses; the brightly colourful clothes adorned ... the sneers & knowing look of gang members ... that was it, I was in for the duration.

Later that year, their single *Complete Control* touched the nether regions of the charts & I finally got to hear them on the Sunday afternoon chart run-down on the radio. I was further enlightened. *Clash City Rockers* &the epic *White*

Man in Hammersmith Palais followed, as did *Tommy Gun* later that year & the purchase of *Give 'em Enough Rope* (£1.50 off a schoolmate's brother who had bought it solely on the production choice of Sandy Pearlman & duly hated the record). I backtracked & found copies of *White Riot* & *Remote Control* still in the racks of our local record shop. Then the iconic game-changer – the first album! I had been staring at the cover of The Clash debut for quite some time in the afore-mentioned local record shop. Suffice to say, like so many fans epiphanies; once I heard that album, I was transfixed. Its impact has lasted a lifetime. I took the record almost everywhere with me; school, youth club disco, mates' houses, you name it. The Clash love affair had been further solidified in earnest.

I did all the typical Clash stuff; I bought the badges (large & small), patches, posters, & all the T-shirts I could afford; I bought the music weeklies, cut out their interviews & photos for scrapbook insertion, copied their hairstyles & had a go at creating my own Clash styled shirts, failing miserably. When I managed to get my hands on an original Alex Michon designed shirt of Joe Strummers, that had been swapped with Joe at a November 77 Sheffield Top Rank gig by a fan, I was over the moon & wore it proudly almost non-stop. I painted *Ignore Alien Orders* in bright green Humbrol model paint on the back of my blazer & wore it to school in defiance of the teachers & their uniform rulings.

By the release of *London Calling*, The Clash had become a finely-tuned raucous & formidable rock 'n roll band; their star was on the ascendency – touching upon worldwide domination. That double LP completely changed my life yet again; it opened me up to so many different & opposing musical styles & genres that my ears had previously been mostly dulled towards or unaware of. Its influence in my life is almost indescribable; such was its huge impact. In due course, across time, with great thanks to that album's diversity of sounds, my tastes would embrace a wide variety of music so tantalisingly eclectic that I would never look back. The following years' flawed but magnificent *Sandinista* was similar in its scope of influence, offering further musical sounds, political observations & lyrical nuances …. And, so the all-encapsulating influence of The Clash continued. I had finally managed to see The Clash on their *London Calling* tour. A date at popular venue the Sheffield Top Rank; a venue that the band had visited twice before: I had read, enviously, a *Record Mirror* review of their July 78 gig there, wishing I could have been there. Their *London Calling* date was another milestone for me. Of huge significance in so many ways, this gig, the sounds of *London Calling* & the manifesto of non-racist, pro-active, pro-creative manifesto of The Clash would steer me through the 80s & beyond, inspiring me to create fanzines, write songs & play in a band & ultimately become a writer many years later. The Clash had given me hope, determination, defiance against the odds & helped forge self-belief when the odds were firmly stacked against me.

Myself & a friend somehow cajoled ourselves onto the guest list for their Sheffield Lyceum gig of October 81 & after the gig met the band – Mick, aside, though I had briefly spoken to him before the gig. Paul & Topper were great, we chatted away with great excitement with them, memory has completely obliterated what was said, but I know it was an enjoyable experience. Joe was surrounded by a gang of punk kids, all vying for his autograph, I got the inside of my leather jacket signed by him & my 1st Clash LP cover T-Shirt; likewise Paul & Topper's autographs. Unfortunately, the photos we had taken with Paul & Topper never turned out. Later, one day, my mum washed that very T-Shirt & proudly stated to me 'Look, your Clash T-shirt has come up lovely in the wash, all those scribbles have completely disappeared & it looks good as new'.

Unfortunately, I never saw The Clash again. A pencilled in date at the Top Rank never appertained & they never played in the Steel City of Sheffield again; a place where they had played their very first live outing supporting Sex

Pistols on American Independence Day, July the 4th, 1976. *Rat Patrol From Fort Bragg* morphed into *Combat Rock* & The Clash won over the United States across sell-out dates at Bonds NYC in 81 & a much-publicised support slot for rock giants the Who at Shea Stadium in 1982. Little did we know, but the lifeline of the Clash was dying, it had been fragile for quite some time, but was now on its way to complete destruction.

1988, The Clash were tragically gone, by a good few years & Joe Strummer was on a nationwide tour against the rich. The band I had been in & left a few years previously, had actually supported Joe & his Latino Rockabilly War band the night before in Doncaster & now I was on my way to see a gig by Joe & his band at Sheffield's Leadmill. A set of new songs & Clash classics enthralled a packed-out & red hot venue. I took photos that night & through the help of my ex-bandmate was taken backstage to meet Joe & the band. Photos were taken & hands shook etc. Then we were invited back to their Hotel for an after show party. The film director, Alex Cox, was there; in fact he is stood in front of me on some of the gig photos I took. The party eventually dwindled down to a handful of the band, Joe, my mate, Tel & myself & my [then] girlfriend, when we were all invited up to Joe's room for further partying: an opportunity of a lifetime & subsequently a dearly cherished memory.

Up in Joe's Hotel room, crates of Holsten Pills & other recreational party accessories were passed around, everyone was smiling, laughing & on the up! I steered myself towards Joe & sat with him, sharing beverages & a fell into a long series of conversations. We spoke about punk, the end of The Clash, the profound influence they had upon me, the failure of 1985's poorly conceived *Cut the Crap* (There were two or three good songs on there, stated Joe, that's all!) & my deep fondness & love for *Sandinista*, which really pleased Joe. At that point, the world had [largely] not quite caught up with the much-maligned triple album expanse of *Sandinista* & as I banged on about its unique musical canvas of world music, Joe sat smiling. Not only was Joe interested in my Clash obsessed ramblings, though, he was genuinely interested in me; what I did in life, what were my aims & ambitions & when I spoke of my defunct fanzine, he kindly offered to help me if I would brave it & move to London & set it back up. I must have sat well into the early hours for a considerable amount of time chatting away to Joe & not once did he appear bored or disinterested; in fact our conversation could have continued even longer. Joe was a true gent, he should still be around; the world still needs him & his like! The sobering cool breeze of a Monday morning, hungover, red-eyed, pasty & wobbly, & I was still in disbelief of the previous night's experience. Though, the prospect of moving to London on Joe's invitation now seemed other-worldly & infeasible to my astonished mind, the offer of such, along with the thoroughly enjoyable & captivating conversation we had shared, was something I knew, right at that point, would enrich the tapestry of my memory bank for decades to come. And, it has, just as the continuing influence of The Clash & all that they stood for, still remains a constant in my life. The Clash gave me hope during a time of insecurity, teenage frustration & misguided anger at the world. The Clash were & are not just a band, they are an ideal, one that they inspire within us & for that & many other reasons. I will always be in love with The Clash! I am currently working on a Clash book project titled Ignore Alien Orders, which will present & celebrate the legacy of The Clash via a collective of fan's experiences, accounts, photos & memorabilia. The book is proposed to be published in 2019 or 2020.

Erhard Grundl, Germany

If you can, imagine a rural bavarian 17-year-old west pockets rebel, living two hours outside of Munich in the very late 1970ties.
The arrival of Punk, mainly the Pistols & The Ramones on the Radio had seamlessly added to my world of Dylan, Stones and The Doors. Somehow The Clash remained on

the sidelines. I thought they were okay but not more. That was maybe due to the fact, that „my" first Clash-Album was "Give'em enough rope".

Saw The Clash live for the first time on May 19th 1981 at the grand Circus Krone in Munich. Sandinista-Tour that was. I remember I had never seen so police-cars and busses in one spot before. So this was going to be a different experience. Before going to that concert I had hit it the hard way: all the other albums, singles & Rude Boy at the movies within a few short days. Looking back from today, right up front at the rails in Circus Krone was a life-changing moment. In the past year I had seen a number of my heroes on stage but when The Clash took to it, I was gone, hypnotized and pleased from the guts. „Ignore Alien Orders" – that was for me. It was very personal message from Joe Strummer. On youtube you can find clips from „my" second Clash-Show in Vienna, in October, same year. During London Calling (from Min 2,22 to 2.26) the cameraman of Austrian television liked zooming upon the rapt face of one Jim Morrison-style guy. That's me.

Joe Strummer and The Clash were pure enthusiasts and therefore the coolest. They defined it. I listen to their music with a smile on my face.

Erhard Grundl ist Mitglied des Deutschen Bundestages - is a German Member of Parliament (MP)

Photo 33

Stephen Taylor, England

DATE 14th January 1980
VENUE The Gaumont, Ipswich
Lets get this straight. We are talking IPSWICH here and a venue that was more akin to promoting the likes of Showaddywaddy, Darts or The Baron Knights.

Ipswich was not renowned for its street cred . The vast bulk of the teenagers of the time were rooted in Deep Purple, Led Zep, Pink Floyd and Yes. The usual pompous self indulgent dross that had helped to spawn Punk 3 + years before.

Luckily the 'Punk' bug had bitten both myself and a few other close mates back in 1977 (when I was just 13). My band from the start was THE JAM but apart from one very early outing to the low key inauspicious Manor Ballroom back in 1977 the band as far as I know didn't venture back to the backwaters of Ipswich again (and who can blame 'em)!

In 1980 I purchased what was for me the ultimate JAM album Setting Sons. Around the same time (late 79) my mate Bill invested in THE CLASH LONDON CALLING. My dabbles with the Clash related to a few singles plus a Canadian version of the first album which came with a free 7" single (now apparently very rare) which I stupidly gave to Bill.

We swapped these albums (temporarily) and I have to admit I was blown away by the varied style and just how different it was from the first album and Give Em Enough Rope. This band were clearly progressing.

By now I was 16. Gigs were an option and when The Clash announced the dates for the 16 Tons Tour the 14th January date was a must.

I remember the night clearly. It was bitterly cold but who cared, it was my FIRST GIG!

First gig, first mistake, our tickets were in the circle but for a relatively short naïve 16 year old this probably wasn't a bad thing.

In actual fact my claim that THE CLASH were the first live band I saw is technically incorrect. It was in fact KIDZ NEXT DOOR who were supporting on the night.

With Jimmy Pursey's brother Robbie on lead vocals and ICF hoodlum (and Jam fanatic) Grant Fleming on Bass they made a reasonable impression on me. Their swan song anthem - Kidz Next Door and Images stuck in my mind. The photos below were from the night and show Robbie and Grant in their power pop Mod splendour!

By now the stalls below were filling up with a retrograde collection of Ipswich Punks determined to play their part. Some 30 minutes later THE CLASH took to the stage and a volley of Gob ensued . Joe ignored it and they crashed into their opening number (I think from the first album).

Track after track followed. A mixture predominantly of tracks from London Calling and The Clash with a couple from Rope (Safe European home and Stay Free I think) and a few singles thrown in for good measure. Pogoing was still prevalent in Ipswich in 1980 and ensued at full pace in the stalls!!

About halfway through the show Joe had had enough of the constant gobbing and I clearly remember him stopping mid song to pick on an Ipswich Herbert about 10 rows back. He pointed at him intimated that gobbing was a couple of years out of date and put him down with a tirade of personal abuse.

The crowd loved it (but still carried on pogoing and gobbing!)

I think the show ended with White Riot although I cannot be certain. If it did it was probably Joe's final salute to The Clash's punk past and was almost certainly lapped up by 'The Ipswich Punx'.

I was blown away.

Bill had heard that you could meet the band if you hung around after the show and despite the cold we made our way (after the dispersal of the crowd) to the stage door down a shady alley at the rear of The Gaumont.

After about 30 freezing minutes the band (well all bar Topper) appeared and we shook hands and chatted. They seemed pretty enthused that a bunch of young school kids were prepared to wait but we were in all honesty amazed that a big band would do such a personal thing (take note

Queen etc) and show interest in who we were and why we liked them.

But that was THE CLASH. Along with THE JAM they were the most down to earth of the 'PuNK' protagonists and both bands had the foresight, the skill and the desire to break free from punk's limitations and progress into acts which are still held in the highest of regards today.

What was clear was that I had now got 'the gig bug' and I followed it up with gigs from Adam & The Ants (supported by the brilliant show stopping GODS TOYS) , Classix Nouveaux (supported by the 2nd phase line up of the Glam / Punk CUDDLY TOYS promoting their great second album Trials And Crosses at the legendary West Runton Pavillion) and U2 (the only one I didn't want to go to and have regretted ever since) all within about 18 months.

My only regret is that I never got to see THE JAM live and I didn't get anything signed by THE CLASH on that night in Ipswich.

It still remains one of the best 3 gigs I have attended (and I have taken in well over 200 since).

When people ask me what was the first gig I attended I am mighty proud to Say ---

THE CLASH

Mauro Zaccuri, Italy

KEYS TO MY HEART: THE CLASH

It was all in my bedroom, what I loved when I was 16, in 1979. A poster showing The Clash in a live concert, a "Davoli" valve amplifier , a low-level electric guitar, stacks of vinyl records with always on top " London Calling ". I had known the Clash thanks to a review of the late '70s on an Italian music magazine called "Ciao 2001". I was immediately intrigued by the description of the group, from the lirics socially committed to the use of reggae in punk music.

From that moment on, it was only visceral love for a group that represented for me the best rock'n'roll band I've ever listened to and seen, really "The only band that mattered". Cool & smart guys. Nobody like them has been able to bring together power, look, emotional charge, anger, effectiveness of lirics and melodies. Nobody like them has been able to mix, leaving his identity intact, punk rock with reggae, ska, dub. They opened a window on the world, a cultural horizon that I could never approach from my view of a little town in the suburs of Milan, Italy. They helped me to get an idea about things, about ourselves, about the world, changed my perspective and my model of thinking making it become an autonomous practice, as if they were proletarian philosophers armed with guitars.

I will thank them forever for this.

"In the time of universal deception, telling the truth is a revolutionary act" (George Orwell).

Art, politics and truth, this was the Clash to me. There was in them the inescapable relationship between politics and truth. Art to be truly (revolutionary) art , must be at the center of social life, it must be true and therefore political. Clash supporter knew that the band described and denounced the "every day truth" without artificial filters. Only for direct experiences (think about "The Clash" album) the words become credible and true. This is probably one of the elements to understand deep inside, the great success of the Clash, along with obviously the talent, great lirics, fantastic look, the charm of the sound, the furious energy of the live. And I also believe that, at least from what I have been able to see and know in these long years, in Italy in particular and probably in other Mediterranean countries, this element "true and social" in the music of the Clash was really fundamental to root the band in the hearts of the fans, together with a romantic component, however, developed in the context just described.In my opinion, the Clash never took, at the political level, any dogmatic or ideological positions. Theirs was an attempt to indicate a path of redemption that passed through the formation of a critical conscience in the young people, the incitement to take position on everyday problems, to be reactive and proactive, to ask questions about the why of things. The Clash encouraged the kids, to use a metaphor, to leave the world of "shadows" and join that of the "sun", to another level of knowledge and dialectics. They did so talking about frustration, rage, bourgeois hypocrisies, lies and corruption of the system, international revolutions, denied rights, violence, war, imperialism, marginalization, but also of pride, identity, solidarity. All this always had at the center, the beloved "guttersnipes" mentioned in "Garageland", the kids, those who really know how things are.

And just like that the Clash became my church, my political movement, my glue. They helped me grow up, not without contradictions, but with some good and necessary convictions.

Another important thing: they stimulated me to play in a band, trying to get out of the shell, to face the adrenaline of the stage communicating with the others.

From West London to the whole world: for real the Clash influenced the lives of thousands of people.

The first concert in Italy of the Clash took place on June 1, 1980 in Bologna in Piazza Maggiore completely full with rockers from all over Italy. It was a free concert organized by the PCI (the Italian Communist Party) in an attempt to reconcile with the young people of that city after the difficulties of the 70s. But the contestation of a part of the public took place anyway and involved the band. The first songs were played by a young drummer who was a component of a support band, as Topper Headon was lost around the Alps and came in big delay.

The following year, May 21, 1981, the Clash played at the Velodrome Vigorelli of Milan as part of the "Mission Impossible Tour" that touched other Italian cities. I was there with another 15,000 fans. In the days before the show, the prefecture of Milan had not given the viability to Vigorelli. Reopened for the occasion, the plant in the eyes of the public authorities did not give sufficient guarantees of security. The organizers and the prefecture fortunately found a compromise and the concert took place anyway. The memory of the famous spaghetti-western intro of Ennio Morricone still gives me goosebumps, then Joe Strummer with "London Calling" intro, cleaned up those who, like me, were negatively surprised by the turning point of Sandinista!.

In my head and in my heart that was "my" Clash concert. There were others of course: in February 1984 at the Milan Palasport, for example, but there wasn't Mick Jones and Topper Headon on stage and it was never the same thing. Then also Strummer in Piazza Reale in Milan in October 1989, just to shout my gratitude to the great Joe.

In the following years I followed the projects of the "after Clash" as every fan has done: the Havana 3AM by Paul Simonon, the BAD by Mick Jones, the solo projects of Joe (I loved the soundtrack of "The Walker"), waiting in vain for a reunion of the band as a salvific moment.

Detonation arrives, many years later, in 1999. Almost at the same time were published the live cd of the Clash "From Here to Eternity" and especially the new the album by Joe Strummer and The Mescaleros "Rock Art and the X Ray Style", the beginning of a new serious project for Joe: new songs, new concerts, still rock'n'roll. Courage, come on !!

A shot of energy that I needed, thanks Joe also for that.

In a torrential rain Joe and the Mescaleros perform, in September 1999, at the Independent Days Festival in Bologna in a short concert. Incredible emotion to see him again on stage, singing every single piece in the rain. But it will be in Milan, at the concert of 4 December 1999 (the only Italian date), that I can completely discover the specific weight of this return of Joe on the stage. The audience was composed by veterans and young fans curious to see the unforgettable frontman of the Clash in action. Once again I have the concrete demonstration of how much Italy loves the Clash and Joe Strummer. People coming from Rome, from Naples, Bologna, Florence singing together the classic anthem. It's a great passion that, I tell myself, deserves to be transferred to the new generations. When the concert ends, the audience still intones the chorus of Bankrobber, like they never want the end of such a special night. From the following year I started seriously thinking about dedicating an Italian website to the Clash and Joe Strummer. I didn't want a mere memorial site, but something alive, as alive and modern was the cultural, musical and social heritage of the Clash.

Thus, on 1st May 2001, after an hard preparation work, Radioclash.it website was born. The history of the Clash, all their lyrics translated into Italian, books and videos, news on Joe Strummer, in-depth articles, interviews and reviews of new band records related to the Clash sounds. I really write a lot, the site was often updated, things flowed in a virtuous spiral, an unstoppable rush of positive energy. A passion that immediately involves a lot of fans spread across Italy: the site is very much visited, we write, we know each other, we do concerts together. The Italian Clash community recognizes itself and was in movement again: my desire was being realized. Not just Italy anyway. I started a contact with the English site of Joe Strummer & Mescaleros, the Strummersite run by Anthony Davie who updated us with all the news of the new course of Joe. But it's not over: in July 2002 I went to London to follow some dates of the Mescaleros tour, and on July 11th, after the concert at Shepherd Bush Empire (thanks again and forever to my good friend Anthony Davie and to Giuseppe Rivela (member of Radio Brixton band), I jumped in the backstage where I finally meet for the first time Joe Strummer. As often happens in these cases I can only say "thank you Joe, thanks for everything", while he offers me and my friend Alessandro Zangarini (always Radio Brixton), a good glass of Italian red wine, showing the known respect towards the fans.

A few months later, the news that you could never expect, cruel and mocking as only life can be in some cases. December 22nd 2002 : "Joe Strummer has died aged 50", on the eve of his third album with The Mescaleros, in a creative and really positive phase of his career. As I wrote with deep effort on the site in those days of great sadness, it is not appropriate to be rhetorical, but the loss of Joe was, for every fan of the Clash, a very hard loss, as you had left a "big brother" that you don't see very often, but which in the meantime has become a symbol of a generation. John Graham Mellor was simply and grandly in my eyes a man who knew how to live his life intensely.

Brave man Joe: he came from the other side of the street, he was not the son of proletarians but the one of an official of the British foreign ministry. Path not simple, that create some problems.

Imagine: in the zero year of punk the leader of the most politicized band came from lower middle class, from private schools. But precisely for this reason the choice to radically change the course of his life was even more fascinating, disruptive, more risky than the other components of the Clash, "working class" in origin. Radical decision, deserving a big respect. He put his heart in the right place, providing his lively intelligence, charisma, great writing, political sensitivity, innate curiosity, high culture base for a project, that of the Clash, destined to deeply affect the history of rock'n 'roll. Also for these reasons I loved Joe Strummer.

The desire to remember Joe Strummer as he deserved , and the desire to compact once more the Italian Clash community, led me to organize the "Joe Strummer Corner" at the Independent Days Festival in Bologna in September 2003, and above all pushed me and Fulvio "Devil" Pinto (drummer and collaborator of the Punkadeka site), together with our great friend Daniele Calesini - to organize in 2004 the first edition of the Italian Tribute to Joe Strummer in Bologna, the city who saw the first Italian concert of the Clash. Thanks to the help of really a lot of people (I cannot fail to mention the members of my band Linea : Silvio-Gianmarco-Federico), 11 editions of the Tribute have been organized (the last one in 2015), always marked by pure passion and a spirit of true brotherhood among the many bands (historical and younger) who came on stage in the memory of Joe Strummer and the Clash. Non-trivial things especially in these years, to be protected as an endangered species. An event that also saw the participation of guests from UK, like different ex Mescaleros and also of Johnny Green, tour manager of the golden days of the Clash. I sincerely believe that Joe deserved this kind of Tribute, and I also think that he would have enjoyed this kind of event in his honor, along with his friends and his fans.

"Even before the brain, is difficult to remove The Clash from the heart" (Alberto Campo, journalist). Things are exactly like that, you cannot remove The Clash from your heart. The passions, the real ones, can remain silent for years and then explode for the most different reasons, as we have seen. And if, as they said, "the future is unwritten", it makes me good to think that there is nothing really precluded, just have the desire to write together, again, somehow, a new page of this fantastic story .

Photo 34

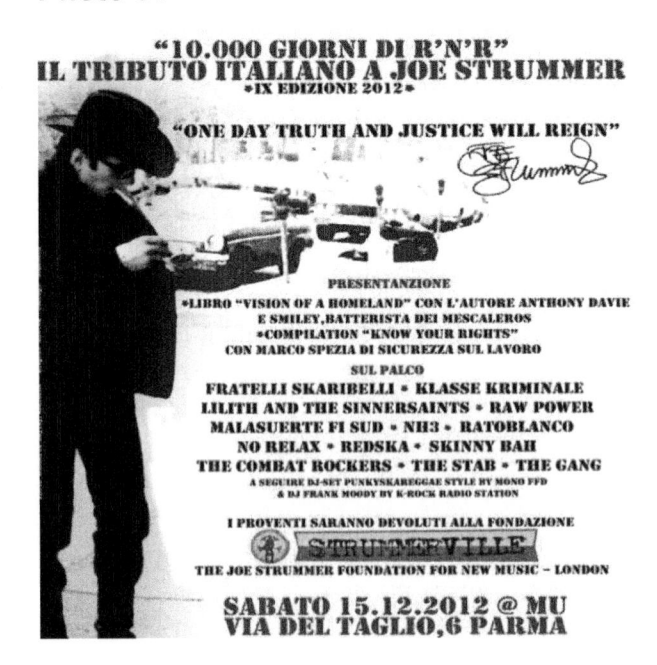

Photo 35

Peter Frawley, New Zealand

It was February 1982, and our heroes were in our far flung part of the world - Auckland, New Zealand.

A contingent of us young punks got together at a home about 2km from the venue. A couple of hours before the show about 20 of us in our best punk gear strolled (" We can do the stroll" song reference!) down the busy Manukau Rd garnering lots of attention - some hostile but we didn't care since we going to see The Clash!

Brett, my mate who I discovered the Clash with, was part of the stroll. We were introduced to the band in 1979 at Dilworth school through a tape of most of the Give 'em enough rope album. It was an epiphany! We would bounce around a small room as if we were possessed - something that will be forever seared into my memory banks.

I had a bet with Brett that the band would open with Clash City Rockers. I lost as it was London Calling but what a great opening.

The whole concert was a blast. But the part that will particularly stay with me was a personal moment I had with Joe. Being a snotty misguided 17 year old, and near the front, I sent a large gob which splattered Joe's arm mid-song. He looked me right in the eyes and gave me a sharp short-armed fingers, then on with the song. All I can say Joe is that it was a gob of love for you and the band.

The Clash will always be the band that matters most to me.

Anthony Davie, England

And finally me!
I am the author of: Vision of a Homeland: The History of Joe Strummer & The Mescaleros
I was going to tell you about the row me and Johnny Green had in Bologna or the Joe/Charles Shaar-Murray story I'm not allowed to tell? Or even how I am currently banned from my grand daughters school and fighting the system's closed ranks to overcome discrimination, quoting Joe left, right & bleedin' centre…I'm definitely not working for their Clampdown.
But, instead I'll tell you about how two old duffers who still love The Clash after first seeing them over 40 years ago.
I work for Royal Mail with a former professional footballer: John Margerison.
John made nearly 100 appearances for Fulham F.C (amongst other clubs) and among his fellow team mates were perhaps two of the worlds greatest ever players in George Best & Bobby Moore.
Now, when we work together I am forever trying to get

info/stories out of John about playing with Messers: Best & Moore, and do you know what? John is always trying to get stories out of me about Joe Strummer & The Clash. John adored The Clash and used to go to a lot of the London gigs.

So, there's two postmen in their little red Fiat van, both wearing their orange hi-vis jackets, one in his late 50's, the other approaching his mid 60's driving along, with *Safe European Home* blasting out on the vans CD player. Both singing out of tune, but happy & content!

Photo 36

Thank you for reading *"This is Joe Public Speaking"* and thereby giving to Great Ormond Street Children's Hospital, London.

Photo Index

1: André Nascimento: Poster Cascais, 30th April 1981

2: Zäta Zettergren: Handwritten message Joe, Ruisrock 4th August 1979

3: Zäta Zettergren: Handwritten message Mick, Ruisrock 4th August 1979

4: Zäta Zettergren: Handwritten message Paul, Ruisrock 4th August 1979

5: Zäta Zettergren: Handwritten message Topper, Ruisrock 4th August 1979

6: Stefan Tews: Himself 1979

7: James Leftwich: Poster Athens 27th July 1985

8: Antonio Bacciocchi: Backstage pass Milan 28th February 1984.

9: Antonio Bacciocchi: The band **Not Moving** that supported The Clash in Milan (Antonio is the drummer)

10: James Burns: Ticket Mayfair, Newcastle 12th June 1980

11: Christopher Downey: with Joe Kent State University 17th October 1982

12: Christopher Downey: Joe & fans Kent State University 17th October 1982

13: Christopher Downey: Mick & fans Kent State University 17th October 1982

14: Nancy Downey: Mick Jones with Christopher Downey 21st Oct 2006

15: Frank Moriarty: Signed *Give 'em Enough Rope* poster

16: Bobo Boggio: Alessandro Zangarini & Giuseppe Rivela

17: Jonathan Ganley: Paul Logan Campbell Centre, Auckland 5th February 1982

18: Jonathan Ganley: Paul Logan Campbell Centre, Auckland 5th February 1982

19: David Zensky: with Joe & fans SUNY Binghamton 2nd October 1982

20: David Zensky: Mick sprays a fans minivan, SUNY Binghamton 2nd October 1982

21: Elliot Kassoff: Mockingbird Hill The Cutting Room, New York 22nd Sept 2018

22: Graham Southard: Personal collection inc: letter from Topper, backstage passes

23: Jeff Freilich: With Joe Detroit Airport March 1980

24: Jeff Freilich: Mick Detroit Airport March 1980

25: Jeff Freilich: Joe Detroit Airport March 1980

26: Jeff Freilich: Backstage pass Motor City Roller Link, Detroit 10th March 1980

27: Jeff Freilich: Mick outside Bonds, New York June 1981

28: Jeff Freilich: Joe outside Bonds, New York June 1981

29: Jeff Freilich: Bonds, New York, June 1981

30: Andy Unger: (White Man) In Hammersmith Palais 7" Yellow sleeve signed copy

31: Scott Parker: Message from Joe Strummer

32: Michele Lupi: Joe Strummer, The Fair Deal, London 11th July 1982

33: Erhard Grundl: Erhard & 1981 Tour poster

34: Mauro Zaccuri: Joe Strummer Tribute gig, Milan 2007

35: Mauro Zaccuri: Joe Strummer Tribute gig, Parma 2012

36: Ellie Davie: Self-portrait, Joe Strummer did for my daughter Ellie 1994

Special thanks: without whose help etc..............

Firstly, to all who contributed. I would like to say a big thanks. It's not the easiest of jobs at times to write, when you have either got a very busy schedule or in my world work all the hours god gave me. So every contribution has been very much appreciated.

Others have also been of great help including my good Canadian friend: Stephen Rioux: big thanks. And whilst talking about Canadians: special thanks to Simon White for letting me use his terrific photograph of The Clash for the front cover.

So, that's it. The end.

Now it's my chance to say a special thanks to my wife Janet, my daughter's Amée & Ellie and my grandchildren Evie & George, plus of course not forgetting:

Ryan "Iron" Steadman, Mum & Stret, Dad & Sheila, Jane, Emma and all the rest of my family in London, Romford, Northants, The Wirral & Australia.

To everyone at Mount Pleasant Sorting Office, London EC1 and these days all the staff at St. James Delivery Office and to postal workers everywhere!

Printed in Great
Britain
by Amazon